Market Demand

FRONTIERS OF ECONOMIC RESEARCH

Series Editors

David M. Kreps   Thomas J. Sargent

Market Demand: Theory and Empirical Evidence

Werner Hildenbrand

Princeton University Press
Princeton, New Jersey

Copyright © 1994 by Princeton University Press
Published by Princeton University Press, 41 William Street,
Princeton, New Jersey 08540
In the United Kingdom: Princeton University Press, Chichester,
West Sussex

Library of Congress Cataloging-in-Publication Data
Hildenbrand, Werner, 1936–
    Market demand: theory and empirical evidence / Werner
Hildenbrand.
        p.   cm. — (Frontiers of economic research)
    Includes bibliographical references and index.
    ISBN 0-691-03428-1
    1. Demand (Economic theory)—Mathematical models. 2. House-
holds—Economic aspects—Mathematical models.   I. Title. II. Series.
    HB801.H5   1994
    338.5′212—dc20   93-5910
                                                                                        CIP

This book has been composed in 10/13 Times Roman

Princeton University Press books are printed on acid-free paper
and meet the guidelines for permanence and durability of the
Committee on Production Guidelines for Book Longevity of the
Council on Library Resources

Printed in the United States of America
10 9 8 7 6 5 4 3 2 1

... *le recours à l'observation systématique tient une place importante, pour montrer lesquelles des spécifications alternatives concevables ont une réalité. L'approche purement microéconomique entretient trop souvent l'illusion qu'on peut se passer de cette référence aux données, alors même que ses résultats négatifs sont autant de preuves qu'on ne peut pas conclure sans faire appel à l'observation.*

Si l'ambition d'une microéconomie générale, recouvrant l'ensemble des phénomènes, est intenable dans les faits, ce n'est pas une raison pour écarter la vision selon laquelle les phénomènes globaux résultent d'actions d'individus et d'entreprises, opérant à l'intèrieur du système économique, c'est-à-dire d'une réalité ayant une importante base microéconomique.

—E. Malinvaud, *Voies de la Recherche Macroéconomique* (1991), p. 147.

Contents

Preface

When I read in the seventies the publications of Sonnenschein, Mantel, and Debreu on the structure of the excess demand function of an exchange economy, I was deeply consternated. Up to that time I had the naive illusion that the microeconomic foundation of the general equilibrium model, which I admired so much, does not only allow us to prove that the model and the concept of equilibrium are logically consistent (existence of equilibria), but also allows us to show that the equilibrium is well determined. This illusion, or should I say rather, this hope, was destroyed, once and for all, at least for the traditional model of exchange economies.

I was tempted to repress this insight and to continue to find satisfaction in proving existence of equilibria for more general models under still weaker assumptions. However, I did not succeed in repressing the newly gained insight because I believe that a theory of economic equilibrium is incomplete if the equilibrium is not well determined.

It is well-known that the main reason for the lack of determinateness of the general equilibrium model lies on the demand side of the economy. Consequently, it is natural, at least as a first step, to try to develop a theory of *market demand* with the aim of establishing some "useful" properties of the market demand function. It was clear from the beginning that the traditional microeconomic foundation of market demand had to be extended.

I believe that the relevant question is not to ask which properties of the individual demand behavior are *preserved* by going from individual to market demand, but rather to analyze which new properties are *created* by the aggregation procedure.

I want to defend in this book the thesis that "sufficient heterogeneity" of a large population of households leads to useful properties of the mean demand of the population. In the defense of this thesis, two hypotheses play a crucial role: "increasing dispersion" (Chapter 3) and "increasing spread" (Chapter 4). To justify these hypotheses I decided to look at empirical data—the Family Expenditure Surveys. This approach—a dialogue between economic modelling and data analysis—has often been suggested in the literature. I am particularly influenced by Malinvaud, as the quotation on the frontispiece shows.

In writing this book I was encouraged and actively supported by many colleagues and friends. I had particularly close collaboration with Jean-Michel Grandmont, Birgit Grodal, Wolfgang Härdle, Kurt Hildenbrand, Michael Jerison, Reinhard John, Alan Kirman, Alois Kneip, Heike Schmidt, and Tom Stoker. I would like to thank all of them for their friendly collaboration.

The various versions of the manuscript were typed by Inge Bassmann, Stephan Hildenbrand, Henrike Peters, and Sabine Randerath. The figures were prepared by Eckart Jäger and Heike Orth. I am grateful to all of them.

Finally, I gratefully acknowledge the financial support from the Deutsche Forschungsgemeinschaft, Sonderforschungsbereich 303 and, in particular, the generous support by the Gottfried-Wilhelm-Leibniz-Förderpreis. Without this financial support I could not have done the kind of research that finally led to this book.

Bonn, May 1993   W.H.

Chapter **1**
Introduction

Pure economics has a remarkable way of producing
rabbits out of a hat—apparently a priori propositions which apparently refer to reality. It is fas-
cinating to try to discover how the rabbits got in;
for those of us who do not believe in magic must
be convinced that they got in somehow.

—J. R. Hicks, *Value and Capital*, (1946), p. 23

1.1   The Law of Market Demand

In this book I shall develop a theory of *market demand*. The principal aim of this theory is to identify the conditions under which the
Law[1] of Demand will hold. I shall defend the thesis that *the Law of
Demand is mainly due to the heterogeneity of the population of households;* the "rationality" of individual households plays only a minor
role. After explaining what I understand by the Law of Demand, it
will become clear that my goal is quite modest. However, I believe,
it is fundamental.

What does the Law of Demand assert? First of all the Law of
Demand does not refer to the demand of an individual household,
but to *market demand*, that is to say, to the *mean demand of a large*

---

[1]A reader who dislikes the term "law" because of the belief that there are no
laws in the social sciences can use the term "monotonicity" instead.

3

population of households, for example, to all private households in Germany or the United Kingdom. To emphasize this, I shall often refer to the Law of Market Demand.

Second, the Law of Market Demand does not assert that for any particular commodity, say h, and any two time periods t and τ, for example the years 1991 and 1992, the actual mean demand per period of that commodity, Q_t^h and Q_τ^h and the actual average prices, p_t^h and p_τ^h, during these periods are related by

$$(p_t^h - p_\tau^h)(Q_t^h - Q_\tau^h) < 0. \qquad (1.1)$$

That is to say, an increase (decrease) in the price of commodity h from period t to period τ is followed by a decrease (increase) in mean demand per period of that commodity. However, the first empirical studies on demand in the nineteenth century analyzed exactly this type of relation.[2]

One might expect that relation (1.1) holds if the two time periods are not far apart from each other and if the prices of all relevant commodities other than commodity h do not change. However, the actual evolution of prices over time would hardly respect such a *ceteris paribus* clause. If all prices change simultaneously there is, of course, no reason why relation (1.1) should hold.

To avoid this *ceteris paribus* clause on prices, one can consider the following weakening of relation (1.1). Consider a comprehensive collection of commodities, say $h = 1, \ldots, l$. Let $p_t = (p_t^1, \ldots, p_t^l)$ denote the vector of actual average prices in period t and let $Q_t = (Q_t^1, \ldots, Q_t^l)$ denote the vector of actual demands per period t. One can now ask whether the vector of prices and the vector of demands for two time periods t and τ are related by

$$(p_t - p_\tau) \cdot (Q_t - Q_\tau) := \sum_{h=1}^{l} (p_t^h - p_\tau^h)(Q_t^h - Q_\tau^h) < 0. \qquad (1.2)$$

---

[2]For example, Engel (1861) considers the average price and harvest of rye for every year from 1846 to 1860 in Prussia. The price p_t and the quantity Q_t is expressed as a percentage deviation from an average. Engel's data show that the relation $(p_{t+1} - p_t)(Q_{t+1} - Q_t) < 0$ holds in 11 out of 14 years.

Similarly, Farquhar and Farquhar (1891) study the demand for potatoes. They compared the annual changes in the harvest with the annual changes in the value of the crop and analyze the relation $(p_{t+1}Q_{t+1} - p_t Q_t)(Q_{t+1} - Q_t) < 0$. They conclude that "Fourteen times out of twenty, an increased crop is followed by a diminished total value, and vice versa." For more details on early studies of consumer behavior, see Stigler (1954).

Relation (1.2) says that the *vector $p_t - p_\tau$ of price changes* and the *vector $Q_t - Q_\tau$ of demand changes point in opposite directions*. This clearly does not imply relation (1.1) for every commodity: For example, in Figure 1.1,

$$(p_t - p_\tau) \cdot (Q_t - Q_\tau) < 0,$$

$$(p_t^1 - p_\tau^1)(Q_t^1 - Q_\tau^1) < 0 \quad \text{yet} \quad (p_t^2 - p_\tau^2)(Q_t^2 - Q_\tau^2) > 0.$$

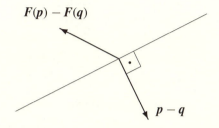

Figure 1.1.

Whether the actual evolution of prices and demand over time satisfies relation (1.2) is an interesting empirical question, which to my knowledge has never been analyzed. However, the Law of Demand, as understood in this book, does not refer to the actual evolution of prices and demand, but to *hypothetical price changes within the same period*. This requires the market demand to be modelled as a *schedule*[3]: If the average price vector in period t were p, then the market demand per period t would be

$$F_t(p) = \begin{cases} F_t^1(p_1, \ldots, p_l) \\ \vdots \\ F_t^l(p_1, \ldots, p_l). \end{cases}$$

This notation emphasizes the dependence of market demand on the price system. Naturally, there are other determinants of demand, like income, tastes, or other household characteristics. If they are not mentioned explicitly in the notation, then this means that these determinants of demand are considered fixed during the period for

---

[3]The schedule notion, that is to say, demand as a function, was introduced as early as 1838 by Cournot, and was popularized by Marshall, who used the term "schedule".

which the market demand function is modelled. I shall say more on these determinants of demand later.

The Law of Demand asserts that the market demand function $F_t(\cdot)$ is *strictly monotone*, i.e.,

$$(p - q) \cdot \big(F_t(p) - F_t(q) \big) < 0 \qquad (1.3)$$

for any two different price vectors p and q (see Figure 1.1).

This clearly implies a downward sloping partial market demand curve for every commodity. Indeed, if only the price of commodity h is changing (all other prices remain fixed), then the inequality (1.3) reduces to

$$(p_h - q_h)\big(F_t^h(p) - F_t^h(q) \big) < 0.$$

Thus, the partial demand curve

$$p_h \mapsto F_t^h(\bar{p}_1, \ldots, p_h, \ldots, \bar{p}_l)$$

is a decreasing function. This partial Law of Demand, however, is much weaker than the Law of Demand, because, in the definition of monotonicity, no restriction is made on the vector of price changes.

I have not yet commented on the nature of the commodities being consumed. It was, however, assumed that the "quantity" and the "price" of a commodity are well-defined. One cannot rule out a priori that the Law of Demand may hold for some commodities or some degree of commodity aggregation and not for others. More details on the nature of the commodities being consumed will be given in Chapter 2, where I distinguish "elementary" (microeconomic) commodities and "commodity aggregates". The composite commodity theorem of Hicks–Leontief, which is explained in Section 2.3, will play an important role, in particular, when I discuss empirical demand data made available by Family Expenditure Surveys.

If the market demand function $F_t(\cdot)$ is differentiable, then the partial demand functions are downward sloping if the partial derivatives $\partial_{p_h} F_t^h(p)$ are negative, that is to say, the diagonal of the Jacobian matrix

$$\partial_p F_t(p) := \Big(\partial_{p_h} F_t^j(p) \Big)_{h,j=1}^{l}$$

is negative. The Law of Demand requires, however, that this Jacobian matrix be *negative definite* for every price vector p (see Appendix 1), which clearly is more demanding than a negative diagonal.

The results (predictions) of partial equilibrium analysis—as everybody knows—depend crucially on the assumption of downward sloping market demand curves, which implies, in particular, a unique and stable partial equilibrium. The Law of Demand plays the same role for a multimarket demand–supply analysis.

A competitive price equilibrium of a multicommodity demand–supply system, $[F(\cdot), S(\cdot)]$, is defined as a solution of the system of l equations

$$
\begin{pmatrix}
F_1(p_1, \ldots, p_l) &=& S_1(p_1, \ldots, p_l) \\
\cdot & & \cdot \\
\cdot & & \cdot \\
\cdot & & \cdot \\
F_l(p_1, \ldots, p_l) &=& S_l(p_1, \ldots, p_l)
\end{pmatrix}.
$$

This equilibrium should be well-determined if one wants to carry out a comparative static analysis. Strict monotonicity of the excess demand system $F(p) - S(p)$ implies that the equilibrium, if it exists, is unique and globally stable with respect to the Walrasian tâtonnement process. Downward sloping partial excess demand functions are not a sufficient condition to derive these results. The Law of Demand is also useful in other applications to price theory, for example, in monopolistic competition, monopoly, or oligopoly price theory. I have chosen competitive price theory as a particularly simple illustration.

If one wants to model the actual evolution over time of an economy by a sequence of "temporary equilibria",[4] then it is crucial that the temporary equilibrium in every period be well-determined. Again, properties of the short-run market demand function F, such as being subject to the Law of Demand, are important.

1.2 Wald's Axiom

The equilibrium of a demand–supply system can be made determinate by a weaker restriction on the excess demand function. This

---

[4]This approach to modelling is analyzed incisively by Malinvaud (1991) in the section "Équilibres intertemporels et temporaires" (pp. 131–135): "... on voit bien que la succession des équilibres temporaires doit fournir à la macroéconomie une meilleur base que l'équilibre temporel."

property was first formulated by Wald in 1936, I shall, therefore, refer to it as Wald's Axiom.[5]

For the market demand function F this axiom asserts that for any two price vectors p and q,

$$p \cdot F(q) \leq q \cdot F(q) \quad \text{implies} \quad q \cdot F(p) \geq p \cdot F(p)$$

or, equivalently,

$$(p - q) \cdot F(q) \leq 0 \quad \text{implies} \quad (p - q) \cdot F(p) \leq 0.$$

Wald's Axiom clearly is a weaker condition on the market demand function F than the Law of Demand, which can be expressed as

$$(p - q) \cdot F(p) < (p - q) \cdot F(q).$$

Consequently, if the expression on the right side of this inequality is nonpositive, then the expression on the left side must be negative.

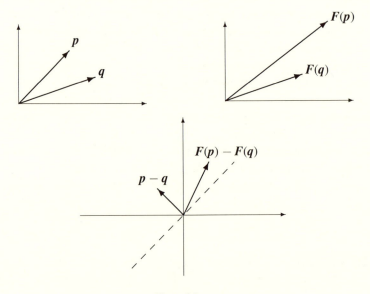

Figure 1.2

---

[5] Wald's original formulation, condition 6 in Wald (1936), is slightly stronger than the definition given here. In the mathematical literature this property is also called quasimonotonicity.

Market Demand

Figure 1.2 shows a situation where Wald's Axiom is satisfied but not monotonicity. Wald's Axiom can be interpreted as a *restricted monotonicity* property of F. Indeed, it is equivalent to $(p - q) \cdot \big(F(p) - F(q)\big) \leq 0$ provided the vector $p - q$ of price changes is orthogonal to $F(q)$, i.e., $(p - q) \cdot F(q) = 0$.

Wald's Axiom for a continuous *excess* demand system $W(p) = F(p) - S(p)$ implies only that the set $\{p \in \mathbb{R}^l_{++} | W(p) = 0\}$ of equilibrium price vectors is a *convex* set; it does not imply that there is at most one solution (see Appendix 2). However, under some additional regularity assumptions one can show that the set of solutions of $W(p) = 0$ is typically (generically) a discrete or even a finite set. In this case, of course, Wald's Axiom implies the uniqueness of the equilibrium price vector.

1.3 Validation of Hypotheses on Market Demand

Does the Law of Market Demand need a justification, or is the Law of Demand and Wald's Axiom *prima facie* plausible or a priori evident?

The *prima facie* plausibility cannot be based on direct experience or empirical observations because the Law of Demand and Wald's Axiom refer to hypothetical situations. Strictly speaking, one can, at best, observe only one point $\big(p_t, F_t(p_t)\big)$ of the postulated market demand function $F_t(\cdot)$. If one believes, on whatever grounds, that the market demand function changes only slowly over time, or does not change at all, even in this case, the empirical data from time series will not exhibit sufficient price variations to test the Law of Demand or Wald's Axiom.[6] The lack of time-invariance of economic relationships poses a fundamental difficulty for an empirical inductive validation of these relationships. Neither can the a priori evidence be derived from introspection since both properties refer to market demand, and introspection can only refer to individual demand, which I shall discuss later.

---

[6]"Au niveau global, l'économist ne peut qu'observer passivement une réalité changeante; de ce fait, les données restent pauvres compte tenu de la complexité et de la variabilité des phénomènes." [Malinvaud (1991), p. 22.] This book contains a very lucid discussion of the fundamental methodological problems in economic theory. As the quotation on the frontispiece shows, I have been greatly influenced in my thinking by the work of Malinvaud.

One can, of course, argue that the foregoing questions are altogether irrelevant; only the conclusions (predictions) that are derived from an assumption have to be tested. In Friedman's words "... the only relevant test of the *validity* of a hypothesis is comparison of its predictions with experience. The hypothesis is rejected if its predictions are contradicted ("frequently" or more often than predictions from an alternative hypothesis); it is accepted if its predictions are not contradicted; great confidence is attached to it if it has survived many opportunities for contradiction."[7] Alas, Friedman's methodological prescription—theory as a tool or an instrument—is hard to apply. What are the precise predictions that are derivable from the Law of Demand? Without additional hypotheses, obviously, no prediction is possible. If the Law of Demand, for example, is embedded in a competitive demand–supply analysis (this seems to be Friedman's framework), then one can think of comparative static results as predictions. It is well-known, however, that comparative static results that are derived solely from the Law of Demand are not specific enough. Testing a theory by its predictions is indeed a difficult task in economics.

Undoubtedly, one has to insist on a justification if one is to model market demand as a monotone function or as a function satisfying Wald's Axiom. Such a justification requires a more explicit definition of market demand that clearly should involve the demand of individual households; after all, market demand is defined as mean demand of households' demand. However, what do we know about the demand behavior of individual households?

1.4   On Individual Behavior: Introspection and Plausibility

The relationship in a given period t between the current average price vector p, the current disposable income x^i, and the current demand

---

[7]Friedman then continues: "To avoid confusion, it should perhaps be noted explicitly that the 'predictions' by which the validity of a hypothesis is tested need not be about phenomena that have not yet occurred, that is, need not be forecasts of future events; they may be about phenomena that have occurred but observations on which have not yet been made or are not known to the person making the prediction." [Friedman (1953), p. 8.] For a critical discussion of Friedman's methodological position, see Malinvaud (1991), Blaug (1980), Caldwell (1982), and the literature referred to in these books.

vector y^i of a household i is described by a "black box" or a function $y^i = f^i_t(p, x^i)$ (see Figure 1.3).

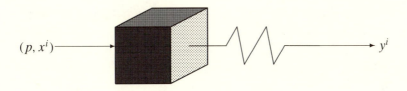

(p, x^i) — — — — y^i

Figure 1.3.

Microeconomics fills this black box by postulating certain models of household behavior. In doing so it is claimed that one derives the relationship f^i from more basic concepts, like preferences and expectations. In this introduction, as a short cut, I take the short-run demand function as a primitive concept. Clearly, the function f^i is typically not homogeneous in (p, x), and does not satisfy the identity $p \cdot f^i(p, x) \equiv x$, since current total expenditure might well be different from current disposable income. More will be said on this topic in Section 2.2.

This unknown functional relationship that is represented by the black box can be viewed either as stochastic or as deterministic. In the former case, a household's demand function $\tilde{f}^i$ is a random function, that is to say, $\tilde{f}^i(p, x^i)$ is a random vector. One can always write the random demand $\tilde{f}^i$ as the sum of the *expected* demand and a *random variable* with expectation zero:

$$\tilde{f}^i(p, x^i) = E\tilde{f}^i(p, x^i) + \left(\tilde{f}^i(p, x^i) - E\tilde{f}^i(p, x^i)\right)$$

$$=: \quad f^i(p, x^i) \quad + \quad \tilde{u}^i(p, x^i).$$

In modelling the behavior of an *individual* household, the random term $\tilde{u}^i(p, x^i)$ might be essential. However, if one is interested in modelling *mean* demand of a *large* population under the hypothesis of weak stochastic interaction among the households, then the individual randomness can be eliminated. Indeed, the *mean demand* of the population is defined by

$$\frac{1}{\#I} \sum_{i \in I} \tilde{f}^i(p, x^i) = \frac{1}{\#I} \sum_{i \in I} f^i(p, x^i) + \frac{1}{\#I} \sum_{i \in I} \tilde{u}^i(p, x^i)$$

and the law of large numbers implies that the random variable

$$\frac{1}{\#I} \sum_{i \in I} \tilde{u}^i(p, x^i)$$

is negligible provided the population is sufficiently large. Thus, for the purpose of modelling market demand of a large population it suffices—if one accepts the assumption of a weak stochastic interaction—to model the demand behavior of an individual household by its *expected* demand function.

How are we to model household demand behavior? Do empirical studies of household behavior establish or at least suggest some general properties of the individual expected demand functions? By properties I naturally think of qualitative predictions about how a household reacts to changes in prices or changes in income. Given the hypothetical nature of the demand function f^i, I am afraid the answer is negative. The empirical studies typically refer to groups of households that are stratified by suitable demographic characteristics like household size, sex, or profession of household head. Empirical analysis typically shows the relevance of these demographic characteristics, but they do not suggest general properties of the individual demand functions. Also, to my knowledge, laboratory experiments have not led, at least up to now, to well established regularities. I am afraid that all properties that have been formulated so far for individual demand functions, for example, the hypothesis of utility maximization or the Weak Axiom of Revealed Preference (which I shall discuss later), are entirely grounded on a priori reasonings. In the face of this fundamental difficulty in justifying properties of individual demand functions, economists[8] often make reference to

---

[8]I shall give several quite lengthy quotations because this point seems to me important. J. N. Keynes (1891) wrote that the assumptions of economics "involve little more than the reflective contemplation of certain of the most familiar of every-day facts."

Robbins (1935) wrote: "The propositions of economic theory, like all scientific theory, are obviously deductions from a series of postulates. And the chief of these postulates are all assumptions involving in some way simple and indisputable facts of experience relating to the way in which the scarcity of goods which is the subject-matter of our science actually shows itself in the world of reality. The main postulate of the theory of value is the fact that individuals can arrange their preferences in an order, and in fact do so.... These are not postulates the existence of whose counterpart in reality admits of extensive dispute once their nature is fully realised. We do not need controlled experiments to establish their validity: they are so much the stuff of "introspection." Some economists see here an essential difference between the natural sciences and economics. It is argued that a physicist can hardly imagine how he would react if he were a molecule. However, every economist makes daily demand decisions. To rely on introspection in justifying a hypothesis has been forcefully criticized by Hutchison (1938).[9]

our everyday experience that they have only to be stated to be recognized as obvious. Indeed, the danger is that they may be thought to be so obvious that nothing significant can be derived from their further examination" (pp. 78, 79).

Koopmans (1957) stated: "The facts of economic life are all around us. Hence much of the factual background of economics can be presupposed without extensive examination or discussion (p. 131).... "The difficulties of verification seem in large part due to the virtual impossibility of experiments under conditions approaching those of real life, and to the presence of many factors simultaneously influencing actual economic developments. In such a situation, we have to exploit all the evidence we can secure, direct and indirect. If, in comparison with some other sciences, economics is handicapped by severe and possibly unsurmountable obstacles to meaningful experimentation, the opportunities for direct introspection by, and direct observation of, individual decision makers are a much needed source of evidence which in some degree offsets the handicap" (p. 140).

Malinvaud (1991) specially emphasizes the role of introspection. The economist "a toutefois un avantage par rapport à ceux qui pratiquent l'induction dans le monde physique. L'activité économique est le fait d'hommes et de femmes, d'entreprises et d'organismes construits par des êtres humains; elle s'exerce à l'intérieur d'un cadre institutionnel défini par nous. Le savant a ainsi une connaissance directe du monde qu'il observe par ailleurs, connaissance fiable malgré les réserves que psychologues ou sociologues pourraient émettre, connaissance dont l'oubli serait dommageable à la compréhension des phénomènes. C'est pourquoi l'économiste analyse les données dont il dispose dans une modèle exprimant sa connaissance directe, préalable des phénomènes...mais la connaissance préalable dont on dispose se situe principalement au niveau microéconomique puisqu'elle concerne les conditions d'activité et les comportements des divers agents. En d'autres termes, la spécification théorique grâce à laquelle on cherche à tirer efficacement parti des résultats de l'observation, trouve l'essentiel de ses fondements dans la compréhension des phénomènes microéconomiques sous-jacents. (pp. 23, 24).

[9]Hutchison (1938) devotes a whole section (pp. 137–143) to introspection: "This is sometimes very crudely, but sufficiently for our purpose, described as follows. Having examined by introspection the marginal utility of different amounts of money income to himself, he perceives that this 'inside experience' is correlated with a certain 'external' behaviour of his as regards money income. He arrives at the conclusion by 'external' observation that his 'external' behaviour regarding money is similar, in general, to everyone else's. He assumes or draws the analogy from this, therefore, that everyone else is 'internally' similar to himself. We again leave on one side the difficulty as to how this 'internal' assumption could conceivably be tested.... At this stage we want simply to emphasize the more obvious point that our economist cannot get any general results by introspection alone, but only by observation of 'external' behaviour.... Further, as the individual introspecting economist is but one, and as he wants results applicable

Everybody who ever tried to model individual behavior knows that it is impossible to avoid a priori assumptions completely. Only some economic methodologists—who, as a matter of fact, perform no modelling themselves, but give prescriptions on how to do so—advise the profession not to use a priori assumptions at all. The best one can do, in my opinion, is to be flexible, to be a methodological pluralist. One should minimize the use of a priori assumptions as far as possible. If, however, they cannot be avoided, one should state them explicitly rather than try to cover them with some pseudoscientific justification.

perhaps to many hundreds, thousands, or millions, it is the recording of 'external' behaviour which must furnish an overwhelming part of the evidence.

One cannot 'feel' (*einfühlen*) oneself or draw analogies into the blue. There must be some 'behaviour' on which to hinge these psychological associations. Words such as 'satisfaction', 'annoyance', and so on, are in fact so used that we verify the presence or absence of these 'emotions' in other people by observing the human body.

We do not wish to become involved in any general discussion as to whether the various processes called *einfühlen* and *verstehen* are or are not useful, significant, or legitimate. These seem to be just the kind of issues over which methodologists and philosophers argue for decades, but the result of which never affects or seems likely to affect any concrete scientific problem.... It may well also be invaluable for the scientist engaged in the preliminary thinking-out of a hypothesis to imagine himself in the place of, say, a trade union leader or a Central Bank director, though this is simply a *Gedankenexperiment* which must be followed up and tested by 'field' investigation...

But if it is imagined that the *Einfühlung* somehow actually adds something of scientific content, something which can conceivably be tested as 'true' or 'false', here it must be pointed out that, on our conception, *Einfühlung* (for which term like *verstehen* there is no translation) begins precisely where the conceivably testable propositions as to people's behaviour, speech, writings, etc., leave off, and if the door is now opened to propositions that can never conceivably be brought to any kind of intersubjective empirical test, but at the same time are supposed to have some kind of scientific validity, the progress of economic science will constantly be obstructed by all sorts of controversies, interminable in their very nature, and there will be no effective barrier against pseudo-science...

With regard to the trustworthiness of propositions recording the results of intro-spection we may allude to maxims like Goethe's 'We know ourselves never by reflection but by action', and Nietzsche's 'Jeder ist sich selbst der Fernste'...

We conclude then that 'introspection', in the sense in which we have described it—the term may be used in other senses—is not really a rival to empirical observation, and that to compare them as two methods and conclude that one is superior to the other is misconceived.... No scientist can rely on introspection alone if he wants results of general applicability, while he can only communicate the results of his introspec-tion...by his behaviour or his written or spoken words. Though, on the other hand, he could *conceivably*, if scarcely in practice, dispense with introspection entirely, it is certainly an invaluable and in fact practically indispensable method for the forming of general hypotheses about one's fellow human beings to observe, first, from a peculiarly intimate but not necessarily more trustworthy or accurate position, oneself—though all such hypotheses must afterwards be tested by empirical investigation."

1.5   Substitution- and Income Effects

A straightforward "microeconomic derivation" of the Law of Market Demand consists in simply postulating the Law of Demand at the level of the individual household, that is to say, in postulating for every household a (strictly) monotone demand function $p \mapsto f^i(p, x^i)$. The market demand function of a population I of households, that is to say, the function

$$F(p) = \tfrac{1}{\#I} \sum_{i \in I} f^i(p, x^i)$$

is then (strictly) monotone, because monotonicity is preserved under addition. For this argument, of course, one needs that the income x^i of every household $i \in I$ is price-independent.

As for the market demand function F, the monotonicity of the household's demand function f^i cannot be tested by observing actual behavior. Why then does one expect, or find it plausible, that the vector Δp of price changes and the vector Δf^i of demand changes for every household point in opposite directions, i.e., $\Delta p \cdot \Delta f^i \leq 0$?

Since the fundamental contribution of Slutsky (1915), one knows that the effect of a price change on demand can be decomposed into a substitution effect and an income effect. If the demand function f^i is differentiable, this can be expressed by the well-known *Slutsky decomposition of the Jacobian matrix*

$$\partial_p f^i(p, x) = Sf^i(p, x) - Af^i(p, x).$$

The matrix

$$Af^i(p, x) := \left(\partial_x f_h^i(p, x) f_k^i(p, x) \right)_{h, k=1}^{l} = \partial_x f^i(p, x) f^i(p, x)^\top$$

is called the matrix of income effects. The matrix $Sf^i(p, x)$ is called the matrix of Slutsky substitution effects and is defined as the Jacobian matrix, evaluated at $q = p$, of the *compensated demand function*[10]

$$q \mapsto f(q, x(q))$$

---

[10]If the demand function would satisfy the budget identity $p \cdot f(p, x) \equiv x$, then the compensated demand is $q \mapsto f(q, q \cdot f(p, x))$. Without the budget identity, one has to define the "compensated income" by

$$x(q) = x - p \cdot f(p, x) + q \cdot f(p, x)$$

in order to obtain the Slutsky decomposition

$$\partial_p f^i(p, x) = Sf^i(p, x) - Af^i(p, x).$$

with

$$x(q) = x - p \cdot f(p, x) + q \cdot f(p, x).$$

For a small price change Δp one therefore obtains

$$\Delta p \cdot \Delta f^i \approx \Delta p \cdot \partial_p f^i(p, x^i) \, \Delta p$$
$$= \Delta p \cdot S f^i(p, x^i) \, \Delta p - \big(\Delta p \cdot \partial_x f^i(p, x^i)\big)\big(\Delta p \cdot f^i(p, x^i)\big).$$

If the vector $\partial_x f^i(p, x^i)$ of marginal propensities to consume is not collinear with the vector $f^i(p, x^i)$ of demand, that is to say, if for some commodity the income elasticity is not equal to 1, then there exist always (see Figure 1.4) vectors Δp of price changes such that

$$\big(\Delta p \cdot \partial_x f^i(p, x^i)\big)\big(\Delta p \cdot f^i(p, x^i)\big) < 0.$$

Consequently, for $\Delta p \cdot \Delta f^i$ to be negative, it is necessary that the Slutsky substitution effect $\Delta p \cdot S f^i(p, x^i)\Delta p$ is sufficiently negative. Why, in general, should this be the case? If the demand behavior of a household is to a large extent determined by habits or tradition, the compensated substitution effect might well be zero or at least very

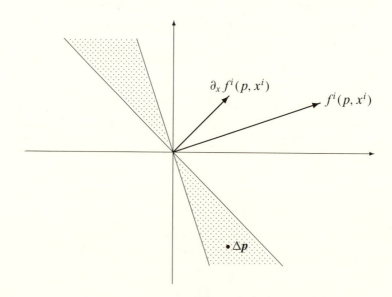

Figure 1.4.

small. Since we are considering compensated demand, the household can still choose the demand vector $f(p, x)$ after the price change and save the same amount as before, i.e., $x - p \cdot f(p, x)$.

There seems to be a general agreement in the profession to exclude—on whatever grounds—a positive Slutsky substitution effect in modelling household's behavior, but this is qualitatively quite different from postulating a *sufficiently strong* negative substitution effect.

If a demand function $f(p, x)$ satisfies the budget identity $p \cdot f(p, x) \equiv x$, then (as is well-known) to exclude positive Slutsky substitution effects, that is to say, to postulate a negative semidefinite Slutsky substitution matrix Sf, is equivalent to assuming that the household's demand function f has the following property: For every (p, x) and (p', x'),

$$p \cdot f(p', x') \leq x \quad \text{implies} \quad p' \cdot f(p, x) \geq x'.$$

Figure 1.5 illustrates a demand function that does not have this property.

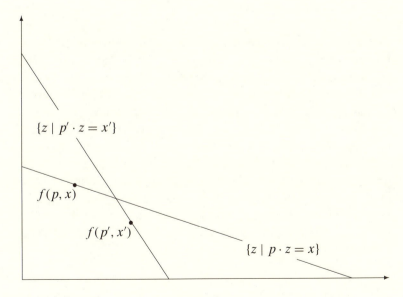

Figure 1.5.

This property of a demand function was first formulated by Samuelson (1938)[11] and is called the *Weak Axiom of Revealed Preference*.

I would prefer to call it the hypothesis of nonpositive Slutsky substitution effects, since the axiom applies to a demand function that might, but need not, be derived from the hypothesis of preference maximization. For details on the theory of demand based on the Axiom of Revealed Preference, see Appendix 3.

There seems to be less general acceptance in the profession for the hypothesis of utility maximization in modelling household's demand, that is to say, to view the household demand function f^i as the result of a utility maximization problem under budget constraints:

$$f^i(p, x) := \arg \max_{p \cdot z \leq x} u^i(z).$$

In any case, the hypothesis of utility maximization implies a nonpositive Slutsky substitution effect—because it implies obviously the Axiom of Revealed Preference—yet it does not imply, in general, a sufficiently strong negative substitution effect to obtain a monotone demand function. For this one needs additonal assumptions on the utility function u^i, in particular, the condition

$$\sigma^i(z) := -\frac{z \cdot \partial^2 u^i(z) z}{z \cdot \partial u^i(z)} < 4,$$

where $\partial^2 u^i(z)$ denotes the matrix of second derivatives of the utility function u^i. For details of this theorem, which is due to Mitjuschin and Polterovich (1978), see Appendix 4.

To my taste, a satisfactory justification of the Law of Market Demand should be based on essentially weaker a priori assumptions on individual demand behavior. Given the hypothetical nature of the Law of Demand, it seems to me impossible to give a deductive validation of the Law of Demand where *all* required hypotheses are supported by empirical evidence or, at least, are in principle falsifiable. My goal therefore is to make the unavoidable a priori assumptions on households' behavior as weak as possible and to base the deductive validation on at least one hypothesis that has good empirical support.

---

[11]To be precise, Samuelson actually formulated a slightly stronger property, i.e., for (p, x) and (p', x') with $f(p, x) \neq f(p', x')$, $p \cdot f(p', x') \leq x$ implies $p' \cdot f(p, x) > x'$.

1.6 Increasing Spread of Households' Demand

The derivation of the Law of Demand that is developed in this book is based on the Slutsky decomposition[12] of the household's demand function f^i:

$$\partial_p f^i(p, x^i) = S f^i(p, x^i) - A f^i(p, x^i).$$

For the Jacobian matrix of the market demand function,

$$F(p) = \tfrac{1}{\#I} \sum_{i \in I} f^i(p, x^i),$$

one then obtains

$$\partial_p F(p) = \tfrac{1}{\#I} \sum_{i \in I} S f^i(p, x^i) - \tfrac{1}{\#I} \sum_{i \in I} A f^i(p, x^i)$$
$$= \bar{S}(p) \qquad - \qquad \bar{A}(p).$$

Hence, the monotonicity of the market demand function F is a consequence of the following two hypotheses:

Hypothesis 1.1: **Negative Average Substitution Effect.** *The average Slutsky substitution effect matrix $\bar{S}$ is negative semidefinite.*

Hypothesis 1.2: **Positive Average Income Effect.** *The average income effect matrix $\bar{A}$ is positive semidefinite.*

I hope that the first hypothesis is accepted without too many qualms by most readers, even though there is certainly no a priori reason why this hypothesis should be expected *under all circumstances.* Actually, for some extreme forms of price expectations it is quite plausible that the hypothesis has to be rejected. I shall discuss the hypothesis in more detail in Section 2.2. This hypothesis is not subject to an empirical test! I have to admit that this certainly is a weak point of the theory of market demand that is presented in this book. The emphasis in this book is put on the second hypothesis, which obviously requires justification. Since the income effect of an individual household typically is not positive semidefinite, why then should the average have this property? To see the reason why this might be so, it is helpful to interpret Hypothesis 1.2 in a different way.

---

[12] For details, see Appendix 2.

The matrix $\bar{A}(p)$ is positive semidefinite if and only if the symmetrized matrix

$$\bar{A}(p) + \bar{A}(p)^\mathsf{T} =: \tilde{M}(p)$$

is positive semidefinite. By definition of the matrix $\tilde{M}$ one obtains

$$\tilde{M}(p) = \frac{1}{\#I} \sum_{i \in I} \partial_x \left(f^i(p, x^i) f^i(p, x^i)^\mathsf{T} \right)$$

$$= \lim_{\Delta \to 0} \frac{1}{\Delta} \left[\frac{1}{\#I} \sum_{i \in I} (f^i(p, x^i + \Delta) f^i(p, x^i + \Delta)^\mathsf{T} \right.$$

$$\left. - f^i(p, x^i) f^i(p, x^i)^\mathsf{T} \right) \right]$$

$$= \lim_{\Delta \to 0} \frac{1}{\Delta} \left[m^2 \{ f^i(p, x^i + \Delta) \}_{i \in I} - m^2 \{ f^i(p, x^i) \}_{i \in I} \right],$$

where $m^2 \{ f^i(p, x^i + \Delta) \}_{i \in I}$ denotes the *matrix of second moments* of the cloud $\{ (f^i(p, x^i + \Delta) \}_{i \in I}$ of demand vectors. Thus, the element (h, j) of this matrix is defined by

$$\frac{1}{\#I} \sum_{i \in I} f^i_h(p, x^i + \Delta) f^i_j(p, x^i + \Delta).$$

The matrix of second moments of any cloud of vectors is always positive semidefinite. The degree of positive definiteness of the matrix of second moments can be interpreted as a measure of *spread around the origin*[13] of the cloud of vectors. This is easily seen for a one-dimensional cloud $\{y^i\}_{i \in I}$ since the following Markov inequality holds for every $\eta > 0$:

$$\frac{1}{\#I} \# \{ i \in I \mid |y^i| \geq \eta \} \leq \frac{m^2 \{y^i\}_{i \in I}}{\eta^2}.$$

Thus, the percentage of points that do not lie in the interval $[-\eta, +\eta]$ is bounded by the second moment of the cloud. I call the cloud $\{y^i\}_{i \in I}$ *more spread* than the cloud $\{z^j\}_{j \in J}$ if the second moment of the first cloud is larger than or equal to the second moment of the second cloud. This definition of spread can be generalized to clouds of vectors of any dimension. The cloud of vectors $\{y^i\}_{i \in I}$ in $\mathbb{R}^l$ is said to be *more*

---

[13] I shall later in Section 1.8 discuss another measure of dispersion that uses the variance instead of the second moment.

spread than the cloud $\{z^j\}_{j \in J}$ in $\mathbb{R}^l$ if the orthogonal projection of these clouds on *every straight line* through the origin is such that the one-dimensional image cloud of $\{y^i\}_{i \in I}$ is more spread than the one-dimensional image cloud of $\{z^j\}_{j \in J}$.

Figure 1.6 shows the one-dimensional image cloud of the two-dimensional cloud $\{y^i\}_{i \in I}$. For more details, see Chapter 4. One can show that the cloud $\{y^i\}_{i \in I}$ is more spread than the cloud $\{z^j\}_{j \in J}$ if and only if the matrix

$$m^2\{y^i\}_{i \in I} - m^2\{z^j\}_{j \in J}$$

is positive semidefinite.

Consequently, Hypothesis 1.2, a positive average income effect, is equivalent to the following hypothesis:

***Hypothesis 1.3:* Increasing Spread of Household's Demand.** *For every sufficiently small $\Delta > 0$, the cloud $\{f^i(p, x^i + \Delta)\}_{i \in I}$ is more spread than the cloud $\{f^i(p, x^i)\}_{i \in I}$.*

In Figure 1.7 the dots describe the cloud $\{f^i(p, x^i)\}_{i \in I}$ and the stars describe the cloud $\{f^i(p, x^i + \Delta)\}_{i \in I}$.

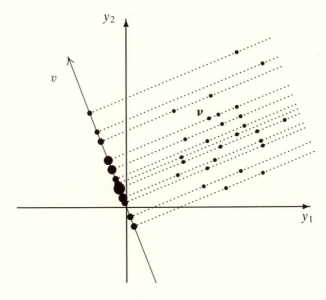

Figure 1.6.

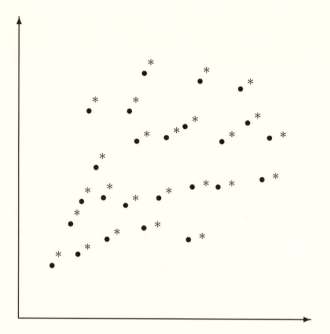

Figure 1.7.

Obviously, both Hypotheses 1.2 and 1.3 are not falsifiable from cross-section data because the vector $\partial_x f^i(p, x)$ of propensities to consume as well as the cloud $\{f^i(p, x^i + \Delta)\}_{i \in I}$ of demand vectors are not observable.

1.7 Family Expenditure Data: Increasing Spread of Conditional Demand

I now consider a "large" population in the sense that one can treat households' income as a continuous variable. Thus, for every level of income x it is assumed that there are households with that income x. These households I call x-households and they are indexed by $I(x) \subset I$, where the index set I now is infinite, even uncountable. Furthermore, I assume that the income distribution is described by a price-independent density ρ. Then one obtains

$$m^2\{f^i(p, x^i)\}_{i \in I} = \int_{\mathbb{R}^+} m^2\{f^i(p, x)\}_{i \in I(x)} \, \rho(x) \, dx.$$

One now compares the spread of x-households' demand, i.e., the cloud $\{f^i(p, x^i)\}_{i \in I(x)}$, with the spread of x-households' demand under the hypothesis that these households have income $x + \Delta$, i.e., the cloud $\{f^i(p, x^i + \Delta)\}_{i \in I(x)}$. In Figure 1.8 these two clouds are illustrated; in Figure 1.8a the households do not save.

For this comparison I would like to use the *observable* cloud $\{f^i(p, x^i)\}_{i \in I(x+\Delta)}$ as a proxy for the *unobservable* cloud

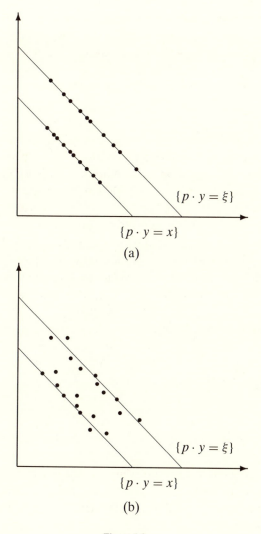

(a)

(b)

Figure 1.8.

$\{f^i(p, x^i + \Delta)\}_{i \in I(x)}$. This leads to two questions: First, is this proxy justifiable, and second, is this proxy useful?

To take the second question first, I observe that a comparison of the spread of the two clouds $\{f^i(p, x^i)\}_{i \in I(x+\Delta)}$ and $\{f^i(p, x^i)\}_{i \in I(x)}$ is, in principle, possible from cross-section data. In particular, the positive definiteness of the matrix

$$m^2\{f^i(p, x^i)\}_{i \in I(x+\Delta)} - m^2\{f^i(p, x^i)\}_{i \in I(x)}$$

can be tested (as I shall show in Chapter 4) by using the data made available by Family Expenditure Surveys. It turns out that on average—over the income distribution—the first cloud is more spread than the second one, that is to say, the matrix

$$M(p, \Delta) := \int_{\mathbb{R}_+} \left(m^2\{f^i(p, x^i)\}_{i \in I(x+\Delta)} - m^2\{f^i(p, x^i)\}_{i \in I(x)} \right) \rho(x)\, dx$$

is positive definite.

This empirical property of cross-section data, which is called *average increasing spread of conditional demand*, is analyzed in detail in Chapter 4. In addition to the empirical evidence (Section 4), I shall also discuss a deductive validation of the property of average increasing spread (Section 4.3) that is based on the heterogeneity— in demand behavior and income—of the population of households. This shows that the proxy is useful for our purpose, but it still lacks a justification. Thus, I have to come back to the first question.

In what sense could the observable cloud $\{f^i(p, x^i)\}_{i \in I(x+\Delta)}$ be a proxy for the unobservable cloud $\{f^i(p, x^i + \Delta)\}_{i \in I(x)}$? Clearly, by appropriate continuity, for sufficiently small $\Delta > 0$, the spread of the two clouds is very similar. However, one needs more than this. The goal is to derive Hypothesis 1.2; hence one has to show that, on average over ρ, the cloud $\{f^i(p, x^i + \Delta)\}_{i \in I(x)}$ is more spread than the cloud $\{f^i(p, x^i)\}_{i \in I(x)}$, i.e., the matrix

$$\tilde{M}(p, \Delta)$$

$$:= \int_{\mathbb{R}_+} \left(m^2\{f^i(p, x^i + \Delta)\}_{i \in I(x)} - m^2\{f^i(p, x^i)\}_{i \in I(x)} \right) \rho(x)\, dx$$

is positive semidefinite. For this comparison I considered the cloud $\{f^i(p, x^i)\}_{i \in I(x+\Delta)}$ and compared the spread of this cloud with the spread of the cloud $\{f^i(p, x^i)\}_{i \in I(x)}$. This lead to the positive definite matrix $M(p, \Delta)$.

Define the matrix $G(p, \Delta)$ by

$$G(p, \Delta)$$

$$:= \int_{\mathbb{R}_+} \left(m^2 \{ f^i(p, x^i + \Delta) \}_{i \in I(x)} - m^2 \{ f^i(p, x^i) \}_{i \in I(x + \Delta)} \right) \rho(x) \, dx.$$

Then one obtains

$$\tilde{M}(p, \Delta) = M(p, \Delta) + G(p, \Delta).$$

It is now clear what is needed to ensure that the matrix $\tilde{M}(p) = \lim_{\Delta \to 0} (1/\Delta) \tilde{M}(p, \Delta)$ is positive semidefinite, i.e., Hypothesis 1.2: the matrix $G(p, \Delta)$ should be "negligible" for sufficiently small $\Delta > 0$, that is to say, $\lim_{\Delta \to 0} (1/\Delta) G(p, \Delta) =: G(p)$ should be negligible. Of course, it would be sufficient to assume that the matrix $G(p)$ is positive semidefinite, yet I can see no reason in support of doing so.

A population of households is called *metonymic*[14], if the matrix $G(p)$ is negligible. This definition is intentionally somewhat vague; negligible means that the positive definiteness of the matrix $M(p)$ is not destroyed by the addition of the matrix $G(p)$. The requirement that the matrix $G(p)$ vanishes exactly describes an "ideal case." The two sets of households $I(x)$ and $I(x + \Delta)$ are disjoint subpopulations. If the distribution of x-households' demand functions (or the distribution of x-households' preferences or demographic characteristics) were identical with the distribution of $(x + \Delta)$-households' demand functions, then, of course, one would obtain

$$m^2 \{ f^i(p, x^i + \Delta) \}_{i \in I(x)} = m^2 \{ f^i(p, x^i) \}_{i \in I(x + \Delta)}$$

and hence, $G(p, \Delta) = 0$. Thus, a sufficient condition for a metonymic population is that the distribution of all relevant determinants of demand—that are different from income—are locally independent of the income level. This local independence condition is not required for every income level, yet it should be satisfied on the average.

The following example might be helpful to understand the condition of metonymy. Consider a population consisting only of one-person households that are either male or female. All males in the

---

[14]*Webster's Dictionary* defines "metonymy" as a "figure of speech that consists in using the name of one thing for that of something else with which it is associated." In the definition of a metonymic population I am using the cloud $\{ f^i(p, x^i) \}_{i \in I(x + \Delta)}$ for the cloud $\{ f^i(p, x^i + \Delta) \}_{i \in I(x)}$.

population have the same demand function $f^{\circlearrowleft}$ and all females have the same demand function $f^{\circlearrowleft}$. Let $\pi(x)$ denote the percentage of males among the x-households. If the function $\pi(x)$ depends on x, for example, if it is an increasing function, then the entire population might not be metonymic. Indeed, the distribution of x-households' demand functions is not independent of the income level x, since this distribution gives the weight $\pi(x)$ to the demand function $f^{\circlearrowleft}$ and the weight $1 - \pi(x)$ to the demand function $f^{\circlearrowleft}$. The matrix $G(p)$ in this example is equal to

$$G(p) = \int \left(f^{\circlearrowleft}(p, x) f^{\circlearrowleft}(p, x)^{\mathsf{T}} - f^{\circlearrowleft}(p, x) f^{\circlearrowleft}(p, x)^{\mathsf{T}} \right) \pi'(x) \rho(x) \, dx.$$

Thus, if the spread of male x-households' demand is different from the spread of female x-households' demand, then the matrix $G(p)$ might well not be negligible. Also, it is clear from this example, that whether the magnitude of the matrix $G(p)$ is significant depends to a large extent on the degree of commodity aggregation. For example, the spread of male and female x-households' demand for ties and bras is expected to be quite different, but does one expect also a difference for the aggregate commodity clothing? The nonmetonymic population in this example can obviously be partitioned into two metonymic subpopulations: males and females. This is all one needs.

In summary, the *hypothesis of a positive average income effect, or equivalently, the hypothesis of increasing spread of household's demand is falsifiable from cross-section data provided the entire population of households can be partitioned into metonymic subpopulations.* Indeed, for every metonymic subpopulation J one can use $m^2\{f^i(p, x^i)\}_{i \in J(x+\Delta)}$ as a proxy for $m^2\{f^i(p, x^i + \Delta)\}_{i \in J(x)}$. Consequently, one can test the hypothesis of increasing spread for every subpopulation, and since this hypothesis is additive, one obtains the hypothesis for the entire population.

1.8 Increasing Dispersion

The hypothesis of *average increasing spread of x-households' demand* [i.e., the positive semidefiniteness of the matrix $\tilde{M}(p, \Delta)$] or its observable counterpart, the hypothesis of *average increasing spread of conditional demand* [i.e., the positive semidefiniteness of the matrix $M(p, \Delta)$] are not *prima facie* plausible, even though, the second hypothesis is empirically well supported by cross-section data. One reason for this lack of intuition is that the *spread* of a cloud of vectors is not easy to visualize. If one replaces the matrix of second moments $m^2\{y^i\}_{i \in I}$ of a cloud of vectors $\{y^i\}_{i \in I}$ by its covariance matrix $\text{cov}\{y^i\}_{i \in I}$, then the degree of positive definiteness of this covariance matrix can be interpreted as a measure of *dispersion around the mean* of the cloud of vectors. I call the cloud $\{y^i\}_{i \in I}$ in $\mathbb{R}$ *more dispersed* than the cloud $\{z^j\}_{j \in J}$ in $\mathbb{R}$ if the *variance* of the first cloud is larger or equal than the variance of the second cloud. The interpretation of this definition is based on Tchebychev's inequality: For every $\eta > 0$,

$$\tfrac{1}{\#I} \#\{i \in I \mid |y^i - \text{mean}\{y^i\}| \geq \eta\} \leq \frac{\text{var}\{y^i\}}{\eta^2}.$$

The cloud of vectors $\{y^i\}_{i \in I}$ in $\mathbb{R}^l$ is called *more dispersed* than the cloud of vectors $\{z^j\}_{j \in J}$ in $\mathbb{R}^l$ if the orthogonal projection of these clouds on every straight line through the origin (see Figure 1.6) is such that the one-dimensional image cloud of $\{y^i\}_{i \in I}$ is more dispersed than the one-dimensional image cloud of $\{z^j\}_{j \in J}$. One can show that the cloud $\{y^i\}_{i \in I}$ is more dispersed than the cloud $\{z^j\}_{j \in J}$ if and only if the matrix

$$\text{cov}\{y^i\}_{i \in I} - \text{cov}\{z^j\}_{j \in J}$$

is positive semidefinite. Recall that the (h, k) element of the matrix $\text{cov}\{y^i\}_{i \in I}$ is defined by

$$\left(\text{cov}\{y^i\}_{i \in I}\right)_{h, k} = \tfrac{1}{\#I} \sum_{i \in I} y_h^i y_k^i - \left(\tfrac{1}{\#I} \sum_{i \in I} y_h^i\right)\left(\tfrac{1}{\#I} \sum_{i \in I} y_k^i\right).$$

Replacing "spread" with "dispersion" in the preceding hypothesis one can now formulate the hypothesis of *(average) increasing dispersion of x-households' demand* and the property of *(average) increasing dispersion of conditional demand*. This property of cross-section data is well supported by empirical evidence as shown in Section 3.3. It generalizes a well-known fact in applied demand analysis that is called heteroscedasticity, that is to say, the variance of x-households' demand for commodity h is *not constant*, but increasing in income (see Figures 3.6 and 3.7).

In the case where the demand function satisfies the budget identity $p \cdot f(p, x) \equiv x$, the hypothesis of increasing dispersion of x-households' demand is weaker than the hypothesis of increasing spread of x-households' demand (for details, see Appendix 5). It

is shown in Chapter 3 that the hypothesis of a negative average substitution effect and the hypothesis of increasing dispersion imply
Wald's Axiom for mean demand.

The concept of dispersion, which is easier to interpret than the
concept of spread, can be used for a deductive validation of the property of average increasing spread of conditional demand, which
is essential—as I have shown—for deriving the Law of Market
Demand.

Indeed, the following decomposition of the matrix $M(p) = \lim_{\Delta \to 0}(1/\Delta)M(p, \Delta)$ holds:

$$M(p) = C_\rho + B(\bar{f}, \rho),$$

where

$$C_\rho := \int_{\mathbb{R}_+} \partial_x \, \text{cov}\{f^i(p, x^i)\}_{i \in I(x)} \, \rho(x) \, dx,$$

$$B(\bar{f}, \rho) := \int_{\mathbb{R}_+} \partial_x \left(\bar{f}(p, x) \bar{f}(p, x)^\mathsf{T} \right) \rho(x) \, dx,$$

and

$$\bar{f}(p, x) := \tfrac{1}{\#I(x)} \sum_{i \in I(x)} f^i(p, x^i)$$

denotes the mean demand of x-households.

Consequently, *the property of average increasing dispersion of conditional demand*, that is to say, the positive semidefiniteness of the
matrix C_ρ *implies the property of average increasing spread of conditional demand*, i.e., the positive semidefiniteness of the matrix $M(p)$,
provided the matrix $B(\bar{f}, \rho)$ is positive semidefinite.

Therefore, under metonymy, the property of average increasing
dispersion of conditional demand and the positive semidefiniteness
of the matrix $B(\bar{f}, \rho)$ imply Hypothesis 1.2, the positive semidefiniteness of the average income effect matrix $\bar{A}$.

The structure of the matrix $B(\bar{f}, \rho)$ is discussed in Section 4.3
and in Appendix 6. It is easy to show that the matrix $B(\bar{f}, \rho)$ is always
positive semidefinite if the density ρ of the income distribution is a
decreasing function on $\mathbb{R}_+$ as illustrated in Figure 1.9.

Estimates of the density of the income distribution (see Figures
2.8 and 2.9) are, however, not decreasing for low income levels. It
is shown in Section 4.3 that for these income distributions one still
obtains a positive semidefinite matrix $B(\bar{f}, \rho)$ if the cross-section
Engel curves $x \mapsto \bar{f}_h(p, x)$ can be approximated on the relevant

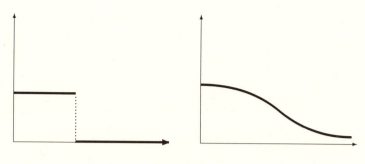

Figure 1.9.

domain of the income distribution by low degree polynomials, for example, polynomials of degree 6.

This completes the short description of the main results of this book.

In Chapter 2, I formulate a microeconomic model of a consumption sector—the μ-model—and explain how certain properties of the market demand function can be falsified, at least in principle, by cross-section data. A short description of the data—the UK Family Expenditure Survey and the French Enquête Budget de Famille—is presented.

In Chapter 3, I discuss various versions of the hypothesis of increasing dispersion. It is shown that the hypothesis of increasing dispersion of the households' demand implies Wald's Axiom for market demand. The empirical support of the various hypotheses of increasing dispersion is discussed in great detail. Finally, in Chapter 4, I discuss the hypothesis of increasing spread and show that this hypothesis implies the Law of Demand. Again, the empirical support of the hypothesis of increasing spread is discussed.

In the Appendices are presented some more or less known mathematical results, which play an important role throughout the book.

Chapter 2

Market Demand

> But economics is not, in the end, much interested in the behaviour of single individuals. Its concern is with the behaviour of groups. A study of indiviual demand is only a means to the study of market demand.

—J. R. Hicks, *Value and Capital*, (1946), p. 34

2.1   The Distribution of Households' Demand

Throughout this book, market demand refers to a large group of households called the *population* of households. These households are considered at a certain *time period*, for example, the year 1992 or the first quarter of 1993. I have in mind households of a certain region, for example, all private households in the United Kingdom. The whole population might be quite heterogeneous. If necessary I shall consider later subpopulations that are stratified in a suitable way. I want to model the *mean demand* function, also called the *market demand*, of this population. Mean demand thus is average demand per household, not per individual.

In the microeconomic theory of demand it is always assumed that all commodities—goods and services—that can be demanded are described by their physical properties in such a way that *quantity* and *price* are well-defined. This is not a harmless assumption, even if it might seem so. Grade A carrots or white sugar are probably commodities of this type; yet even tea is more problematic.[1] Food or dairy products and clothing or footwear are not commodities in this sense. It is obvious that this notion of commodities—called *microeconomic* or *elementary commodities*—requires a very detailed description of the physical properties, and consequently, one has to consider a very large number l of elementary commodities. For the pure theory this does not cause any complication since the high dimension of the commodity space $\mathbb{R}^l$ does not create any problem as long as it is finite. However, difficulties do occur, in fact, if one wants to confront the theory with actual demand statistics. Family expenditure surveys, for example, that are available for many countries, do not refer to these elementary commodities. They report for every household in the sample the *expenditure* (in money, say DM or ECU) on various consumption categories, like food, housing, or clothing. For example, the category "food" is composed of a wide variety of items, for which a detailed list is given: potatoes (raw, crisp, tinned, and frozen chips), tomatoes (fresh, canned, bottled, and frozen, not tomato juice), etc. More details on family expenditure surveys are given in Section 2.4.

I shall explain later in Section 2.3 of this chapter to what extent such expenditure data can be used to falsify certain hypotheses in the pure theory of demand with reference to elementary commodities as described in the preceding text.

Let me now explain the basic concepts of microeconomic demand theory that I shall draw upon in the rest of the book. From now on I will assume that $\mathbb{R}^l$ denotes the space of elementary commodities.

I denote by y^i the commodity vector in $\mathbb{R}^l$ that is chosen by household i of the given population G during the given time period. Thus, y^i describes *current* consumption. The value of this consumption vector y^i with respect to the prevailing price system $p \in \mathbb{R}^l$, i.e.,

---

[1]"The question where the lines of division between different commodities should be drawn must be settled by convenience of the particular discussion. For some purposes it may be best to regard Chinese and Indian teas, or even Souchong and Pekoe teas, as different commodities; and to have a separate demand schedule for each of them. While for other purposes it may be best to group together commodities as distinct as beef and mutton or even as tea or coffee, and to have a single list to represent the demand for the two combined; but in such a case of course some convention must be made as to the number of ounces of tea which are taken as equivalent to a pound of coffee." Marshall (1920), p. 100.

$\sum_{k=1}^{l} p_k y_k^i =: p \cdot y^i$, is the current *total expenditure* on all commodities (goods and services) of household i and is denoted by e^i. The current *disposable income* is denoted by x^i. The collection $\{y^i, x^i\}_{i \in G}$ and p represents the ideal cross-section data. One expects that the collection of vectors $\{y^i\}_{i \in G}$ depends on the prevailing price system p, expected future prices, current and expected income, and past consumption, as well as on certain household characteristics that might be observable (like household composition, geographical region, religion, occupation, sex, etc.) or unobservable (like preferences). One cannot decide from these observations alone whether the current total expenditure e^i depends on the price vector p, whether household i has chosen the commodity vector y^i *given* current total expenditure e^i, or whether e^i is simply the consequence of the decision y^i, and hence, depends on p and x^i. For many households current total expenditure e^i is different from current disposable income x^i. For example, according to the UK Family Expenditure Survey[2] for the year 1985, average (over the whole population) disposable income per week is £174.67 and average total expenditure on goods and services per week is £161.87. If one stratifies the population by income classes (income, not disposable income!), then the average (over the income class) weekly disposable income and total expenditure are given in Table 2.1.

The population of households is assumed to be very large and heterogeneous. Therefore, it is convenient and appropriate to describe the collection $\{y^i\}_{i \in G}$ of demand vectors by its *distribution* on the commodity space $\mathbb{R}^l$. This distribution depends on p and is denoted by $\nu(p)$. Thus, for any subset B in $\mathbb{R}^l$, $\nu(p)(B)$ describes the relative number of households in the population whose demand vector y^i lies in B, i.e.,

$$\nu(p)(B) := \tfrac{1}{\#G} \cdot \#\{i \in G \mid y^i \in B\}.$$

The distribution $\nu(p)$ is called the *distribution of household demand* at the price system p.

Clearly, the mean of the distribution $\nu(p)$ of household demand is just the market demand of the population, which I shall denote by $F(p)$. This notation indicates that emphasis is put on the dependence of market demand on the price system. Then the typical question is:

---

[2] For a definition of total expenditure on goods and services, disposable income, and income see Section 2.4.

Table 2.1.

Income Group	Total Expenditure per Week (£)	Disposable Income per Week (£)	Total Number of Households Observed
[0, 40]	43.71	33.93	368
[40, 50]	46.43	44.11	362
[50, 65]	64.61	57.75	418
[65, 80]	78.01	70.78	428
[80, 100]	94.69	86.46	429
[100, 125]	113.15	102.89	430
[125, 150]	127.20	120.32	456
[150, 175]	139.64	137.40	464
[175, 200]	154.31	155.16	449
[200, 225]	170.43	172.52	392
[225, 250]	173.72	190.29	417
[250, 300]	197.24	216.28	681
[300, 350]	226.45	252.66	551
[350, 400]	249.38	292.01	354
[400, 500]	297.62	338.01	445
[500, ∞]	383.46	502.82	368
Average over the whole population			
216.23	161.87	174.67	7012

Source: FES-Report 1985, Tables 5, 8, 22 (pp. 8, 24, 66)

If at the prevailing price system p the market demand is $F(p)$, what would be the market demand $F(q)$ if the price system were q? This question refers to a hypothetical situation since both price systems p and q refer to the same period and the same population. Surely, one only expects a qualitative answer to this type of question. As explained in the Introduction, I am particularly interested whether a price change from p to q that induces a demand change from $F(p)$ to $F(q)$ satisfies

$$(p - q) \cdot \left(F(p) - F(q)\right) < 0,$$

that is to say, the vector $(p-q)$ of price changes and the vector $F(p) - F(q)$ of changes in market demand point in opposite directions. The Law of Demand asserts that this holds for any price change.

If one wants to know how the distribution $v(p)$ and, hence the market demand $F(p)$ depends on the price system p, one has to make assumptions on hypothetical situations because one can observe the distribution $v(p)$ only at the prevailing prices. If one makes assumptions on hypothetical situations, one is building a theory. Theory is not a description of facts; it deals with hypothetical or not yet observed situations. The difficulty at present is, of course, that one does not know how the distribution $v(p)$ of household demand depends on the price system p. Consequently, we have to *model how the distribution $v(p)$ is generated*. Traditional microeconomics gives a hypothetical answer to this question.

Remark.   Before I explain how traditional microeconomics closes this gap, I would like to mention that I do not know of any successful alternative for modelling directly the dependence of $v(p)$ on p. There is, of course, the well-known example of Becker (1962). In this example it is assumed that the collection $\{y^i\}_{i \in G}$ of demand vectors at the price system p is a very large random sample from a hypothetical smooth distribution $\tilde{v}(p)$ on $\mathbb{R}^l_+$. Since the sample is very large one can use this hypothetical distribution $\tilde{v}(p)$ instead of the sample distribution $v(p)$ (Glivenko–Cantelli theorem). Consider now for every price vector p the conditional distribution $\tilde{v}(p|x)$ of $\tilde{v}(p)$ on the expenditure set $B(p, x) = \{z \in \mathbb{R}^l_+ \mid p \cdot z = x\}$, and assume that for every expenditure level x, this conditional distribution $\tilde{v}(p|x)$ is the *uniform distribution* on $B(p, x)$! This amounts to saying that all households who spend x choose "at random" and stochastically independently in the expenditure set $B(p, x)$. Then, the market demand function of a large population is approximately equal to the mean of $\tilde{v}(p)$, which is equal to

$$F(p) = \frac{\bar{x}}{l} \begin{pmatrix} \frac{1}{p_1} \\ \vdots \\ \frac{1}{p_l} \end{pmatrix},$$

where $\bar{x}$ denotes the mean (over the whole population) of total expenditure. Hence the Jacobian matrix $\partial_p F(p)$ is a diagonal matrix with negative elements on the diagonal. Thus the Law of Demand holds.

For this specific result on the dependence of mean $v(p)$ on p one does not actually need the unplausible restrictive assumption that $v(p|x)$ is the uniform distribution. What is needed is that the random vector of expenditure shares, $s^i_h = p_h y^i_h / x^i$ $(h = 1, \ldots, l)$, have a distribution that is independent of the price system. Indeed, consider a sequence $i = 1, 2, \ldots$ of households with random demand vectors y^i. Assume now that the random expenditure share,

$$s_h^i = \frac{p_h y_h^i}{x^i}, \qquad h = 1, \ldots, l,$$

is such that its expectation $E s_h^i$ *does not depend on the price system* p! This amounts to assuming that the random demand y_h^i for commodity h of household i who spends x^i is equal to $(x^i/p_h)s_h^i$. Furthermore, assume that the law of large numbers applies to the sequence (y^i), i.e.,

$$\frac{1}{n} \sum_{i=1}^{n} (y^i - Ey^i)$$

converges to zero (either in probability or almost everywhere). Then, for large n, the random mean demand is approximately equal to

$$\frac{1}{p_h} \left(\frac{1}{n} \sum_{i=1}^{n} x^i E s_h^i \right) =: F_h(p).$$

Hence the Jacobian matrix $\partial_p F(p)$ is a negative diagonal matrix. If the expected expenditure share $E s_h^i$ does not depend on the individual households i, as in Becker's example, i.e., $E s_h^i = \beta_h$ for every i, then one obtains for the market demand the Cobb–Douglas demand function

$$F_h(p) = \frac{\bar{x}}{p_h} \beta_h.$$

The question, of course, is why should the expected expenditure share $E s_h^i$ be price independent?

2.2 A Microeconomic Model: The Distribution of Households' Characteristics

It is a well-established empirical fact (see for example Table 2.1), that for many households total expenditure $e^i = p \cdot y^i$ in the current period is different from current disposable income x^i. The difference $x^i - p \cdot y^i =: s(p, x)$ is called current savings and can be positive (saving) or negative (dissaving). Consequently, the commodity vector y^i, demanded by household i in the current period, has to be modelled as the result of an intertemporal decision problem. Many economists view this intertemporal decision problem as a multiperiod preference maximization problem under budget constraints and uncertainty. Formulating this intertemporal decision problem in full generality is quite complex. It requires a specification of the planning horizon, i.e., the number of periods that are considered in the preference maximization, a specification of the intertemporal preference relation, and a specification of the intertemporal budget constraints that involves expectations about future income, future prices, and future interest rates. This decision problem is often simplified by assuming sufficient separability of the preference relation. I do not think that it is very useful if I write down such an intertemporal decision problem. For the present analysis only *current period demand* matters, even though this current period demand is part of a larger decision problem. Expenditure in the current period, of course, then depends on many things: current and expected future prices, current and expected future income, time preference, etc.

Without much justification I take the usual shortcut and consider the *current period demand* vector y^i as a *function* $f^i(p, x)$ in the *current period price vector* p and *current period (disposable) income* x^i. Thus all determinants of demand other than p and x^i—past consumption, price-income expectations, etc.—are summarized in the function f^i. It follows, in particular, that different households will have different demand functions. Current income x^i is assumed to be exogenous; hence, current income is independent of the current price system.

Every household is then described by a short-run (current) *demand function* f^i and a level of *current disposable income* x^i. I shall refer to (x^i, f^i) as the *household characteristics*.

To define a microeconomic model of a large and heterogeneous population of households, one has first to specify the *space $\mathscr{F}$ of admissible demand functions*. The *space of household characteristics* then is defined by the Cartesian product

$$\mathbb{R}_+ \times \mathscr{F}.$$

Every household is now described by a point (x^i, f^i) in the space $\mathbb{R}_+ \times \mathscr{F}$, which is illustrated in Figure 2.1. Households that differ either in demand behavior or in current income are represented by different points in $\mathbb{R}_+ \times \mathscr{F}$.

A *distribution* μ on the space of household characteristics $\mathbb{R}_+ \times \mathscr{F}$ now induces, for every price vector $p \in \mathbb{R}_{++}^l$, the

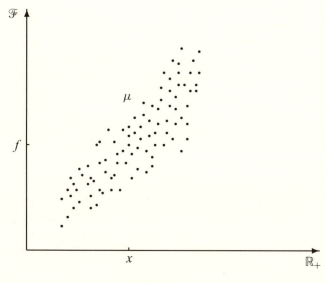

Figure 2.1.

distribution $v(p)$ of household demand on the commodity space $\mathbb{R}^l$. Indeed, the distribution $v(p)$ is defined as the image measure of μ under the mapping $(x, f) \longmapsto f(p, x) = y$. That is to say,

$$v(p)\{B\} = \mu\{(x, f) \in \mathbb{R}_+ \times \mathcal{F} \mid f(p, x) \in B\}.$$

The mean of the distribution $v(p)$ was called the market demand at the price system p. In terms of the distribution μ one obtains the following definition:

Definition. The market demand of a distribution μ of household characteristics in $\mathbb{R}_+ \times \mathcal{F}$ is defined by

$$F(p) := \int_{\mathbb{R}_+ \times \mathcal{F}} f(p, x) \, d\mu.$$

Note that the market demand function $F(\cdot)$ depends on the distribution μ and should more correctly be denoted by $F(p, \mu)$ or $F_\mu(p)$. However, as long as the distribution μ of household characteristics is fixed, μ is dropped in the notation.

Remark. This definition of market demand requires a technical remark, since I would like to apply this definition for more general distributions than those that are concentrated on finitely many characteristics in $\mathbb{R}_+ \times \mathscr{F}$. In such cases, the space $\mathscr{F}$ of admissible demand functions has to be defined more carefully. The simplest way is to assume that $\mathscr{F}$ is finite. If one finds this too restrictive, then one can assume that $\mathscr{F}$ is a *closed* subset in the space of all continuous demand functions endowed with the topology of uniform convergence on compact subsets. In both cases, the space $\mathscr{F}$, and hence the product space $\mathbb{R}_+ \times \mathscr{F}$, is a complete separable metric space. Now one can consider any distribution (i.e., positive, normalized, σ-additive measure) on the Borelian subsets of the complete separable metric space $\mathbb{R}_+ \times \mathscr{F}$. I shall always assume that the marginal distribution of current disposable income x of such a distribution μ has a finite mean and that the integral defining mean demand, $F(p) = \int_{\mathbb{R}_+ \times \mathscr{F}} f(p, x) \, d\mu$, is well-defined and finite.

It will be convenient in the sequel to assume that the income distribution has a *density*, which is always denoted by ρ. Since I am interested only in large populations that are heterogeneous in income, this assumption can easily be justified. Also it is convenient to assume that the support, supp(ρ), of the income distribution is an interval, that is to say, $\{x \in \mathbb{R}_+ \mid \rho(x) > 0\}$ is an interval.

For every level of current disposable income x in the support of the income distribution, one can consider the subpopulation of all households with current disposable income x. I call this subpopulation the "x-households." The mean demand $\bar{f}(p, x)$ of all x-households is defined by

$$\bar{f}(p, x) := \int_{\mathscr{F}} f(p, x) \, d\mu|x,$$

where $\mu|x$ denotes the conditional distribution on $\mathscr{F}$ of x-household demand functions. The function $\bar{f}(p, \cdot)$ of supp(ρ) into $\mathbb{R}^l$ is called the *cross-section Engel function* and the function $\bar{f}_h(p, \cdot)$ is called the *cross-section Engel curve* for commodity h. Note that the function $\bar{f}$ depends on the distribution μ and should more correctly be denoted by $\bar{f}^\mu$.

With this notation, for the market demand function one obtains

$$F(p) = \int_{\mathbb{R}_+} \bar{f}(p, x)\rho(x) \, dx.$$

In the definition of market demand,

$$F(p) = \int_{\mathbb{R}_+ \times \mathscr{F}} f(p, x) \, d\mu,$$

the variables over which it is integrated are the demand function f and the level of current disposable income x. The following change in notation will sometimes clarify the presentation. Assume that the admissible demand functions in $\mathcal{F}$ are parametrized by a parameter α in some set $\mathcal{A}$. Thus, instead of f in $\mathcal{F}$ I shall write now f^α with $\alpha \in \mathcal{A}$. This is no restriction since the parameter space $\mathcal{A}$ can be any complete separable metric space (for example, the space of all admissible demand functions itself). I now replace everywhere $\mathcal{F}$ by $\mathcal{A}$. Thus, the distribution μ is defined on the space of household characteristics $\mathbb{R}_+ \times \mathcal{A}$ and market demand is defined by

$$F(p) = \int_{\mathbb{R}_+ \times \mathcal{A}} f^\alpha(p, x)\, d\mu.$$

This integral is now taken over the variables α and x.

If one wants to describe individual behavior as preference maximization under budget constraints, then one can parametrize the demand functions by preference relations. Thus, the parameter space $\mathcal{A}$ is replaced by the set $\mathcal{P}$ of binary relations on $\mathbb{R}_+^l$, which are complete, transitive, smooth, and strongly convex. Every such relation $\precsim$ determines a continuously differentiable demand function $f^{\precsim}$ in the variables p and x by the hypothesis of preference maximization under budget constraints. The set $\mathcal{P}$ can be endowed with a metric such that $\mathcal{P}$ becomes a complete separable metric space.

A distribution μ on $\mathbb{R}_+ \times \mathcal{P}$, i.e., a joint distribution of preferences and income, then defines the microeconomic model of a population.

N.B. If in the future I refer to the μ-model, I shall always assume that the following assumptions are satisfied.

Standard Assumptions for the μ-Model

Assumption 1. *The distribution μ is defined on a complete separable metric space $\mathbb{R}_+ \times \mathcal{A}$ of household characteristics, i.e., μ is a probability measure on the σ-field of Borelian subsets of $\mathbb{R}_+ \times \mathcal{A}$.*

Assumption 1 is of a rather technical nature. It avoids certain measure theoretical complications. For example, it follows that for every x in the support of the income distribution, a conditional distribution $\mu|x$ on $\mathcal{A}$ always exists.

Assumption 2. *There exists a density ρ of the marginal distribution of income, the mean income $\bar{x} = \int_{\mathbb{R}_+} x\rho(x)\, dx$ is finite.*

Assumption 2 can easily be justified for a large and heterogeneous population.

Assumption 3. *The household demand functions $f^\alpha(p, x)$ are continuous in (α, p, x) and continuously differentiable in p and x; furthermore, differentiation with respect to prices and integration is interchangeable (Leibniz rule),*

$$\partial_p \int_{\mathbb{R}_+ \times \mathcal{A}} f^\alpha(p, x) \, d\mu = \int_{\mathbb{R}_+ \times \mathcal{A}} \partial_p f^\alpha(p, x) \, d\mu$$

and

$$\partial_p \int_{\mathcal{A}} f^\alpha(p, x) \, d\mu | x = \int_{\mathcal{A}} \partial_p f^\alpha(p, x) \, d\mu | x.$$

Whether continuity or differentiability of household demand functions is an acceptable assumption depends very much on the nature of the commodities. On an aggregate level (see the Hicks–Leontief composite commodity theorem, Section 2.3), this seems to be an acceptable approximation. The assumption that Leibniz rule can be applied for differentiation with respect to prices is not restrictive because, by assumption, the distributions μ and $\mu|x$ do not depend on the price vector p.

Assumption 4. *The hypothesis of a nonpositive average substitution effect, i.e., the average Slutsky substitution matrix*

$$\bar{S}(p) = \int_{\mathbb{R}_+ \times \mathcal{A}} Sf^\alpha(p, x) \, d\mu,$$

is negative semidefinite.

Assumption 4 is of a different nature than the other assumption made so far since it is an a priori hypothesis on the demand behavior of the households that is formulated in terms of the Slutsky substitution matrices of the short-run demand functions.

To understand what is implicitly assumed on the demand behavior and the formation of expectations one has to go back to the definition of the Slutsky substitution matrix.

The situation is simple for a household who does not save, that is to say, the short-run demand function $f(p, x)$ of this household satisfies the budget identity $p \cdot f(p, x) = x$ for all p, x in a neighborhood of the the prevailing price system $\bar{p}$ and the current income $\bar{x}$. In this case, it is well-known (Appendix 3) that the Slutsky substitution matrix $Sf(\bar{p}, \bar{x})$ at $(\bar{p}, \bar{x})$ is negative semidefinite if and only if the demand function f satisfies in a neighborhood U of $(\bar{p}, \bar{x})$ the Weak Axiom of Revealed Preference, i.e., for every (p, x) and (p', x') in U,

$$p' \cdot f(p, x) \leq x' \quad \text{implies} \quad p \cdot f(p', x') \geq x.$$

The standard example for this case is a household whose demand function is the solution of an *atemporal utility maximization* problem:

$$f(p, x) = \arg \max_{p \cdot y \leq x} U(y).$$

Let us now consider a household who saves; then, the budget-identity does not hold. Consequently, the short-run demand function of such a household must be viewed as a multiperiod *temporal* decision problem. In this case, the Slutsky substitution matrix $Sf(p, x)$ is defined as the Jacobian matrix, evaluated at $q = p$, of the "compensated" demand function

$$q \mapsto f(q, x(q)),$$

where the "compensated income" is defined by

$$x(q) = x - p \cdot f(p, x) + q \cdot f(p, x).$$

Thus,

$$Sf(p, x) = \partial_q f(q, x(q)) \,|_{q=p}.$$

With this compensated income $x(q)$ the household can save the same amount as before the price change, i.e., $x - p \cdot f(p, x)$, and can still buy the old consumption vector $f(p, x)$ at the new price vector q. Of course, if the price change from p to q effects the next period price expectation, then the expected purchasing power in the next period of the saving $x - p \cdot f(p, x)$ is not the same. Thus, the term "compensated income" might be misleading. The reason I have defined the compensated income $x(q)$ by $x - p \cdot f(p, x) + q \cdot f(p, x)$ is simply that this definition implies the Slutsky decomposition of the Jacobian matrix

$$\partial_p f(p, x) = Sf(p, x) - Af(p, x),$$

where the matrix $Sf(p, x)$ is defined previously and $Af(p, x) := \partial_x f(p, x) f(p, x)^{\mathsf{T}}$ is the usual income effect matrix.

The assumption of a negative semidefinite Slutsky substitution matrix $Sf(p, x)$ amounts to assuming that the compensated demand function $q \mapsto f(q, x(q))$ is monotone at $q = p$, i.e.,

$$(p - q) \cdot (f(p, x) - f(q, x(q))) \leq 0$$

for all q in a neighborhood of p.

I have now to clarify the circumstances under which the temporal decision problem leads to a negative semidefinite Slutsky substitution matrix $Sf(p, x)$.

If the demand behavior of a household is modelled as the solution of a multiperiod *temporal* utility maximization problem, then the current demand depends on current prices and current income, as well as on *expected* future prices and interest rates and expected future income. If these expectations were exogenous, that is to say, if they do not depend on current prices and current income, then one can show that the hypothesis of temporal utility maximization implies that the Slutsky substitution matrix $Sf(p, x)$, as defined previously, is negative semi-definite. However, typically the expectations on future prices and income depend on current prices and current income. In this case the hypothesis of temporal utility maximization alone does not imply a non-positive Slutsky substitution effect. As long as one does not formulate specific assumptions on the formation of expectations the hypothesis of temporal utility maximization does not imply any useful property of the short-run demand function. This discussion should clarify why I claimed in the Introduction that there are certainly no a priori reasons why the Slutsky substitution matrix of the short-run demand function should be negative semidefinite in all circumstances.

Assumption 4 does not require that the Slutsky substitution matrix be negative semidefinite for *every* household; only the *average* (over the whole population) of these matrices is assumed to be negative semidefinite. This alone, of course, does not justify Assumption 4. For the time being, Assumption 4 is taken simply for granted; the assumption is not submitted to an empirical test, nor do I have a satisfactory deductive justification. I hope one can do better one day!

Examples

I shall now describe two examples of μ-models. In Chapters 3 and 4, I shall refer to these examples to illustrate the hypothesis and assumptions on which I shall base the theory of market demand that is developed in this book.

To obtain an example for a μ-model one has first to specify the *distribution of income*. Then one has to specify the *conditional distribution $\mu|x$ of x-household demand functions* for every x in the support of the income distribution.

Example 1: Assume that the income distribution has a density ρ satisfying Assumption 2. Consider a finite collection $\{f^1, \ldots, f^n\}$ of demand functions satisfying the first part of Assumption 3 and assume that the Slutsky substitution matrix $Sf^i(p, x)$ is negative semidefinite. Let $\pi_i(x) \geq 0$ with $\sum_{i=1}^n \pi_i(x) = 1$ for every $x \in \text{supp}(\rho)$. The number $\pi_i(x)$ is interpreted as the fraction of x-households with demand function f^i. It is now clear how the conditional distribution $\mu|x$ of x-household demand functions is defined:

$$\mu|x(f^i) = \pi_i(x).$$

The density ρ and the conditional distributions $\mu|x$, $x \in \text{supp}(\rho)$, define a μ-model that satisfies the standard assumptions. Note that Assumption 1 and the second part of Assumption 3 are trivially satisfied because $\mathcal{A} = \{1, \ldots, n\}$ is a finite set.

The cross-section Engel function is

$$\bar{f}(p, x) = \sum_{i=1}^n \pi_i(x) f^i(p, x).$$

Note that $\bar{f}$ is, in general, not homogeneous in (p, x) even though all functions f^i are homogeneous in (p, x).

The market demand function F is

$$F(p) = \int_0^\infty \sum_{i=1}^n \pi_i(x) f^i(p, x)\rho(x)\, dx.$$

Example 2: **The Model of Grandmont (1992).** Grandmont (1992) starts from the assumption that a large population of households can be decomposed into particular subpopulations, called *types*. A type consists of many households, all of them have the same income, yet their demand functions are different (heterogeneity of consumption behavior or preferences). Furthermore, they are different in a well-defined specific way: there exists a demand function $g(p, \xi)$ such that for every household there is a vector $\alpha \in \mathbb{R}_+^l$, which determines the demand function of this household by the formula

$$f^\alpha(p, \xi) = T_\alpha g(T_\alpha p, \xi),$$

where T_α denotes the diagonal matrix with α on the diagonal. Thus, the demand functions of all households of a given type are parametrized by vectors α in $\mathbb{R}_+^l$. This is illustrated in Figure 2.2 for a generating function g that satisfies $p \cdot g(p, x) \equiv x$.

Note that if the generating demand function g is derived from a preference relation $\precsim$ (or utility function u), then f^α is derived from the preference relation $\precsim^\alpha$ defined by

$$z \succsim^\alpha y \quad \text{if and only if} \quad T_{1/\alpha} z \succsim T_{1/\alpha} y$$

[or the utility u^α defined by $u^\alpha(z) = u(T_{1/\alpha} z)$], where $T_{1/\alpha}$ denotes the diagonal matrix with $1/\alpha_k$ on the kth row.

For a complete description of a type, one has to specify the distribution of the parameter α, which is done by a density η on $\mathbb{R}_+^l$.

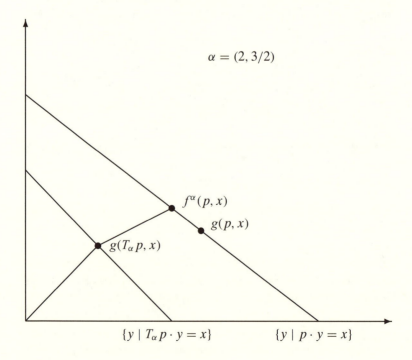

Figure 2.2.

In summary, a type of households is defined by the common level, x, of income, the generating demand function g, and the density η on $\mathbb{R}_+^l$. The mean demand of the type $[x, g, \eta]$ is then defined by

$$\int_{\mathbb{R}_+^l} f^\alpha(p, x)\eta(\alpha)\, d\alpha,$$

where $f^\alpha(p, x) = T_\alpha g(T_\alpha p, x)$.

The entire population might consist of many types with the same income level x, yet different generating functions g or densities η. To simplify the notation I shall assume that x-households consists of only *one* type $[x, g_x, \eta_x]$. Note that the generating demand function $g(p, \xi)$ and the density $\eta(\alpha)$ of the type of x-households can depend on the income level x. Thus, the mean demand of all x-households is given by

$$\bar{f}(p, x) = \int_{\mathbb{R}_+^l} T_\alpha g_x(T_\alpha p, x)\eta_x(\alpha)\, d\alpha,$$

and market demand F of the entire population is equal to

$$F(p) = \int_{\mathbb{R}_+} \left[\int_{\mathbb{R}_+^l} T_\alpha g_x(T_\alpha p, x)\eta_x(\alpha)\, d\alpha \right] \rho(x)\, dx.$$

To see that Grandmont's model is actually an example of a μ-model, one must define the parameter space $\mathcal{A} = \mathbb{R}_+^l \times G$, where G is a closed set of generating demand functions $g_x(p, \xi)$. A distribution μ on $\mathbb{R}_+ \times \mathcal{A}$ then must have the property that the conditional distribution $\mu|x$ is concentrated on $\mathbb{R}_+^l \times \{g_x\}$. Consequently, one can identify the conditional distribution $\mu|x$ on $\mathcal{A}$ with the density η_x on $\mathbb{R}_+^l$.

The standard assumptions on the μ-model can easily be expressed in terms of the generating demand functions g_x and the densities η_x, which define the type of x-households. Only Assumption 4 merits special attention. If one assumes that the generating demand function g of the type of x-households satisfies the Weak Axiom of Revealed Preference, then, as it is easy to verify, the demand functions f^α also have this property. Thus, in this case, Assumption 4 is trivially satisfied.

The interesting point is that Grandmont *does not assume* that the generating demand function g satisfies the Weak Axiom of Revealed Preference. Then, of course, none of the Slutsky substitution matrices $Sf^\alpha(p, x)$ needs to be negative semidefinite. Consequently, in general, there is no reason why Assumption 4 should be satisfied.

However, one can show (a proof follows) that for every differentiable generating demand function $g(p, \xi)$, which is homogeneous in (p, ξ), i.e., $g(\lambda p, \lambda \xi) = g(p, \xi)$, $\lambda > 0$, and satisfies the budget identity $p \cdot g(p, \xi) \equiv \xi$, the *average Slutsky substitution matrix*

$$\bar{S}(p, x) = \int_{\mathbb{R}^l_+} Sf^\alpha(p, x)\eta(\alpha)\, d\alpha$$

is *"nearly" negative semidefinite if the density η is differentiable and vanishes on the boundary of $\mathbb{R}^l_+$, and if the following expression $(*)$ is sufficiently small:*

$$\max_k \int_{\mathbb{R}^l_+} \left|\partial_{\alpha_k}\big(\alpha_k\eta(\alpha)\big)\right| d\alpha. \qquad (*)$$

Let γ denote the density of $\log \alpha = (\log \alpha_1, \ldots, \log \alpha_l)$. If γ is differentiable on $\mathbb{R}^l$, then one easily verifies that

$$\int_{\mathbb{R}^l} \left|\partial_{\beta_k}\gamma(\beta)\right| d\beta = \int_{\mathbb{R}^l_+} \left|\partial_{\alpha_k}\big(\alpha_k\eta(\alpha)\big)\right| d\alpha.$$

Thus, the expression $(*)$ is arbitrarily small if the density γ is sufficiently "flat" in the sense of Grandmont, that is to say, if $\max_k \int_{\mathbb{R}^l} \left|\partial_{\beta_k}\gamma(\beta)\right| d\beta$ is sufficiently small.

Grandmont's example shows that Assumption 4 of the standard assumptions is actually weaker than assuming that all Slutsky substitution matrices are negative semidefinite.

The assumption of a sufficiently "flat" density of $\log \alpha$ is very powerful; it implies that the market demand has surprisingly strong properties. It suffices to explain this for the mean demand of one type of households. Let

$$s_h^\alpha(p, x) := \frac{1}{x} p_h f_h^\alpha(p, x)$$

denote the *expenditure share* on commodity h and

$$\bar{s}_h(p, x) := \int_{\mathbb{R}^l_+} s_h^\alpha(p, x)\eta(\alpha)\, d\alpha$$

denote the *mean expenditure share* on commodity h of the type $[x, g, \eta]$. Since $f_h^\alpha(p, x) = \alpha_h g_h(T_\alpha p, x)$, one obtains

$$\bar{s}_h(p, x) = \frac{1}{x} \int_{\mathbb{R}^l_+} p_h\alpha_h g_h(T_\alpha p, x)\eta(\alpha)\, d\alpha,$$

and by substituting $\alpha_h = \beta_h/p_h$, this implies

$$\bar{s}_h(p, x) = \frac{1}{x} \int_{\mathbb{R}_+^l} \beta_h g_h(\beta, x) \frac{1}{p_1} \cdots \frac{1}{p_l} \eta\left(\frac{\beta_1}{p_1}, \ldots, \frac{\beta_K}{p_l}\right) d\beta.$$

If one computes the partial derivative $\partial_{p_i} \bar{s}_h(p, x)$ and substitutes again $\beta_i = \alpha_i p_i$, then one obtains

$$\partial_{p_i} \bar{s}_h(p, x) = -\frac{1}{x p_i} \int_{\mathbb{R}_+^l} p_h \alpha_h g_h(T_\alpha p, x) \partial_{\alpha_i}(\alpha_i \eta(\alpha)) d\alpha,$$

and, hence,

$$\left| \partial_{p_i} \bar{s}_h(p, x) \right| \leq \frac{1}{p_i} \int_{\mathbb{R}_+^l} \left| \partial_{\alpha_i}(\alpha_i \eta(\alpha)) \right| d\alpha.$$

A sufficiently "flat" density of $\log \alpha$ then implies that all elements of the matrix $\partial_p \bar{s}(p, x)$ are nearly zero, and, consequently, *the Jacobian matrix $\partial_p \bar{f}(p, x)$ is nearly diagonal with a negative diagonal* since

$$\partial_{p_i} \bar{f}_h(p, x) = \frac{x}{p_h} \partial_{p_i} \bar{s}_h(p, x) \quad \text{for } i \neq h$$

and

$$\partial_{p_h} \bar{f}_h(p, x) = -\frac{1}{p_h} \bar{f}_h(p, x) + \frac{x}{p_h} \partial_{p_h} \bar{s}_h(p, x) \quad \text{for } i = h.$$

This result on the structure of the Jacobian matrix $\partial_p \bar{f}(p, x)$ can now be used to prove the foregoing claim that the average Slutsky substitution matrix

$$\bar{S}(p, x) := \int_{\mathbb{R}_+^l} Sf^\alpha(p, x) \eta(\alpha) d\alpha$$

is nearly negative semidefinite if the density of $\log \alpha$ is sufficiently "flat".

By the Slutsky decomposition it follows that

$$\bar{S}(p, x) = \partial_p \bar{f}(p, x) + \int_{\mathbb{R}_+^l} (\partial_x f^\alpha(p, x)) f^\alpha(p, x)^\mathsf{T} \eta(\alpha) d\alpha.$$

If $f^\alpha(p, x)$ is homogeneous, one obtains

$$\partial_x f^\alpha(p, x) = -\frac{1}{x} \sum_{k=1}^{l} p_k \partial_{p_k} f^\alpha(p, x).$$

It follows from the definition of the demand functions f^α that

$$p_i\, \partial_{p_i} f_i^\alpha(p, x) = \alpha_i\, \partial_{\alpha_i} f_i^\alpha(p, x) - f_i^\alpha(p, x)$$

and

$$p_k\, \partial_{p_k} f_i^\alpha(p, x) = \alpha_k\, \partial_{\alpha_k} f_i^\alpha(p, x) \quad \text{if } k \neq i.$$

Consequently one obtains

$$\int_{\mathbb{R}_+^l} \partial_x \left(f^\alpha(p, x) f^\alpha(p, x)^\top \right) \eta(\alpha)\, d\alpha$$

$$= \frac{2}{x} \int_{\mathbb{R}_+^l} f^\alpha(p, x) f^\alpha(p, x)^\top \eta(\alpha)\, d\alpha$$

$$- \frac{1}{x} \sum_{k=1}^l \int_{\mathbb{R}_+^l} \alpha_k \partial_{\alpha_k} \left(f^\alpha(p, x) f^\alpha(p, x)^\top \right) \eta(\alpha)\, d\alpha.$$

If the density μ is differentiable on $\mathbb{R}_+^l$ and vanishes on the boundary, then partial integration yields

$$\int_{\mathbb{R}_+^l} \partial_x \left(f^\alpha(p, x) f^\alpha(p, x)^\top \right) \eta(\alpha)\, d\alpha$$

$$= \frac{2}{x} \int_{\mathbb{R}_+^l} \left(f^\alpha(p, x) f^\alpha(p, x)^\top \right) \eta(\alpha)\, d\alpha$$

$$+ \frac{1}{x} \sum_{k=1}^l \int_{\mathbb{R}_+^l} \left(f^\alpha(p, x) f^\alpha(p, x)^\top \right) \partial_{\alpha_k} \left(\alpha_k \eta(\alpha) \right) d\alpha.$$

The second matrix becomes arbitrarily small if the density of $\log \alpha$ is sufficiently "flat".

Consequently, it remains to show that the matrix

$$B := \begin{pmatrix} -\dfrac{\bar{f}_1}{p_1} & & 0 \\ & \ddots & \\ 0 & & -\dfrac{\bar{f}_l}{p_l} \end{pmatrix} + \frac{1}{x} \int f^\alpha(p, x) f^\alpha(p, x)^\top \eta(\alpha)\, d\alpha$$

is negative semidefinite. This follows from a well-known result on diagonal dominance of matrices since all off-diagonal elements of the matrix B are nonnegative and since the budget identity $p \cdot f^\alpha(p, x) = x$ implies that

$$p_i b_{ii} = - \sum_{\substack{j=1 \\ j \neq i}}^l p_j b_{ij}.$$

In the following chapters, I shall use Grandmont's model as a non-trivial example of a μ-model that satisfies the general hypotheses (Increasing Dispersion of Household Demand, Section 3.1, and Increasing Spread of Household Demand, Section 4.1) on which I shall base the theory of market demand.

2.3 Hicks–Leontief Composite Commodity Theorem

The μ-model was defined with respect to the microeconomic commodity space $\mathbb{R}^l$ of a large number l of elementary commodities. As I mentioned at the beginning of this chapter, family expenditure surveys refer to "composite commodities" and not to these elementary commodities. A link between these two notions of commodities is given by the Hicks–Leontief composite commodity theorem, that will be explained now.

Let $\mathcal{P} = \{P_1, P_2, \ldots, P_K\}$ denote any *partition* of the set of elementary commodities $\{1, \ldots, l\}$, i.e.,

$$\{1, \ldots, l\} = P_1 \cup \cdots \cup P_K$$

and

$$P_k \cap P_j = \emptyset, \quad k \neq j.$$

For example, the subset P_1 (P_2, P_3, ..., respectively) describes all elementary commodities that belong to the category "food" ("clothing", "housing", ..., respectively).

Consider any price system $\bar{p} \in \mathbb{R}^l$, called the *base price* system or the *current price* system. For every vector $\pi \in \mathbb{R}^K_{++}$ define the vector $\bar{p}_\pi$ in $\mathbb{R}^l_{++}$ by multiplying all prices of $\bar{p}$ that belong to the partition P_k with π_k ($k = 1, \ldots, K$). This defines a *cone* $C(\bar{p}, \mathcal{P})$ of price systems in $\mathbb{R}^l_{++}$. For every two price systems p and q in $C(\bar{p}, \mathcal{P})$ it follows that $p_h/p_i = q_h/q_i$ if h and i belong to the same subset P_k. Clearly, the finer the partition, the larger the cone.

Given any demand function

$$f: \mathbb{R}^l_{++} \times \mathbb{R}_+ \longmapsto \mathbb{R}^l,$$

$$(p, x) \longmapsto f(p, x).$$

For every base price system $\bar{p}$ and any partition $\mathscr{P} = (P_1, \ldots, P_K)$, a "reduced" or "composite commodity" demand function

$$\varphi : \mathbb{R}_{++}^K \times \mathbb{R}_+ \longmapsto \mathbb{R}^K,$$

$$(\pi, x) \longmapsto \varphi(\pi, x)$$

is defined by

$$\varphi_1(\pi, x) := \sum_{h \in P_1} \bar{p}_h f_h(\bar{p}_\pi, x)$$

$$\vdots$$

$$\varphi_K(\pi, x) := \sum_{h \in P_K} \bar{p}_h f_h(\bar{p}_\pi, x).$$

Thus, in the reduced demand function φ the *quantity* of the composite commodity $k \in K$ is measured by the *total expenditure on all elementary commodities in P_k evaluated with respect to the base price system $\bar{p}$*. The price level (with respect to $\bar{p}$) of the composite commodity k is π_k.

For every partition $\mathscr{P} = \{P_k\}_{k \in K}$ and every base price vector $\bar{p}$, one defines the linear mapping of $\mathbb{R}^l$ into $\mathbb{R}^K$ by

$$(y_1, \ldots, y_l) \longmapsto \left(\sum_{h \in P_1} \bar{p}_h y_h, \ldots, \sum_{h \in P_K} \bar{p}_h y_h \right).$$

The matrix representing this linear mapping is

$$P = (p_{kj})_{\substack{k=1,\ldots,K \\ j=1,\ldots,l}}$$

where $p_{kj} = \bar{p}_j$ of $j \in P_k$ and $p_{kj} = 0$ if $j \notin P_k$. Then one obtains for the reduced household demand function

$$\varphi^\alpha(\pi, x) = P f^\alpha(\bar{p}_\pi, x)$$

and for the reduced market demand

$$\phi(\pi) = \int P f^\alpha(\bar{p}_\pi, x) \, d\mu = P F(\bar{p}_\pi).$$

The Hicks–Leontief *composite commodity theorem* says that *the reduced demand function $\varphi(\pi, x)$ satisfies the hypothesis of utility maximization or the Weak Axiom of Revealed Preference if the original demand function $f(p, x)$ has these properties*.

Furthermore, if $\phi(\pi)$ denotes the reduced market demand function, then one easily verifies that

$$(\pi - \pi') \cdot \big(\phi(\pi) - \phi(\pi')\big) = (p_\pi - p_{\pi'}) \cdot \big(F(p_\pi) - F(p_{\pi'})\big).$$

Consequently, *the reduced market demand function ϕ is monotone if and only if the original market demand function F is monotone on the cone $C(\bar{p}, \mathcal{P})$*. The Law of Demand for the market demand function F is falsified if it is falsified for some reduced market demand function ϕ. The coarser the partition $\mathcal{P}$ of the set of elementary commodities, that is to say, the higher the level of commodity aggregation, the less demanding it is to require that the reduced market demand function satisfy the Law of Demand. The empirical test of the Law of Demand that is offered in this book is based for each data set on one partition only. It would be interesting to use different partitions and/or different degrees of commodity aggregation. Such a sensitivity analysis with different and finer partitions presently is being carried out; hopefully, the results will be available soon.

The μ-model can be considered on any level of commodity aggregation. If the underlying commodity space is the space $\mathbb{R}^l$ of elementary commodities, then I shall speak of the *microeconomic μ-model*. For *every partion $\mathcal{P}$ of the set of elementary commodities* and for *every base price system $\bar{p}$*, a reduced μ-model, which I also shall call the *composite commodity μ-model is defined*; the underlying commodity space is then $\mathbb{R}^K$, where the number K of composite commodities is typically much smaller than the number l of elementary commodities. If the standard assumptions are satisfied for one partition $\mathcal{P}$, then they are satisfied for any coarser partition. *If in the following chapters I refer to family expenditure surveys, then I always have a suitably reduced demand system in mind*; this goes without saying. Also it should be clear that any hypothesis on the microeconomic level that specifies the demand functions $f^\alpha(p, x)$ and the distribution μ should be preserved under aggregation; otherwise such a hypothesis can never be falsified by empirical evidence.

2.4 Family Expenditure Surveys: The Data

United Kingdom Family Expenditure Survey

The Family Expenditure Survey (FES) is based on a representative sample of private households in the United Kingdom in every year since 1957. The survey is well documented in the *Family Expenditure Survey Handbook* (Kemsley et al., 1980).

A *private household* comprises one person living alone or a group of people living at the same address having meals prepared together and with common housekeeping. Resident domestic servants are included. People living in hostels, hotels, boarding houses, or institutions are excluded.

The sample size of the FES is approximately 7000 households per year, which amounts to about 0.05% of all households in the United Kingdom. About 11,000 addresses are randomly selected every year. The response rate varies slightly from year to year, but it is approximately 68 percent. A household is included in the FES sample if every member aged 16 and over is willing to cooperate, that is to say, to give information on expenditure and income. The households are assured that the information they provide is treated as strictly confidential. Information on expenditure is collected partly by interview and partly by records kept by individual members of the household. Details of income, with minor exceptions, are obtained by interview. Information is recorded in a household schedule, income schedule, and a diary record book. In the diary record-book each spender maintains a detailed record of expenditures during 14 consecutive days. The periods for the diary record book and interviews are spread evenly over the year.

Details on such important topics as sample design, spacing of fieldwork over time, interviewers' work, confidentiality, response rates, conceptual problems of definitions, reliability, and other topics are discussed in the *Family Expenditure Survey Handbook*.

The Family Expenditure Survey contains detailed information on household characteristics, like household size and composition, occupation, age, etc. I give no details on household characteristics since I do not stratify the population of households by these characteristics. I am mainly interested in expenditure and income.

Total expenditure represents current expenditure on goods and services (given in pounds sterling per week). Total expenditure, defined in this way, excludes those recorded payments that are really savings or investments (e.g., purchases of national savings certificates, life insurance premiums, contributions to pension funds). Similarly, income tax payments, national insurance contributions, and mortgage and other payments for the purchase of, or major additions to, dwellings are excluded. Expenditure data are collected in the diary record book and on the household schedule. Informants are asked to record in the diary any payments made during the 14 days of record-keeping, whether or not the goods and services paid for have been received. Special instructions are given in the following cases:

- Goods supplied from a household's own shop or farm
- Hire purchase, credit sales agreements, and transactions financed by loans repaid by installments
- Credit card transactions
- Income tax
- Rented dwellings
- Owner-occupied dwellings
- Rent-free dwellings
- Second-hand goods and partial exchange transactions
- Business expenses

For consumption items, which are frequently purchased, expenditure is computed exclusively from recorded expenditures during the 14 days in the diary record book.

If for a consumption item, there is a commitment to make regular payments at regular intervals, then information from interviews also is used to compute the expenditure. Examples are housing costs covering rent, gas, and electricity through credit meters, telephone in the accommodation occupied by the household, various licenses including vehicle licenses and insurance, and payments by means of standing orders to banks.

Expenditures on goods and services are grouped in the following nine consumption categories (abbreviations used in the subsequent figures and tables are given in brackets):

1. Housing (Housing)
2. Fuel, light, and power (Fuel)
3. Food and nonalcoholic beverages (Food)
4. Clothing and footware (Clothing)

5. Durable household goods (Durables)
6. Services (Services)
7. Transport and vehicles (Transport)
8. Alcohol and tobacco (Alcohol)
9. Other goods and miscellaneous (Other Goods)

Each of these nine consumption categories is composed of a wide variety of items (with components separately identified) for which a detailed list is given. For example:

Housing: households renting unfurnished accommodation (rent, water, and sewerage charges, insurance, expenditure by households on repair, maintainance, and decoration...), households renting furnished accommodation, households living rent-free, households living in their own dwellings, expenditure on repairs, maintainance, and decoration
Fuel: gas, electricity, coal and coke, fuel oil, and other fuel and light
Food: bread, flour, biscuits, cakes, breakfast and other cereals, beef and veal, mutton and lamb, pork, bacon and ham, poultry, fish, etc.
Durables: furniture, floor coverings, soft furnishings and household textiles, television, video and audio equipment (including repairs but not rental), gas and electric appliances, china, glass, cutlery, hardware, ironmongery, electric appliances, insurance of contents of dwelling

The expenditure data consists of a "cloud" of vectors η^i in $\mathbb{R}^9$. This cloud $\{\eta^i\}$ is very spread, since households differ in income and since y^i refers to the expenditure during a randomly chosen two week period. Figure 2.3 illustrates this expenditure cloud in the plane Food-Housing.

Figure 2.4a and b illustrate the Food expenditure cloud and Alcohol expenditure cloud; expenditure is plotted against income.

The average expenditure on these nine consumption categories varies greatly. For example, in the year 1985, average expenditure on the nine consumption categories in percentage of average total expenditure is as follows:

Housing	16.1%
Fuel	6.1%

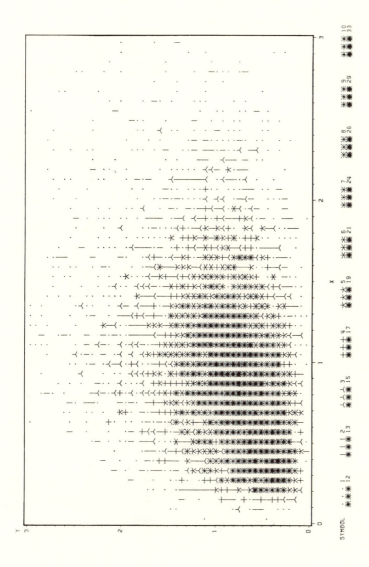

Figure 2.3 Sunflower Plot: Food versus Housing, 1973

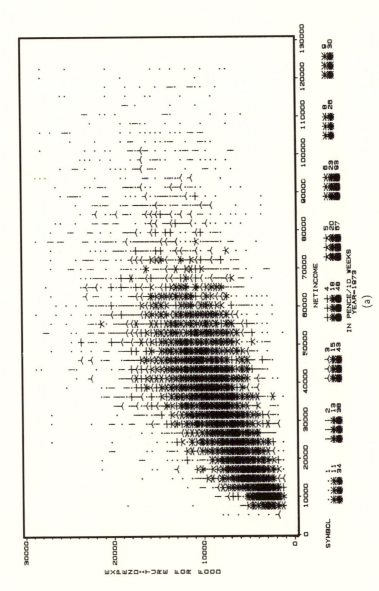

Figure 2.4   Sunflower Plot: (a) Income versus Food

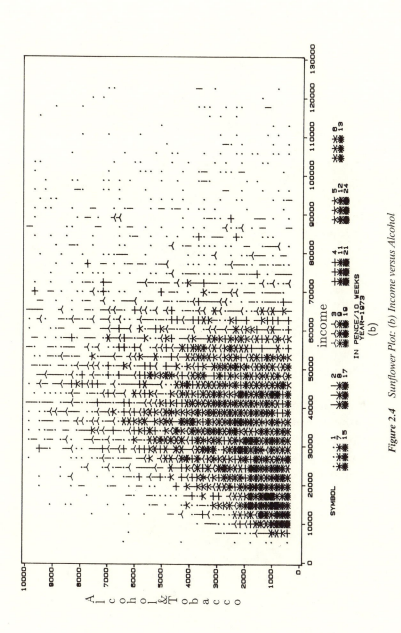

Figure 2.4 Sunflower Plot: (b) Income versus Alcohol

Food	20.2%
Clothing	7.4%
Durables	7.2%
Services	12.0%
Transport	15.2%
Alcohol	7.6%
Other goods	8.2%

The evolution over time of these expenditure percentages is shown in Figure 2.5.

Household expenditure on a particular consumption category depends very much on the level of the household's total expenditure. This dependence is illustrated in Figure 2.6. The total expenditure level (normalized such that 1 corresponds to the average total expenditure) is plotted on the horizontal axes and the expenditure on a particular consumption category in percentage of total expenditure is plotted on the vertical axes. The dots, of course, do not represent individual households but an average of households, because it is not meaningful to show a plot of 7000 households. The regression curve shows well the general dependence.

In Figure 2.7 is illustrated the evolution over time of the *statistical Engel curve* for Food, that is to say, the regression curve if one plots expenditure on Food against total expenditure. Again a dot stands for an average of households.

The standard concepts of *income* in the survey is *gross weekly cash income* and *disposable income*. Disposable income is defined as gross weekly cash income less the statutory deductions and payments of income tax (taking refunds into account) and national insurance contributions. The following sources of income are considered

- Wages and salaries
- Self-employment
- Investments
- Annuities and pensions
- Social security benefits
- Imputed income from owner/rent-free occupancy

The following are excluded from the assessment of income:

- Money received by one member of the household from another

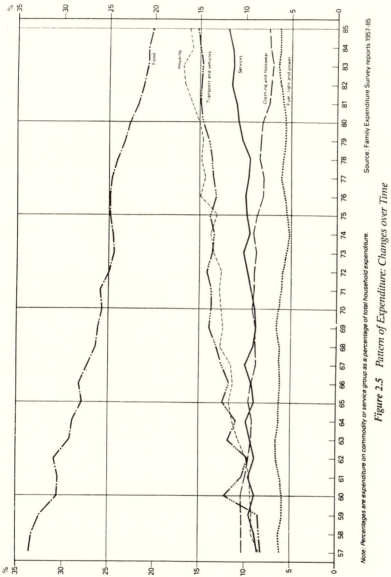

Food

Housing

Transport and vehicles

Services

Clothing and footwear

Fuel, light and power

Note: Percentages are expenditure on commodity or service group as a percentage of total household expenditure.

Source: Family Expenditure Survey reports 1957-85

Figure 2.5 Pattern of Expenditure: Changes over Time

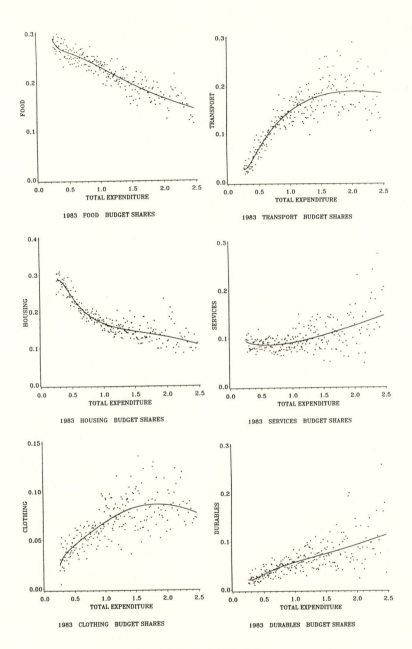

Figure 2.6. *Budget Share Curves*

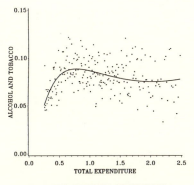

1983 ALCOHOL AND TOBACCO BUDGET SHARES

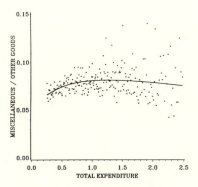

1983 MISC / OTHER GOODS BUDGET SHARES

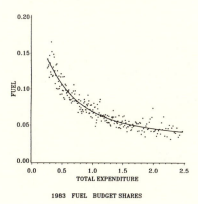

1983 FUEL BUDGET SHARES

Figure 2.6.   *(Continued)*

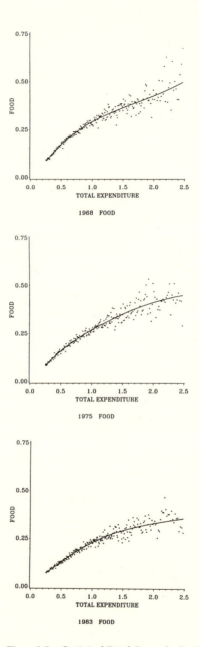

Figure 2.7. *Statistical Engel Curves for Food*

- Withdrawals of savings, receipts from maturing insurance policies, proceeds from sale of financial and other assets, winning from betting, lump-sum gratuities, and windfalls such as legacies
- The value of educational grants and scholarships not paid in cash
- The value of income in kind, including the value of goods received free and the abatements in cost of goods received at reduced prices, other than the imputed value of owner/occupied and of rent-free accommodation
- Loans and money received in money repayment of loans

There is a large variation among the households between gross income, disposable income, and total expenditure. The averages over the whole sample in 1985 are £216.23, £174.67 and £161.87 per week, respectively (see Table 2.1). The distribution of disposable income for the year 1973 is shown in Figure 2.8.

Due to inflation the income distributions change very much from year to year. If in every year the disposable income of every household is divided by the sample mean (thus, average disposable income is normalized to 1), then one obtains the normalized income distributions as shown in Figure 2.9.

The FES is not designed to produce data on savings, either directly or indirectly. Total expenditure as explained previously does not cover all outgoings nor is the income definition comprehensive for all sources of financing expenditure. Direct savings information is available for only a few specific items. To compare expenditure with income and attribute the difference to savings or dissavings is not a reliable estimate. Income and expenditure are not collected over

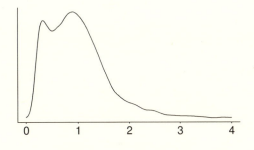

Figure 2.8. *Income Density, 1973*

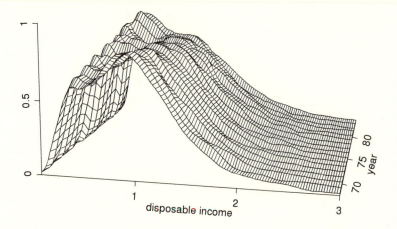

Figure 2.9.   *Income Densities for 1968–83*

a common time period. Much of the expenditure data relates to the 14 days of record-keeping following the preliminary interview, whereas all the income information is retrospective to that date and relates to a much longer period, often a full year. This explains to a large extent the great dispersion in Figure 2.10, where total expenditure is plotted against disposable income.

The French Enquête Budget de Famille

The structure of the French Enquête Budget de Famille (EBF) is quite similar to the UK Family Expenditure Survey even though there are naturally some differences. A description of the EBF is given in several documents of the French Institut National de la Statistique et des Etudes Economiques. I shall only comment on some essential differences that are relevant for the data analysis presented in this book.

As in the UK FES, the survey contains information on house-hold characteristics, expenditure on goods and services, and in-come. The survey is not yearly, but every five years: 1979, 1984–5 and 1989. The sample size is larger; it varies from 9000 to 12,000 households. The specification of consumption items differs some-what from that used in the UK FES, and is more detailed. The list of consumption items of the French EBF is grouped into the

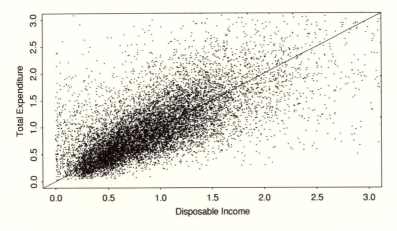

Figure 2.10. *Disposable Income versus Total Expenditure, 1984*

following 14 consumption categories (abbreviations are given in brackets):

1. Food at home (Food 1)
2. Food outdoors (Food 2)
3. Nonalcoholic beverages (Beverage)
4. Alcoholic beverages (Alcohol)
5. Clothing (Clothing)
6. Footware (Footware)
7. Housing (Housing)
8. Fuel, light, and power (Fuel)
9. Durable household goods and domestic services (Durables)
10. Hygiene and health (Health)
11. Transport and communication (Transport)
12. Tobacco (Tobacco)
13. Culture and leisure (Culture)
14. Other goods and miscellaneous (Other Goods)

I do not think that it is necessary to describe in detail the difference of these 14 consumption categories with the 9 consumption categories of the UK FES. As an example I just mention that holiday expenditure is included in the consumption category "Culture" in the French EBF, whereas holiday expenditure is not separately distinguished in the UK FES, where expenditure while away

from home is classified according to the standard coding frame
for expenditure items.

Household Expenditure Data and the Distribution
of Household Demand: Errors in the Data

I want to use the data from the UK and the French Family Expenditure Survey to estimate the distribution $v(p)$ of household demand
at the prevailing price system. It is clear that household demand then
refers to the same composite commodities that are used in the expenditure survey. Thus I consider a reduced μ-model as explained
in Section 2.3. In this section the price vector is always the prevailing
price vector $\bar{p}$, and I drop $\bar{p}$ in the notation. To shorten the notation,
I shall denote the composite commodity demand by $f^\alpha(x)$ instead
of $Pf^\alpha(\bar{p}, x)$, where P is the matrix defined by the partition $\mathscr{P}$ of
elementary commodities and the base price system $\bar{p}$ as explained in
Section 2.3.

In both family expenditure surveys every household in the
sample keeps records of expenditures only for *two consecutive
weeks*, which are choosen at random during the year. If $\eta^i \in \mathbb{R}^K$
denotes the vector of expenditures (in current prices $\bar{p}$) on the
K consumption categories of household i, then this vector would
most likely be somewhat different if the household had been
asked to keep records in another two-week period; in particular,
$26\eta^i$ does not necessarily represent the composite commodity
demand $y^i = Pf^i(\bar{p}, x^i)$ of household i in the reduced μ-model
if the household demand functions refer to average demand
per year.

By the sample design a household is randomly assigned to a two-
week period during the year; thus the observed expenditure vector η^i
can be considered as a realization of a random vector $\tilde{\eta}^i$ with expec-
tation $\mathbb{E}\tilde{\eta}^i = 1/26y^i$. Furthermore, the random vectors $\{\tilde{\eta}^i\}_{i \in S}$ in the
sample can be assumed to be stochastically independent. Depending
on the type of consumption category and the way the information on
expenditure is obtained, the random deviation

$$\tilde{u}^i := \tilde{\eta}^i - y^i$$

might be negligible or have to be modelled explicitly. If there are
many items in the consumption category that are all purchased quite

frequently (for example, in the case of Food), then the random deviation can most likely be neglected. Also, if there is a commitment
to make regular payments at regular intervals, then, as previously
explained, expenditure is computed from interviews and, again, the
random deviation can be neglected. The deviation $\tilde{u}^i$, however, can
be quite important for consumption categories if purchases of the
consumption item are infrequent and if there are no commitments
to make regular payments, like in the case of Durables.

For a large "representative" sample S of the population I (which
includes a representative spacing of two-week periods) one obtain

$$\frac{1}{\#S} \sum_{i \in S} 26\eta^i \approx \frac{1}{\#S} \sum_{i \in S} 26\mathbb{E}\tilde{\eta}^i$$

$$= \frac{1}{\#S} \sum_{i \in S} y^i \approx \frac{1}{\#I} \sum_{i \in I} y^i$$

yet the *distribution of the data* $\{26\eta^i\}_{i \in S}$ is not necessarily "similar" to
the *distribution of household demand* (in the reduced μ-model) if the
household demand functions refer to a one-year period, even though
the two distributions have approximately the same mean. One might
expect that the observed distribution of the data $\{26\eta^i\}_{i \in S}$ will
be more heterogeneous than the distribution of the yearly expenditures $\{y^i\}_{i \in I}$.

Alternatively, one can interpret the demand functions in the
μ-model as household demand referring to a specified two-week
period τ during the year. Thus, every household has 26 demand functions $f^{i,\tau}(p, x)$ (which need not be the same). Formally, this amounts
to increasing the population. The parameter α over which one takes
the mean then describes all relevant determinants of demand including the particular two-week period to which the demand function
f^α refer. The diary record book and household demand functions
now refers to the same period. The assumption that the family expenditure survey is a representative sample is now, of course, more
demanding.

The discussion up to now implicitly assumed that all households
in the sample correctly report their expenditures. It might well be that
some households make mistakes in writing down expenditures or that
some consciously underreport expenditures on particular items.
If one assumes that these "errors" can be modelled as random

variables, then the observed expenditure data η^i of household i is

$$\eta^i = y^i + u^i,$$

where u^i denotes a realization of a random error $\tilde{u}^i$. The essential difference from the preceding situation (where the "random error" was due to the two-week recording period) is that now the assumption of an unbiased error, i.e., $\mathbb{E}\tilde{u}^i = 0$, has to be rejected. Typically, if there is a deviation at all, one expects that the households underreport, that is to say, the expected error $\mathbb{E}\tilde{u}^i$ is a negative vector.

In order to analyze the influence of the random error in the data one has to model more explicitly the data generating process. The population of households is modelled, as explained in Section 2.2, by the distribution μ on the space of households' characteristics $\mathcal{A} \times \mathbb{R}_+$. We assume now that the demand vector of a household with characteristics (α, x) can only be observed up to a random error $\tilde{u}_{\alpha, x}$, that is to say,

$$f^\alpha(x) + u_{\alpha, x},$$

where $u_{\alpha, x}$ is a realization of a random vector $\tilde{u}_{\alpha, x}$ in $\mathbb{R}^K$. Let $\delta_{\alpha, x}$ denote the distribution (on $\mathbb{R}^K$) of the random variable $\tilde{u}_{\alpha, x}$, which typically depends on the characteristics (α, x).

The stochastic model of the data generating process is defined by the probability measure $\mu \otimes \delta$ on the space $\mathcal{A} \times \mathbb{R}_+ \times \mathbb{R}^K$; the *marginal* distribution on $\mathcal{A} \times \mathbb{R}_+$ of $\mu \otimes \delta$ is equal to μ and the conditional distribution on $\mathbb{R}^K$ of $\mu \otimes \delta$ given (α, x) is equal to $\delta_{\alpha, x}$.

The data set is considered as a large random sample of the random variable $(\alpha, x, u) \mapsto f^\alpha(p, x) + u$ with respect to the probability distribution $\mu \otimes \delta$ on $\mathcal{A} \times \mathbb{R}_+ \times \mathbb{R}^K$.

The *distribution of households demand with error* in the data, that is to say, the image distribution on $\mathbb{R}^K$ of $\mu \otimes \delta$ under the mapping $(\alpha, x, u) \mapsto f^\alpha(x) + u$, is denoted by ν_{error}. The question now is whether *the distribution ν_{error} of households demand with error is more heterogeneous than the distribution ν of households demand without error.*

As mentioned already in the Introduction and as explained in detail in Chapters 3 and 4, one can measure the degree of heterogeneity of a distribution ν on $\mathbb{R}^K$ either by the *covariance matrix*, cov ν, or by the *matrix of second moments*, $m^2\nu$. In the first case, I speak of *dispersion* and in the second, of *spread*. I call the distribution ν_{error} *more dispersed (more spread)* than the distribution ν if

$\text{cov}\, v_{\text{error}} - \text{cov}\, v(m^2 v_{\text{error}} - m^2 v)$ is positive semidefinite. For a motivation and more details see Chapters 3 and 4.

In order to answer the foregoing question one has to compute the covariance matrix

$$\text{cov}\, v_{\text{error}} = \text{cov}_{\mu \otimes \delta}(f^{\alpha}(x) + u)$$

and the matrix of second moments

$$m^2 v_{\text{error}} = m^2_{\mu \otimes \delta}(f^{\alpha}(x) + u).$$

One obtains

$$\text{cov}\, v_{\text{error}} - \text{cov}\, v = \text{cov}_{\mu \otimes \delta}(u) + V + V^{\mathsf{T}}$$

and

$$m^2 v_{\text{error}} - m^2 v = m^2_{\mu \otimes \delta}(u) + W + W^{\mathsf{T}},$$

where the matrices V and W are defined by

$$V := \text{cov}_{\mu}\big(f^{\alpha}(x), \mathbb{E}\tilde{u}_{\alpha, x}\big),$$
$$W := \mathbb{E}_{\mu}\big(f^{\alpha}(x)\mathbb{E}\tilde{u}^{\mathsf{T}}_{\alpha, x}\big),$$

which is equal to

$$V + F(p)U^{\mathsf{T}} \quad \text{with} \quad U := \mathbb{E}_{\mu \otimes \delta}\tilde{u}.$$

Consequently, for *unbiased errors*, i.e., $\mathbb{E}\tilde{u}_{\alpha, x} = 0$, the distribution v_{error} of households demand with error in the data is more dispersed and more spread than the distribution v of households demand without error in the data, because in this case $V = 0$ and $W = 0$ and the matrices $\text{cov}_{\mu \otimes \delta}(u)$ and $m^2_{\mu \otimes \delta}(u)$ are positive semidefinite. The definition of the distribution $\mu \otimes \delta$ implies for unbiased errors $\text{cov}_{\mu \otimes \delta}(u) = \mathbb{E}_{\mu} \text{cov}\, \tilde{u}_{\alpha, x}$.

The situation is different for *biased errors* in the data, i.e., $\mathbb{E}\tilde{u}_{\alpha, x} \neq 0$. In this case the errors in the data do not necessarily increase the dispersion or spread.

Example: **Deterministic Underreporting.** Assume that for every consumption category k the "error" is proportional to demand, i.e.,

$$\big(\tilde{u}_{\alpha, x}\big)_k = -\tau_k f^{\alpha}_k(x) \quad \text{with } 0 \leq \tau_k \leq 1,$$

and τ_k does not depend on (α, x). In matrix notation,

$$\tilde{u}_{\alpha, x} = -D_\tau f^\alpha(x),$$

where D_τ denotes a diagonal matrix with $\tau_1, \ldots, \tau_K$ on the diagonal. Then one obtains

$$\text{cov } v_{\text{error}} = \text{cov}_\mu \left(f^\alpha(x) - D_\tau f^\alpha(x) \right)$$
$$= D_{1-\tau} \text{cov}_\mu \left(f^\alpha(x) \right) D_{1-\tau}.$$

Thus, if $\tau_1 = \cdots = \tau_K$, then the distribution v_{error} *is less dispersed* than the distribution v. However, in general, no comparison of dispersion is possible, if the factors $\tau_1, \ldots, \tau_K$ are not identical.

The distribution v_{error} is still *more dispersed* than the distribution v if there is no correlation between demand $f^\alpha(x)$ and expected error $\mathbb{E}\tilde{u}_{\alpha, x}$ within the whole population, i.e., $V = 0$. However, I believe that the typical case is rather

$$\text{cov}_\mu \left(f_k^\alpha(x), \mathbb{E}_k \tilde{u}_{\alpha, x} \right) < 0.$$

Indeed, if there is a bias in the error for consumption category k, then there is typically underreporting of expenditure, i.e., $\mathbb{E}_k \tilde{u}_{\alpha, x} < 0$, which is likely to be proportional to the amount of expenditure on that consumption category. Thus, the diagonal elements of the matrix V are likely to be nonpositive and the matrix V has a tendency to be negative semidefinite. For example, if $\mathbb{E}_k \tilde{u}_{\alpha, x} = -\tau\% f_k^\alpha(x)$, i.e., the expected underreporting on consumption category k is $\tau\%$, then one obtains $V_{kk} = -\tau \text{var}_\mu(f_k^\alpha(x)) < 0$. Consequently, if there is a correlation between demand $f^\alpha(x)$ and expected error $\mathbb{E}\tilde{u}_{\alpha, x}$, then it is not clear whether the matrix

$$\text{cov}_{\mu \otimes \delta}(u) + V + V^\top$$

is positive semidefinite, that is to say, one cannot unambiguously conclude that v_{error} is more dispersed than v.

The same conclusion holds if one compares the spread of the distribution v_{error} and v. Indeed, for biased errors in the data with $\mathbb{E}\tilde{u}_{\alpha, x} < 0$, the diagonal elements of the matrix W are likely to be negative and, hence, the matrix $m^2 v_{\text{error}} - m^2 v$ is not necessarily positive semidefinite.

In conclusion, only in the case of *unbiased errors* in the data—which seems not to be the typical case—the distribution v_{error} of households demand with error is more dispersed and more spread than the distribution v of households demand without error. In the case of *biased errors* in the data, one has to model the error structure explicitly if one wants to compare the dispersion or the spread of the two distributions v_{error} and v.

Chapter 3

Increasing Dispersion

> ... the preference hypothesis only acquires a *prima facie* plausibility when it is applied to a statistical average [...] to assume that an actual person, the Mr. Brown or Mr. Jones who lives round the corner, does in fact act in such a way does not deserve a moment's consideration.
>
> —J. R. Hicks, *A Revision of Demand Theory*, (1956), p. 55

In this chapter I shall try to answer the following question: Under what circumstances does the *mean demand* of a large population of households satisfy Wald's Axiom?

In the Introduction I explained why an economic theorist might be interested in deriving Wald's Axiom for mean demand. Wald's Axiom for the excess demand of a multicommodity competitive demand–supply system seems to be the weakest assumption, which implies that the equilibrium price system is generically well-determined. For details I refer to Appendix 2.

Wald's Axiom for the mean demand $\bar{f}(p, x)$ of a population with identical income x asserts that for any two price vectors p and q,

$$p \cdot \bar{f}(q, x) \leq q \cdot \bar{f}(q, x) \quad \text{implies} \quad q \cdot \bar{f}(p, x) \geq p \cdot \bar{f}(p, x).$$

If the budget identity $p \cdot \bar{f}(p, x) \equiv x$ were satisfied for the demand function $\bar{f}$, then Wald's Axiom would become a special case of the

Weak Axiom of Revealed Preference,

$$p \cdot \bar{f}(q, x) \leq x \quad \text{implies} \quad q \cdot \bar{f}(p, x) \geq x.$$

It is well-known that the hypothesis of utility maximization (and hence the Weak Axiom of Revealed Preference) for individual demand does not imply Wald's Axiom for mean demand even in the case of identical income. Figure 3.1 illustrates this claim.

If the mean demand function $\bar{f}(\cdot, x)$ is differentiable, then Wald's Axiom is equivalent to the negative semidefiniteness of the Jacobian matrix $\partial_p \bar{f}(p, x)$ on the hyperplane $\bar{f}(p, x)^{\perp}$ for every price vector p (Appendix 2). The hypothesis of preference maximization or the Weak Axiom of Revealed Preference implies that the Jacobian matrix $\partial_p f^{\alpha}(p, x)$ of the individual demand function $f^{\alpha}(p, x)$ is negative semidefinite on the hyperplane $f^{\alpha}(p, x)^{\perp}$ (Appendix 3).

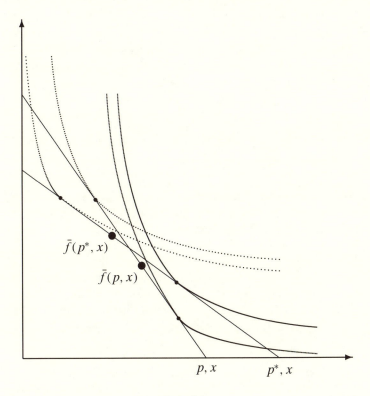

$\bar{f}(p^*, x)$

$\bar{f}(p, x)$

$p, x \qquad\qquad p^*, x$

Figure 3.1.

This, however, does not imply that

$$\partial_p \bar{f}(p, x) = \int_{\mathcal{A}} \partial_p f^\alpha(p, x) \, d\mu | x$$

is negative semidefinite on the hyperplane

$$\bar{f}(p, x)^\perp = \left(\int_{\mathcal{A}} f^\alpha(p, x) \, d\mu | x \right)^\perp.$$

If one insists in deriving Wald's Axiom from assumptions that are expressed exclusively in terms of the individual demand functions (or individual preferences)—I call this the microscopic microeconomic[1] approach—then very restrictive assumptions are needed to obtain the desired result; for example, that individual demand functions are linear in income, i.e., $f^\alpha(p, x) = x f^\alpha(p, 1)$.

An alternative approach consists in making assumptions on the population of households as a whole, that is to say, on the *distribution* of households' demand functions—I call this the macroscopic microeconomic approach. If the households' demand functions are not identical—and always I have this case in mind—then one needs a certain form of *heterogeneity* of the population of households. It is this form of heterogeneity that I shall formulate in the next section.

3.1 The Hypothesis of Increasing Dispersion of Households' Demand

All households in the population with income equal to x were called in the previous chapter the x-households. The distribution of the x-households' demand is denoted by

$$\nu(p|x).$$

Thus, $\nu(p|x)$ is a distribution on the commodity space $\mathbb{R}^l$ and is formally defined in the μ-model as the image distribution on $\mathbb{R}^l$ of the conditional distribution $\mu|x$ on $\mathcal{A}$ under the mapping $\alpha \mapsto f^\alpha(p, x)$.

---

[1] "Est dite microéconomique toute théorie qui prétend respecter dans ses formulations abstraites l'individualité de chaque bien et the chaque agent," Malinvaud (1991), p. 22.

Imagine now what x-households would demand if their income were increased to ξ. I am again interested in the distribution of these demand vectors. Thus, let

$$\tilde{v}(\xi, x, p)$$

denote the distribution of x-households' demand *under the hypothesis* that their income is ξ. The hypothesis that the income of the x-households is ξ is a *Gedankenexperiment* or, one might say *counterfactual*. To link this distribution with the distribution μ of households' characteristics, one can define $\tilde{v}(\xi, x, p)$ formally as the image distribution of the conditional distribution $\mu|x$ on $\mathcal{A}$ given the income level x under the mapping $\alpha \longmapsto f^{\alpha}(p, \xi)$ of $\mathcal{A}$ into $\mathbb{R}^l$. Obviously, the definition of the distribution $\tilde{v}(\xi, x, p)$ involves *unobservable* situations. Only the distribution $\tilde{v}(x, x, p)$, that is to say, the conditional distribution $v(p|x)$ of x-households' demand, is observable. Figures 3.2a and b illustrate these distributions; Figure 3.2a refers to the case where households do not save.

Let me now informally state a hypothesis on which I would like to base the theory of market demand:

Hypothesis: *The "dispersion" (around the mean) of x-households' demand increases if the income of all x-households is increased to $x + \Delta$, that is to say, the distribution $\tilde{v}(x + \Delta, x, p)$ is "more dispersed" than the distribution $\tilde{v}(x, x, p)$ if $\Delta > 0$.*

Actually I shall need only a weakened version of this hypothesis for the central results in this book. Instead of requiring that for *every* income level in the relevant domain of the income distribution the dispersion of x-households' demand is increasing, I shall require only that *on average* the dispersion of x-households' demand is increasing, where the average is taken with respect to the income distribution. The first hypothesis shall be called *Hypothesis 1** and the weakened version shall be called *Hypothesis 1*.

To give a precise meaning to these hypotheses, I have to define the partial ordering "more dispersed" for distributions on $\mathbb{R}^l$, which shall be defined in terms of the covariance matrices of the distributions.

For one-dimensional distributions the ordering "more dispersed" around the mean can easily be defined by larger variance. The interpretation of the variance of the distribution v on $\mathbb{R}$ as a

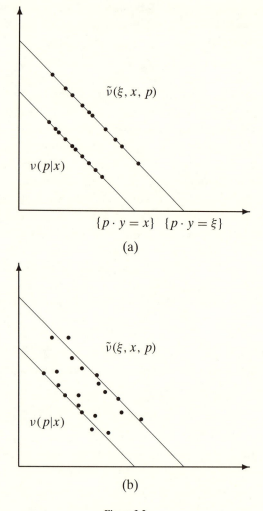

$$\tilde{v}(\xi, x, p)$$

$$v(p|x)$$

$$\{p \cdot y = x\} \quad \{p \cdot y = \xi\}$$

(a)

$$\tilde{v}(\xi, x, p)$$

$$v(p|x)$$

(b)

Figure 3.2.

measure of dispersion around the mean is based on Tchebychev's inequality, which says that for every $\eta \geq 0$,

$$v\{y \in \mathbb{R} \mid |y - \text{mean } v| \geq \eta\} \leq \frac{\text{variance } v}{\eta^2}.$$

Clearly, if the variance of v_2 is larger than the variance of v_1, this does not imply that for every $\eta \geq 0$,

$$v_1\{y \in \mathbb{R} \mid |y - \text{mean } v_1| \geq \eta\} \leq v_2\{y \in \mathbb{R} \mid |y - \text{mean } v_2| \geq \eta\}.$$

These inequalities would define a stronger concept of "more dispersedness". Of course, one can think of alternative ways to measure *dispersion* around the mean, but using the variance turns out to be the appropriate way for the purpose of this chapter. Thus, from now on *the distribution v_2 on $\mathbb{R}$ is said to be more dispersed around the mean than the distribution v_1 on $\mathbb{R}$ if the variance of v_2 is greater than or equal to the variance of v_1.*

For distributions on $\mathbb{R}^l$ one can define the partial ordering "more dispersed" by requiring that in any direction the variance is larger. To be more precise, consider any linear mapping from $\mathbb{R}^l$ into $\mathbb{R}$, i.e., $y \mapsto v \cdot y$ for some v in $\mathbb{R}^l$. This linear mapping can be visualized in the case where $|v| = 1$ by the orthogonal projection on the straight line generated by v. The one-dimensional image distribution of the distribution v with respect to this linear mapping is illustrated in Figure 3.3.

It is well-known that the variance of the one-dimensional image distribution of the distribution v with respect to this linear mapping is given by

$$v \cdot (\operatorname{cov} v)\, v,$$

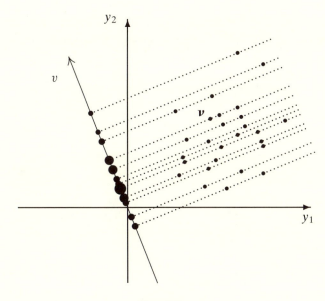

Figure 3.3.

where $\operatorname{cov} v$ denotes the $l \times l$ matrix whose element (j, k) is given by

$$(\operatorname{cov} v)_{j, k} := \int_{\mathbb{R}^l} y_j y_k \, dv - \int_{\mathbb{R}^l} y_j \, dv \cdot \int_{\mathbb{R}^l} y_k \, dv,$$

which is equal to

$$\int_{\mathbb{R}^l} (y_j - \bar{y}_j)(y_k - \bar{y}_k) \, dv,$$

where $\bar{y}_h = \int_{\mathbb{R}^l} y_h \, dv$ denotes the mean value.

Consequently, v_2 is defined to be *more dispersed* than v_1 *in the direction v* if

$$v \cdot (\operatorname{cov} v_2)v \geq v \cdot (\operatorname{cov} v_1)v.$$

This motivates the following definition:

Definition. The distribution v_2 on $\mathbb{R}^l$ is said to be *more dispersed* than the distribution v_1 on $\mathbb{R}^l$ if the matrix

$$\operatorname{cov} v_2 - \operatorname{cov} v_1$$

is positive semidefinite .

There is a nice geometric representation of the partial ordering "more dispersed".

For every covariance matrix $Q = \operatorname{cov} v$ of a distribution v on $\mathbb{R}^l$ one defines the *ellipsoid of dispersion* (also called ellipsoid of concentration) by

$$\operatorname{Ell}(Q) = \{y \in \mathbb{R}^l \mid v \cdot y \leq 1 \text{ for every } v \in \mathbb{R}^l \text{ such that } v \cdot Qv \leq 1\}.$$

Thus the ellipsoid of dispersion $\operatorname{Ell}(Q)$ is defined as the polar of the covariance ellipsoid $\{v \in \mathbb{R}^l \mid v \cdot Qv \leq 1\}$. If the covariance matrix Q is nonsingular, then one can show that

$$\operatorname{Ell}(Q) := \{v \in \mathbb{R}^l \mid v \cdot Q^{-1}v \leq 1\}.$$

The ellipsoid of dispersion of a one-dimensional distribution v with $\operatorname{var} v = \sigma^2$ is simply the interval $[-\sigma, +\sigma]$. For a two-dimensional distribution v, with

$$\operatorname{cov} v = \begin{pmatrix} \sigma_1^2 & r\sigma_1\sigma_2 \\ r\sigma_1\sigma_2 & \sigma_2^2 \end{pmatrix}$$

(r denotes the coefficient of correlation, i.e., $r = \text{cov } v_{12}/\sigma_1 \cdot \sigma_2$) the ellipsoid of dispersion is illustrated in Figure 3.4.

One easily verifies that the ellipsoid of dispersion of v_1 is contained in the ellipsoid of dispersion of v_2 if and only if the covariance ellipsoid of v_1 contains the covariance ellipsoid of v_2, which is equivalent to the positive semidefiniteness of the difference $\text{cov } v_2 - \text{cov } v_1$. Consequently, we obtain

$$v_2 \text{ is more dispersed than } v_1$$

if and only if

$$\text{Ell}(\text{cov } v_1) \subset \text{Ell}(\text{cov } v_2).$$

Now I can give a formal statement of the hypothesis of increasing dispersion.

Hypothesis 1*: Increasing Dispersion of x-Households' Demand.
The distribution $\tilde{v}(x + \Delta, x, p)$ is more dispersed than the distribution $v(p|x)$ if $\Delta > 0$. In particular, the matrix

$$\partial_\xi \text{ cov } \tilde{v}(\xi, x, p)|_{\xi=x} =: \tilde{C}(x, p)$$

is positive semidefinite for all x in the support of ρ.

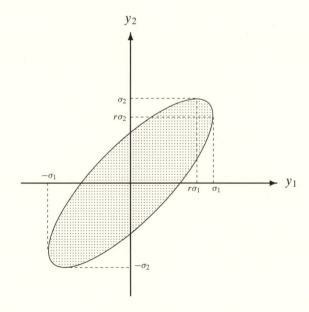

Figure 3.4.

Hypothesis 1: **Average Increasing Dispersion of *x*-Households' Demand..** *The matrix*

$$\int_{\mathbb{R}_+} [\text{cov } \tilde{v}(x + \Delta, x, p) - \text{cov } v(p|x)]\rho(x)\,dx$$

is positive semidefinite if $\Delta > 0$. *In particular,*

$$\tilde{C}_\rho(p) := \int_{\mathbb{R}_+} \tilde{C}(x, p)\rho(x)\,dx$$

is positive semidefinite.

Obviously, Hypothesis 1* implies Hypothesis 1, which is substantially weaker.

Remark 1. Let me emphasize that the hypothesis of increasing dispersion of *x*-households' demand does not imply a specific restriction on the behavior of any particular individual household. The hypothesis refers to the subpopulation of *x*-households, and this subpopulation is thought of as being large. More precisely, I would like to emphasize here—but postpone the detailed discussion to the next section where I shall discuss some examples—that Hypothesis 1* is very restrictive if the number of different *x*-households is *smaller than the number l of commodities*. This does not seem to me to be the typical case. On the relevant domain of the income distribution the population of *x*-households is large and one can expect that this population is heterogeneous.

Remark 2. Hypothesis 1* implies in particular that the dispersion is increasing in the directions $1_k = (0, \ldots, 1, \ldots, 0)$ and p. Consequently,

$$\text{cov}_{\mu|x}\left(f_k^\alpha(p, x), \partial_x f_k^\alpha(p, x)\right) \geq 0$$

and

$$\text{cov}_{\mu|x}\left(e^\alpha(p, x), \partial_x e^\alpha(p, x)\right) \geq 0.$$

Thus, Hypothesis 1* implies that *for the population of x-households there is a nonnegative correlation* between the demand $f_k^\alpha(p, x)$ and the propensity to consume $\partial_x f_k^\alpha(p, x)$ for every commodity k, and a *non-positive correlation* between the expenditure $e^\alpha(p, x)$ and the propensity to save $\partial_x s^\alpha(p, x)$, where $s^\alpha(p, x) = x - e^\alpha(p, x)$.

Remark 3. If all demand functions satisfy the budget identity $p \cdot f^{\alpha}(p, x) \equiv x$, then the increase in dispersion of x-households' demand can never be *strict in all directions.* In this case it follows that

$$\text{cov } \tilde{v}(\xi, x, p)\,p \equiv 0,$$

and consequently

$$p \cdot \tilde{C}(x, p)\,p \equiv 0.$$

Slightly more general, if all x-households save the same amount, then the matrix $\tilde{C}(x, p)$ in Hypothesis 1* can never be positive definite because its maximal rank is $l - 1$.

Remark 4. The hypothesis of increasing dispersion is defined with respect to a given commodity space $\mathbb{R}^l$. Consider any partition $\mathcal{P}$ of $\{1, \ldots, l\}$ and any base price vector $\bar{p}$ and the corresponding reduced (composite commodity) μ-model, as explained in Section 2.3. If Hypothesis 1* or 1 is satisfied, then they are also satisfied for every reduced μ-model. This follows from the definition in Section 2.3 of the reduced μ-model, which is defined with respect to a partition $\mathcal{P}$ of the set of elementary commodities and the base price vector $\bar{p}$. Let $\tilde{v}_p(x + \Delta, x, \pi)$ denote the distribution of x-households composite commodity demand under the hypothesis that income is increased to $x + \Delta$. By definition of the reduced μ-model, distribution $\tilde{v}_p(x + \Delta, x, \pi)$ is the image distribution of $\tilde{v}(x + \Delta, x, \bar{p}_\pi)$ under the linear mapping P of $\mathbb{R}^l$ into $\mathbb{R}^K$, which was defined in Section 2.3. Consequently, by a well-known result, one obtains

$$\text{cov } \tilde{v}_p(x + \Delta, x, \pi) = P \text{ cov } \tilde{v}(x + \Delta, x, \bar{p}_\pi)P^{\mathsf{T}},$$

and hence,

$$\tilde{C}_P(x, \pi) = P\tilde{C}(x, \bar{p}_\pi)P^{\mathsf{T}}$$

and

$$\tilde{C}_{\rho, P}(x, \pi) = P\tilde{C}_\rho(x, \bar{p}_\pi)P^{\mathsf{T}}.$$

Thus, if Hypothesis 1* or 1 is satisfied for the microeconomic commodity space $\mathbb{R}^l$, it is also satisfied for every composite commodity space $\mathbb{R}^K$. Are there any a priori reasons why the hypothesis of increasing dispersion would be rejected for some level of commodity aggregation but not for another?

Up to now I considered the conditional distribution $v(p|x)$ of x-households' demand and then I compared this distribution with the hypothetical distribution $\tilde{\nu}(x + \Delta, x, p)$ of x-households' demand under the hypothesis that the x-households income is increased to $x + \Delta$.

Now I consider the distribution $\nu(p)$ of *all* households' demand and compare this distribution with a hypothetical distribution $\tilde{\nu}(\Delta, p)$, which is obtained by assuming that the income of *every* household is increased by $\Delta > 0$. More formally, $\tilde{\nu}(\Delta, p)$ is the image distribution of μ on $\mathcal{A} \times \mathbb{R}_+$ with respect to the mapping

$$(\alpha, x) \longmapsto f^\alpha(p, x + \Delta).$$

With this notation I can now formulate the following hypothesis:

Hypothesis 2:   Increasing Dispersion of All Households' Demand.   *For all directions v that are orthogonal to $F(p)$, the distribution $\tilde{\nu}(\Delta, p)$ is more dispersed than the distribution $\nu(p)$, if $\Delta > 0$. In particular, the matrix*

$$\tilde{C}(p) = \partial_\Delta \operatorname{cov} \tilde{\nu}(\Delta, p)|_{\Delta=0}$$

is positive semidefinite on the hyperplane $F(p)^\perp$.

Clearly, the foregoing Remarks 1 and 4 also apply to Hypothesis 2.

Remark 5.   In Hypothesis 1* increasing dispersion is required in *all directions*. Why then in the formulation of Hypothesis 2 is increasing dispersion required *only* in directions that are orthogonal to market demand $F(p)$?

The reason is that the assumption of a matrix $\tilde{C}(p)$ turns out to be very restrictive. Indeed, this follows from purely theoretical arguments, and more importantly, increasing dispersion in *all* directions is rejected by empirical tests as I shall show in Section 3.3.

One formal reason is that even for the trivial example of a μ-model where all household demand functions are linear in income, i.e., $f^\alpha(p, x) = x f^\alpha(p, 1)$, it does not follow, in general, that the dispersion of all households' demand is increasing in directions that are not orthogonal to $F(p)$. Yet the market demand of such a μ-model satisfies Wald's Axiom because in this example the market demand is even monotone.

There is, however, another reason. If the μ-model is interpreted as modelling *short-run* demand, then households' demand functions

f^α typically do not satisfy the budget identity $p \cdot f^\alpha(p, x) \equiv x$. If, however, one also wants to consider the μ-model as a model for *intertemporal* demand, like in general equilibrium theory, then the budget identity $p \cdot f^\alpha(p, x) \equiv x$ holds for all household demand functions. In this case the stronger version of Hypothesis 2 has an unpleasant implication, as I shall show in succeeding text. Surely I do not want to exclude an intertemporal interpretation of the μ-model, even though the presentation in this book emphasizes the short-run interpretation. Since I am mainly interested in testing the hypothesis with data from family expenditure surveys, I have to interpret the μ-model as a model for short-run demand, and hence I cannot require the budget identity.

I now want to show that increasing dispersion of all household demand in every direction together with the budget identity for household demand functions implies that

$$\text{cov}_\mu \left(\partial_x f_k^\alpha(p, x), x \right) = 0,$$

that is to say, for every commodity k, marginal propensity to consume and total expenditure are uncorrelated within the whole population.

Indeed, the budget identity $p \cdot f^\alpha(p, x) \equiv x$ implies that

$$p \cdot \text{cov}_\mu \left(\partial_x f^\alpha(p, x), f^\alpha(p, x) \right) p = 0;$$

hence,

$$p \cdot \tilde{C}(p) p = 0.$$

If the symmetric matrix $\tilde{C}(p)$ is assumed to be positive semidefinite, then this implies, by a well-known result, that $\tilde{C}(p) p = 0$. The budget identity implies that

$$\text{cov}_\mu \left(f^\alpha(p, x), \ \partial_x f^\alpha(p, x) \right) p = 0.$$

Consequently one obtains

$$0 = \text{cov}_\mu \left(\partial_x f^\alpha(p, x), f^\alpha(p, x) \right) p$$
$$= \text{cov}_\mu \left(\partial_x f^\alpha(p, x), x \right),$$

which proves the claim.

The following proposition shows the implication of Hypothesis 1* and Hypothesis 2 on mean demand.

Proposition 1.   *Let μ be a distribution on the space of households' char-*
acteristics $\mathbb{R}_+ \times \mathcal{A}$ satisfying the standard assumptions. Then Hypothesis
1* implies that the cross-section demand function $\bar{f}(\cdot, x)$ satisfies Wald's
Axiom, and Hypothesis 2 implies that the market demand F satisfies
Wald's Axiom.

Proof.   The cross-section demand function $\bar{f}$ is defined by

$$\bar{f}(p, x) = \int_{\mathcal{A}} f^\alpha(p, x) \, d\mu | x.$$

Since one can apply Leibniz' rule, we obtain for the Jacobian matrix
of $\bar{f}(p, x)$,

$$\partial_p \bar{f}(p, x) = \int_{\mathcal{A}} \partial_p f^\alpha(p, x) \, d\mu | x.$$

By the Slutsky decomposition of $\partial_p f^\alpha(p, x)$, i.e.,

$$\partial_p f^\alpha(p, x) = Sf^\alpha(p, x) - \left(\partial_x f^\alpha(p, x)\right) f^\alpha(p, x)^\top,$$

one obtains

$$\begin{aligned}
\partial_p \bar{f}(p, x) &= \int_{\mathcal{A}} Sf^\alpha(p, x) \, d\mu | x - \int_{\mathcal{A}} \left(\partial_x f^\alpha(p, x)\right) f^\alpha(p, x)^\top \, d\mu | x \\
&= \qquad \bar{S}(p, x) \qquad\qquad - \qquad\qquad \bar{A}(p, x).
\end{aligned}$$

The matrix $\bar{A}(p, x)$ will be decomposed into two matrices by using
the definition of covariance:

$$\begin{aligned}
\text{cov}_{\mu | x} &\left(\partial_x f_k^\alpha(p, x), f_j^\alpha(p, x)\right) \\
&= \int_{\mathcal{A}} \partial_x f_k^\alpha(p, x) f_j^\alpha(p, x) \, d\mu | x \\
&\quad - \int_{\mathcal{A}} \partial_x f_k^\alpha(p, x) \, d\mu | x \int_{\mathcal{A}} f_j^\alpha(p, x) \, d\mu | x.
\end{aligned}$$

Then one obtains

$$\begin{aligned}
\partial_p \bar{f}(p, x) &= \bar{S}(p, x) - \left(\int_{\mathcal{A}} \partial_x f^\alpha(p, x) \, d\mu | x\right) \bar{f}(p, x)^\top \\
&\quad - \text{cov}_{\mu | x}\left(\partial_x f^\alpha(p, x), f^\alpha(p, x)\right).
\end{aligned}$$

The first matrix, $\bar{S}(p, x)$, is negative semidefinite by the Standard
Assumption 4 on households' behavior. The second matrix has rank

1 and its null space is equal to $\bar{f}(p, x)^\perp$. Hence it remains to discuss the third matrix,

$$Q(x, p) := \operatorname{cov}_{\mu|x}\left(\partial_x f_i^\alpha(p, x), f_j^\alpha(p, x)\right)_{i,j}.$$

Because

$$\operatorname{cov} \tilde{v}(\xi, x, p) = \operatorname{cov}_{\mu|x}\left(f_i^\alpha(p, \xi), f_j^\alpha(p, \xi)\right)_{i,j},$$

one obtains

$$\partial_\xi \operatorname{cov} \tilde{v}(\xi, x, p) = \operatorname{cov}_{\mu|x}\left(\partial_\xi f_i^\alpha(p, \xi), f_j^\alpha(p, \xi)\right)$$
$$+ \operatorname{cov}_{\mu|x}\left(f_i^\alpha(p, \xi), \partial_\xi f_j^\alpha(p, \xi)\right).$$

Hence,

$$\tilde{C}(x, p) = Q + Q^\mathsf{T}.$$

Hypothesis 1* therefore implies that the matrix Q is positive semidefinite. Thus I have shown that the Jacobian matrix $\partial_p \bar{f}(p, x)$ is negative semidefinite on the hyperplane $\bar{f}(p, x)^\perp$. By the lemma in Appendix 2 this implies that $\bar{f}(\cdot, x)$ satisfies Wald's Axiom.

Analogously one obtains

$$\partial_p F(p) = \bar{S}(p) - \left(\int \partial_x f^\alpha(p, x)\, d\mu\right) F(p)^\mathsf{T}$$
$$- \operatorname{cov}_\mu\left(\partial_x f_i^\alpha(p, x), f_j^\alpha(p, x)\right).$$

As before we consider the matrix

$$Q = \operatorname{cov}_\mu\left(\partial_x f_i^\alpha(p, x), f_j^\alpha(p, x)\right).$$

Because

$$\operatorname{cov} \tilde{v}(\Delta, p) = \operatorname{cov}_\mu\left(f_i^\alpha(p, x + \Delta), f_j^\alpha(p, x + \Delta)\right),$$

one obtains

$$\partial_\Delta \operatorname{cov} \tilde{v}(\Delta, p) = \operatorname{cov}_\mu\left(\partial_x f_i^\alpha(p, x + \Delta), f_j^\alpha(p, x + \Delta)\right)$$
$$+ \operatorname{cov}_\mu\left(f_i^\alpha(p, x + \Delta), \partial_x f_j^\alpha(p, x + \Delta)\right).$$

Hence,

$$\tilde{C}(p) = Q + Q^\mathsf{T}.$$

Hypothesis 2 therefore implies that $Q + Q^\top$ is positive semidefinite on $F(p)^\perp$. Thus I showed that the Jacobian matrix $\partial F(p)$ is negative semidefinite on the hyperplane $F(p)^\perp$, which implies Wald's Axiom (Appendix 2).

Q.E.D.

Wald's Strict Axiom for Market Demand

The assumptions in Proposition 1 do not imply that the market demand function F satisfies Wald's Strict Axiom. However, as I shall now show, there is only a small step from Proposition 1 to the very useful stronger conclusion that F satisfies even Wald's Strict Axiom.

Indeed, I have shown in the proof of Proposition 1 that for every v that is orthogonal to $F(p)$ one has

$$v \cdot \partial_p F(p)v = v \cdot \bar{S}(p)v - v \cdot Q(p)v.$$

Now, a sufficient condition for Wald's Strict Axiom is that the Jacobian matrix $\partial_p F(p)$ is negative definite on the hyperplane $F(p)^\perp$ (Appendix 2). Thus, one obtains

$$v \cdot \partial_p F(p)v > 0$$

for $v \perp F(p)$ with $v \neq 0$, if either $v \cdot Q(p)v > 0$ or $v \cdot \bar{S}(p)v < 0$.

The first case amounts to assuming a strengthening of Hypothesis 2. That is to say, one assumes that the matrix

$$\partial_\Delta \operatorname{cov} \tilde{v}(\Delta, p)|_{\Delta=0}$$

is *positive definite* on the hyperplane $F(p)^\perp$ (not just positive semidefinite as in Hypothesis 2). This strengthening of Hypothesis 2, which seems to me quite acceptable, is called Hypothesis 2+. Thus, the standard assumptions on the μ-model and Hypothesis 2+ imply that the market demand function F satisfies Wald's Strict Axiom.

In the second case one uses a nonzero Slutsky substitution effect. Up to now I only used the assumption that the average Slutsky substitution matrix $\bar{S}(p)$ is negative semidefinite. If now one assumes that the matrix $\bar{S}(p)$ satisfies $v \cdot \bar{S}(p)v < 0$ for every v that is not collinear with p, then Hypothesis 2 implies Wald's Strict Axiom. I have excluded a vector that is collinear with p because $\bar{S}(p)p = 0$ if all household demand functions satisfy the budget identity. Thus, by the additional assumption $v \cdot \bar{S}(p)v$ can only be zero for $v = \lambda p$, yet in this case,

$$v \cdot \bar{A}(p)v = \int \partial_x \left(p \cdot f^\alpha(p, x) \right) d\mu \cdot \left(p \cdot F(p) \right),$$

which can be assumed to be positive. Hence I have shown that Hypothesis 2 and a nonzero average substitution effect implies Wald's Strict Axiom.

The relationship between Hypotheses 1 and 2 is described by the following lemma:

Lemma. *For every $v \in \mathbb{R}^l$ that is orthogonal to $F(p)$, it follows that*

$$v \cdot \tilde{C}(p)v = v \cdot \tilde{C}_\rho(p)v + 2v \cdot \tilde{U}(p)v,$$

where the matrix $\tilde{U}(p)$ is defined by

$$\tilde{U}(p) := \int_{\mathbb{R}_+} \left[\left(\int_{\mathcal{A}} \partial_x f^\alpha(p, x) \, d\mu | x \right) \left(\int_{\mathcal{A}} f^\alpha(p, x) \, d\mu | x \right)^\mathsf{T} \right] \rho(x) \, dx.$$

Consequently, Hypothesis 1, the average increasing dispersion of x-households' demand, contributes to the positive semidefiniteness of $\tilde{C}(p)$ on $F(p)^\perp$, but does not imply it, because the matrix $\tilde{U}$ need not be positive semidefinite on $F(p)^\perp$. Hence, assuming that $\tilde{C}(p)$ is positive semidefinite on $F(p)^\perp$ amounts to assuming a sufficiently strong average increase in dispersion in those directions v where $v \cdot \tilde{U}v$ is negative.

The matrix $\tilde{U}(p)$ looks frightening, and, in general, nothing can be said about positive definiteness of this matrix. Clearly, if the household demand functions are linear in income, then is the matrix $\tilde{U}(p)$ positive semidefinite? I shall show in the next section that in Grandmont's example the matrix $\tilde{U}(p)$ is approximately positive semidefinite. More will be said on the matrix $\tilde{U}$ in Chapter 4.

Proof of the Lemma. By the definition of the covariance matrix one obtains

$$\mathrm{cov}\,\tilde{v}(\Delta, p) = \int_{\mathbb{R}_+ \times \mathcal{A}} f^\alpha(p, x + \Delta) f^\alpha(p, x + \Delta)^\mathsf{T} \, d\mu$$

$$- \int_{\mathbb{R}_+ \times \mathcal{A}} f^\alpha(p, x + \Delta) \, d\mu \cdot \int_{\mathbb{R}_+ \times \mathcal{A}} f^\alpha(p, x + \Delta)^\mathsf{T} \, d\mu.$$

The first matrix on the right hand side is equal to

$$\int_{\mathbb{R}_+} \left[\int_{\mathscr{A}} f^\alpha(p, x + \Delta) f^\alpha(p, x + \Delta)^\mathsf{T} d\mu | x \right] \rho(x) \, dx$$

$$= \int_{\mathbb{R}_+} \left[\text{cov}_{\mu|x} \, f^\alpha(p, x + \Delta) + \left(\int_{\mathscr{A}} f^\alpha(p, x + \Delta) \, d\mu | x \right) \right.$$

$$\left. \cdot \left(\int_{\mathscr{A}} f^\alpha(p, x + \Delta) \, d\mu | x \right)^\mathsf{T} \right] \rho(x) \, dx.$$

Taking now the derivative of cov $\tilde{v}(\Delta, p)$ with respect to Δ and evaluating this derivative at $\Delta = 0$, one obtains

$$\tilde{C}(p)$$

$$= \int_{\mathbb{R}_+} \left[\tilde{C}(x, p) + \left(\int_{\mathscr{A}} \partial_x f^\alpha(p, x) \, d\mu | x \right) \left(\int_{\mathscr{A}} f^\alpha(p, x) \, d\mu | x \right)^\mathsf{T} \right.$$

$$\left. + \left(\int_{\mathscr{A}} f^\alpha(p, x) \, d\mu | x \right) \left(\int_{\mathscr{A}} \partial_x f^\alpha(p, x) \, d\mu | x \right)^\mathsf{T} \right] \rho(x) \, dx$$

$$- \left(\int \partial_x f^\alpha(p, x) \, d\mu \right) F(p)^\mathsf{T} - F(p) \left(\int \partial_x f^\alpha(p, x) \, d\mu \right)^\mathsf{T}.$$

Hence if v is orthogonal to $F(p)$, then one obtains

$$v \cdot \tilde{C}(p)v = v \cdot \tilde{C}_\rho(p)v + 2v \cdot \tilde{U}(p)v,$$

which proves the lemma.   Q.E.D.

3.2   Examples

The following examples of distributions of x-households' demand functions might be helpful for understanding the content and restrictiveness of the hypothesis of increasing dispersion.

Example 1:   The reader will easily find robust examples of distributions μ on the space of households' characteristics that do not satisfy Hypothesis 1* at least for some levels of expenditure. In this formal sense, Hypothesis 1* is restrictive.

For example, taking up Example 1 of Chapter 2, consider a population consisting of two types of households with demand function f^1

and f^2, respectively. For the income level x the fraction of households of type one is denoted by $\pi(x)$. Thus, in this example, the *support* of the conditional distribution $\mu|x$ does not depend on x, however the conditional distribution $\mu|x$ depends on x; $\mu|x\{f^1\} = \pi(x)$ and $\mu|x\{f^2\} = 1 - \pi(x)$. One easily verifies that

$$\operatorname{cov} \tilde{v}(\xi, x, p) = \pi(x)\big(1 - \pi(x)\big)$$
$$\cdot \big(f^1(p, \xi) - f^2(p, \xi)\big)\big(f^1(p, \xi) - f^2(p, \xi)\big)^{\mathsf{T}}$$

and

$$\tilde{C}(x, p) = \pi(x)\big(1 - \pi(x)\big)\big(uw^{\mathsf{T}} + wu^{\mathsf{T}}\big)$$

where

$$u = \partial_x f^1(p, x) - \partial_x f^2(p, x)$$

and

$$w = f^1(p, x) - f^2(p, x).$$

Consequently, $\tilde{C}(x, p)$ is positive semidefinite if and only if the vectors u and w are positively collinear (i.e., $u = \lambda w$ with $\lambda \geq 0$).

If there are only two commodities and if the demand–expenditure curves $f^1(p, \cdot)$ and $f^2(p, \cdot)$ look like in Figure 3.5, then $\tilde{C}(x, p)$ is *positive* semidefinite for $x < x_1$ and $x_2 < x$ and *negative* semidefinite for $x_1 < x < x_2$. Indeed, if there are only two commodities, then the budget identity implies that the vectors u and w are collinear, because the vectors are orthogonal to the price vector p. Furthermore, if the distance between $f^1(p, x)$ and $f^2(p, x)$ is increasing with x, then the vectors u and w are positively collinear.

Depending on the income distribution it might well happen in this example that Hypothesis 1 holds, i.e.,

$$\int_{\mathbb{R}_+} \tilde{C}(x, p)\rho(x)\, dx$$

is positive semidefinite.

Now assume that there are three or more commodities and that the two demand–expenditure curves $f^1(p, \cdot)$ and $f^2(p, \cdot)$ do not lie in a plane. In this case the budget identity no longer implies that the vectors u and w are collinear. Consequently, if the vectors $f^1(p, x) - f^2(p, x)$ and $\partial_x f^1(p, x) - \partial_x f^2(p, x)$ are not collinear, then $\tilde{C}(x, p)$ cannot be positive semidefinite, hence Hypothesis 1* will not be satisfied. This shows that Hypothesis 1* is very

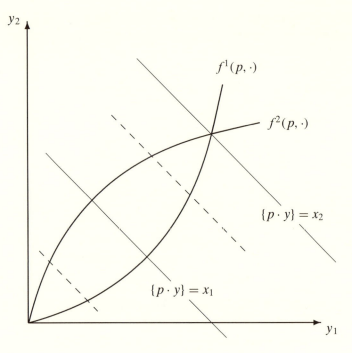

y_2

$f^1(p, \cdot)$

$f^2(p, \cdot)$

$\{p \cdot y\} = x_2$

$\{p \cdot y\} = x_1$

y_1

Figure 3.5.

restrictive if the number of types of households is less than the number of commodities. This, however, is not a relevant case.

Example 2: A trivial example where all three hypotheses are satisfied is the case where *households' demand functions f^α* are linear in income, i.e.,

$$f^\alpha(p, x) = x f^\alpha(p, 1).$$

Indeed, in this case $\partial_x f^\alpha(p, x) = (1/x) f^\alpha(p, x)$, and one easily verifies that

$$\tilde{C}(x, p) = \frac{2}{x} \operatorname{cov} v(p|x).$$

Thus, Hypothesis 1*, and hence Hypothesis 1, is satisfied because the covariance matrix $\operatorname{cov} v(p|x) = \operatorname{cov}_{\mu|x}\left(f^\alpha(p, x)\right)$ is positive semidefinite. Also it is clear that the matrix $\tilde{U}(p)$ of the lemma is positive semidefinite. Consequently, by the lemma, Hypothesis 2 is also satisfied.

Example 3: Now I consider the example of Grandmont (1992) that I described in Chapter 2. In this example the support of the conditional distribution $\mu|x$ consists of all demand functions $f^\alpha(p, \xi)$, $\alpha \in \mathbb{R}^l_+$, which are obtained by the expression

$$f^\alpha(p, \xi) := T_\alpha g(T_\alpha p, \xi),$$

where $g(p, \xi)$ is some given homogeneous demand function that might depend on the expenditure level x, and T_α is a diagonal matrix with α_k on the kth row, thus $T_\alpha y = (\alpha_1 y_1, \ldots, \alpha_l y_l)^\mathsf{T}$.

The distribution $\mu|x$ on this class of demand functions is then given by a distribution on $\mathbb{R}^l_+$, which is assumed to have a density denoted by η. In this example, one obtains

$$\tilde{C}(x, p) = \partial_x \operatorname{cov}_\eta\big(f^\alpha(p, x)\big).$$

To check whether Hypothesis 1* is satisfied, I shall now compute the matrix $\partial_x \operatorname{cov}_\eta(f^\alpha)$. If $f^\alpha(p, x)$ is homogeneous, one obtains

$$\partial_x f^\alpha(p, x) = -\frac{1}{x} \sum_{k=1}^{l} p_k\, \partial_{p_k} f^\alpha(p, x)$$

and consequently

$$\partial_x \operatorname{cov}_\eta(f^\alpha)_{i,j} = -\frac{1}{x}\left[\sum_{k=1}^{l} \operatorname{cov}_\eta\big(p_k\, \partial_{p_k} f_i^\alpha(p, x),\, f_j^\alpha(p, x)\big)\right.$$
$$\left. + \sum_{k=1}^{l} \operatorname{cov}_\eta\big(f_i^\alpha(p, x),\, p_k\, \partial_{p_k} f_j^\alpha(p, x)\big)\right].$$

From the definition of the demand function f^α one obtains (Grandmont, Lemma 1.2.)

$$p_i\, \partial_{p_i} f_i^\alpha(p, x) = \alpha_i\, \partial_{\alpha_i} f_i^\alpha(p, x) - f_i^\alpha(p, x)$$

and

$$p_k\, \partial_{p_k} f_i^\alpha(p, x) = \alpha_k\, \partial_{\alpha_k} f_i^\alpha(p, x) \quad \text{if } k \neq i.$$

Hence

$$\partial_x \operatorname{cov}_\eta(f^\alpha) = \frac{1}{x}\Bigg[2\operatorname{cov}_\eta(f^\alpha)$$

$$-\sum_{k=1}^{l}\int_{\mathbb{R}^l}\alpha_k\,\partial_{\alpha_k}\big(f^\alpha(p,x)f^\alpha(p,x)^\mathsf{T}\big)\eta(\alpha)\,d\alpha$$

$$+\left(\int\alpha_k\,\partial_{\alpha_k}f^\alpha(p,x)\eta(\alpha)\,d\alpha\right)\bar{f}(p,x)^\mathsf{T}$$

$$+\,\bar{f}(p,x)\left(\int\alpha_k\,\partial_{\alpha_k}f^\alpha(p,x)\eta(\alpha)\,d\alpha\right)^\mathsf{T}\Bigg].$$

If the density η is differentiable on $\mathbb{R}^l_+$ and vanishes on the boundary, then partial integration yields

$$\int_{\mathbb{R}^l_+}\alpha_k\,\partial_{\alpha_k}\big(f^\alpha(p,x)f^\alpha(p,x)^\mathsf{T}\big)\eta(\alpha)\,d\alpha$$

$$=-\int_{\mathbb{R}^l_+}\big(f^\alpha(p,x)f^\alpha(p,x)^\mathsf{T}\big)\partial_{\alpha_k}\big(\alpha_k\eta(\alpha)\big)\,d\alpha.$$

The matrix $\partial_x \operatorname{cov}_\eta(f^\alpha)$ is positive semidefinite if it is positive semidefinite on the hyperplane $\bar{f}(p,x)^\perp$; this follows from the budget identity.

Consequently, the matrix $\partial_x \operatorname{cov}_\eta(f^\alpha)$ is positive semidefinite if the matrix

$$2\operatorname{cov}_\eta(f^\alpha)+\sum_{k=1}^{l}\int_{\mathbb{R}^l_+}\big(f^\alpha(p,x)f^\alpha(p,x)^\mathsf{T}\big)\partial_{\alpha_k}\big(\alpha_k\eta(\alpha)\big)\,d\alpha$$

is positive semidefinite. Clearly, the covariance matrix $\operatorname{cov}_\eta\big(f^\alpha(p,x)\big)$ is positive semidefinite. Furthermore, all elements of the second matrix become arbitrarily small if the density η is such that

$$\max_k\int_{\mathbb{R}^l_+}\big|\partial_{\alpha_k}\big(\alpha_k\eta(\alpha)\big)\big|\,d\alpha$$

is small. As shown in Chapter 2, this is the case if the density η of the distribution of α is such that $\log\alpha$ has a sufficiently "flat" density. Thus I have shown that for a sufficiently "flat" density of $\log\alpha$ the matrix $\partial_x \operatorname{cov}_\eta(f^\alpha)$ is nearly positive semidefinite. In the case where $\operatorname{cov}_\eta(f^\alpha)$ is actually positive definite on $\bar{f}(p,x)^\perp$, which essentially means that the generating demand function g is not of Cobb–Douglas type, then it follows that $\partial_x \, \text{cov}_\eta(f^\alpha(p, x))$ is positive semidefinite provided the density η of the distribution of α is such that $\log \alpha$ has a sufficiently "flat" density.

Finally, I want to show that the matrix $\tilde{U}(p)$ of the lemma is approximately positive definite provided the density of $\log \alpha$ is sufficiently "flat". For this, one first computes the marginal propensity to consume

$$\partial_x f^\alpha(p, x) = \frac{1}{x} f^\alpha(p, x) - \frac{1}{x} \sum_{k=1}^{l} \alpha_k \, \partial_{\alpha_k} f^\alpha(p, x).$$

Thus, in this example, *individual* households' marginal propensity to consume, $\partial_x f^\alpha(p, x)$, and demand, $f^\alpha(p, x)$, are, in general, not collinear. If one computes now the *average* marginal propensity to consume of all x-households, i.e.,

$$\overline{\partial_x f}(p, x) = \int_{\mathbb{R}^l} \partial_x f^\alpha(p, x) \eta(\alpha) \, d\alpha,$$

one obtains from the preceding expression for the marginal propensity to consume and partial integration that

$$\overline{\partial_x f}(p, x) = \frac{1}{x} \bar{f}(p, x) + \frac{1}{x} \sum_{k=1}^{l} \int_{\mathbb{R}^l} f^\alpha(p, x) \partial_{\alpha_k} (\alpha_k \eta(\alpha)) \, d\alpha.$$

Hence if the density η (which might depend on x) of the distribution of α is such that $\log \alpha$ has a sufficiently flat density, then the second term on the right hand side becomes arbitrarily small. Thus, in that case, the vectors $\overline{\partial_x f}(p, x)$ and $\bar{f}(p, x)$ are "approximately" collinear. This then implies that the matrix $\tilde{U}(p, x) = \partial_x \bar{f}(p, x) \bar{f}(p, x)^\top$ is "approximately" positive definite.

3.3 Empirical Evidence of Increasing Dispersion of Households' Demand

Hypothesis 1*, the increasing dispersion of x-households' demand, refers to hypothetical situations. Indeed, as I explained before, the distribution

$$\tilde{v}(x + \Delta, x, p)$$

is unobservable from cross-section data, because what x-households would demand if they could spend $x + \Delta$ cannot be observed. Using cross-section data one can estimate, for example, cov $\tilde{v}(x, x, p)$ and cov $\tilde{v}(x + \Delta, x + \Delta, p)$, but not cov $\tilde{v}(x + \Delta, x, p)$. A pure economic theorist might have no difficulty with Hypothesis 1*; it is well defined and, after all, the hypothesis can be interpreted and is not implausible. Indeed, in my opinion, there are many other hypotheses that the profession is used to accepting and that seem to me less plausible, for example, the hypothesis of rational behavior in its various forms.

However, the a priori plausibility of a hypothesis is not a sufficient justification if one is interested in a descriptive theory, that is to say, in positive economics. A hypothesis should also have empirical content. Consequently, a hypothesis should be falsifiable, at least in principle, even if this requires some ideal circumstances that are never precisely satisfied in practice.

I shall now discuss to what extent one can link the foregoing hypotheses to cross-section data. This will be done in the following three steps:

1. *Formulation of Observable Properties.* First I shall formulate three properties of the distribution $v(p)$ of households' demand that are the observable counterparts to Hypotheses 1*, 1, and 2. Strictly speaking these properties are also hypotheses: hypotheses on—at least in principle—observable distributions of cross-section data. Since I want to distinguish clearly these hypotheses from Hypotheses 1*, 1, and 2, I call them properties.
2. *Empirical Evidence.* Then I shall discuss the empirical support of these properties.
3. *Metonymy.* Finally I shall argue under what circumstances these properties imply the hypotheses.

Formulation of Observable Properties

The following three properties of the distribution $v(p)$ of households' demand describe the observable counterparts to Hypotheses 1*, 1, and 2, respectively.

Property 1: **Increasing Dispersion of Conditional Demand.** *The dispersion of the conditional distribution $v(p|x)$ is increasing in income x on the relevant domain of the income distribution. In particular, the matrix*

$$\partial_x \operatorname{cov} v(p|x) =: C(x, p)$$

is positive semidefinite.

Property 1: **Average Increasing Dispersion of Conditional Demand.**
The matrix

$$\int_{\mathbb{R}_+} (\operatorname{cov} v(p|x + \Delta) - \operatorname{cov} v(p|x))\, \rho(x)\, dx$$

is positive semidefinite if $\Delta > 0$. *In particular, the matrix*

$$\int_{\mathbb{R}_+} \partial_x \operatorname{cov} v(p|x)\rho(x)\, dx =: C_\rho(p)$$

is positive semidefinite.

The distribution $v(p)$ on $\mathbb{R}_+^l$ of all households' demand has been "decomposed" into the conditional distributions $v(p|x)$ and the marginal distribution ρ of income. If now for every $x \geq \Delta$ one keeps the conditional distribution $v(p|x)$, but replaces the marginal distribution by $\rho(x - \Delta)$, $\Delta > 0$, then this defines a new distribution

$$v(\Delta, p) \quad \text{on } \mathbb{R}_+^l,$$

which I shall call the Δ-*shift of the distribution* $v(p)$. A formal definition of the distribution $v(\Delta, p)$ is: For every measurable subset M of $\mathbb{R}_+^l$, let

$$v(\Delta, p)(M) := \int_0^\infty v(p|x)(M)\rho(x - \Delta)\, dx.$$

In terms of this distribution $v(\Delta, p)$, I can now formulate the following property:

Property 2: *For all directions v that are orthogonal to $F(p)$ the distribution $v(\Delta, p)$ is more dispersed than the distribution $v(p)$, if $\Delta > 0$. In particular, the matrix*

$$\partial_\Delta \operatorname{cov} v(\Delta, p)|_{\Delta=0} =: C(p)$$

is positive semidefinite on the hyperplane $F(p)^\perp$.

Strictly speaking, Properties 1*, 1, and 2 are not properties of the distribution $v(p)$ alone, because the conditional distribution $v(p|x)$ is obtained by stratifying the *population of households* by disposable income.

Of course, one can also stratify the population by *total expenditure* $e = p \cdot f(p, x)$. In this case one considers for every expenditure level e the conditional distribution of $v(p)$ on the expenditure set $B(p, e) = \{z \in \mathbb{R}_+^l \mid p \cdot z = e\}$. I shall denote this distribution by $\dot{v}(p|e)$ and denote the density of the distribution of total expenditure by $\dot{\rho}$.

Thus, Properties 1*, 1, and 2 can also be formulated with respect to *total expenditure e* instead of disposable income x. The corresponding matrices are denoted by $\dot{C}(e, p)$, $\dot{C}_{\dot{\rho}}(p)$, and $\dot{C}(p)$.

One expects that the increase in dispersion is more pronounced if one conditions on total expenditure e rather than on disposable income x, because only part of the increase in income is actually used for consumption. For example, if all x-households spend the same amount, i.e., $e^\alpha(p, x) = e(p, x)$ is independent of α, then

$$C(x, p) = \dot{C}(e(p, x), p)\, \partial_x e(p, x),$$

and $\partial_x e(p, x) < 1$, if the marginal propensity to save is positive.

The empirical findings, indeed, will show that Properties 1* and 1 are better supported by the data if one conditions on total expenditure rather than on disposable income. It is, however, not clear whether this empirical fact can be used for deriving Wald's Axiom or the Law of Demand. If households do actually save—and only in this case is there a difference between the two ways of conditioning—then the distribution $\dot{\rho}$ of expenditure e is not price-independent. The price independence of the income distribution, however, is an essential assumption for the approach of this book.

Before I discuss in the next section the question of whether Properties 1*, 1, and 2 are consistent with the available data, that is to say, whether some or all are rejected by a statistical test, I should first carefully discuss the question of whether these properties are possibly a logical consequence of their definitions, or at least, to what extent the definitions imply a "tendency" in favor of these properties. Otherwise, it is possible that I claim empirical content of something that actually has none.

For this discussion I choose the case where Properties 1*, 1, and 2 are considered with respect to total expenditure. The case of disposable income is analogous. Thus, let v be *any smooth distribution* on $\mathbb{R}_+^l$ and let $v|x$ denote the conditional distribution of v on the set $\{y \in \mathbb{R}^l \mid p \cdot y = x\}$, where p is any vector in $\mathbb{R}_+^l$.

By definition, the matrix $\operatorname{cov} v|x$ is positive semidefinite and $(\operatorname{cov} v|x)\, p = 0$. Consequently, zero is always an eigenvalue of the matrices $\operatorname{cov} v|x + \Delta - \operatorname{cov} v|x$ and $\partial_x \operatorname{cov} v|x$, yet nothing follows for the sign of the other eigenvalues; in particular, all other eigenvalues can be positive or negative (see Example 1 in Section 3.2). There is no tendency in favor of Property 1* that is due to its definition.

The situation is somewhat different with Properties 1 and 2. Whether these properties hold for an arbitrary smooth distribution v on $\mathbb{R}^l_+$ depends to a large extent on the density ρ of the distribution of the parameter x with respect to which one conditions; in the case under discussion, this is $x = p \cdot y$, i.e., total expenditure. Indeed, one can show (see the proof of the lemma in Chapter 4) that *for any smooth distribution v on $\mathbb{R}^l_+$, the matrix*

$$C_\rho = \int_{\mathbb{R}_+} \partial_x \operatorname{cov} v|x \,\rho(x)\, dx$$

is positive semidefinite and the matrix

$$C = \partial_\Delta \operatorname{cov} v(\Delta)|_{\Delta=0}$$

is positive semidefinite on the hyperplane mean $v^\perp$ provided the density ρ is a decreasing function on $\mathbb{R}_+$. If the density ρ is not decreasing, then the matrix C_ρ or C might, but need not be positive semidefinite. This result shows that for decreasing densities ρ of total expenditure or disposable income, Properties 1 and 2 are tautological. However, estimates of these densities clearly show (see Figure in 2.9) that these densities are not decreasing functions on $\mathbb{R}_+$. Consequently, Properties 1 and 2 are not a logical consequence of their definitions; they have empirical content. The plausibility of these properties is certainly increased by the foregoing mathematical result for decreasing densities, but, definitely, I still have to show that Properties 1 and 2 pass a statistical test with actual data.

Empirical Evidence

If "ideal microeconomic" cross-section data were available [i.e., the quantity demanded (per period) of *all elementary* commodities and the disposable income for a large random sample of households], then one could develop statistical tests for the three properties. For example, one could estimate the covariance matrix $\operatorname{cov} v(p|x)$ of the conditional distribution for various income levels $x_1 < x_2 < \cdots$

provided there are sufficiently many households in the sample with these income levels. Then one can check whether the dispersion of the estimates of the conditional distributions $v(p|x_1)$, $v(p|x_2) \cdots$ is increasing. Unfortunately, ideal microeconomic cross-section data are not available.

Family expenditure data that are available refer, however, to expenditure (in current prices) on consumption categories, where each consumption category is defined by a detailed list of items (see Section 2.4). Therefore, I defined in Section 2.3 for every partition $\mathcal{P}$ of the set of elementary commodities and every base price system $\bar{p}$, the composite commodity μ-model. Properties 1*, 1, and 2 can only be tested for such a reduced μ-model because only these data are available. Clearly, if the microeconomic μ-model (with commodity space $\mathbb{R}^l$) satisfies Property 1*, 1, or 2, then the reduced μ-model (with commodity space $\mathbb{R}^K$) also satisfies these properties. Consequently, if for one reduced μ-model, Property 1*, 1, or 2 is falsified, then this property is falsified for the microeconomic μ-model.

It should be clear that Properties 1*, 1, and 2 for a reduced μ-model can only be tested *at the prevailing price system* with respect to which the expenditure data are obtained. Thus, in different periods the base price system is not the same.

In this section I shall drop the price vector p, since this is always the prevailing price vector, and I shall write $v(x)$, v_Δ, $C(x)$, C_ρ, and C for $v(p|x)$, $v(\Delta, p)$, $C(x, p)$, $C_\rho(p)$ and $C(p)$, respectively.

As explained in Section 2.4, there are 9 composite commodities in the UK Family Expenditure Survey and 14 composite commodities in the French Enquête Budget de Famille. Surely one could choose different numbers of composite commodities, but the data are available in this form, and this is the only reason why I have chosen for the present analysis $K = 9$ for the UK FES data and $K = 14$ for the French EBF data. Alternative aggregation levels should also be analyzed.

One can, of course, question the reliability of the data from family expenditure surveys.[2] Since not all households that are selected in the sample participate in the survey, there is a nonparticipation bias. The accepted view among the users of these data is that house-

---

[2]A discussion of the reliability of the FES data can be found in Kemsley et al. (1980), Chapter 14.

hold expenditure on the various consumption categories are quite reliable—with the exception of underreporting of Alcohol and Tobacco and Consumer Durables. At the end of this section I take up the discussion of errors in the data which I mentioned already in Section 2.3. However, doubt on the reliability is justified in the case of disposable income.[3] Even if the household would report absolutely correctly, the item "disposable income" in the survey does not cover all income sources. If now one stratifies expenditure on consumption by disposable income, then one has to be aware that there might be considerable noise in the data. For this reason, I consider in the following text Properties 1*, 1, and 2 with respect to both disposable income and total expenditure.

In every year there are some households whose total expenditure is several times greater than their disposable income. Some of these households are clear outliers. Since the estimation procedure is quite sensitive to outliers, I have decided to eliminate from the data all households who spend three times more than their disposable income if the estimates refer to disposable income. In the case of estimates that refer to total expenditure, no outliers are eliminated.

The results of the statistical data analysis of the UK FES and the French EBF are presented in the following order:

1. *Estimates of the conditional variance curve*: $x \mapsto \operatorname{cov} v(x)_{hh}$ for a selection of composite commodities h.
2. *Estimates of the ellipsoid of dispersion*:
   - Ell cov $v(x)$ for different income levels x
   - Ell cov v_Δ for different values of $\Delta > 0$
   for a selection of pairs of composite commodities.
3. *Statistical tests of Property 1**:
   - A test for the hypothesis that the distribution $v(x + 0.5\bar{x}_t)$ is more dispersed than the distribution $v(x)$ for the values $x = 0.5\bar{x}_t$, $x = \bar{x}_t$, and $x = 1.5\bar{x}_t$.
   - A test for the hypothesis of increasing dispersion of conditional demand at the income level $x = 0.25\bar{x}_t$, $0.75\bar{x}_t$, $1.25\bar{x}_t$, and $2\bar{x}_t$.
4. *Statistical tests of Property 1*: Estimates of the smallest eigenvalue of the matrix C_ρ with confidence bounds.

---

[3]See, e.g., Atkinson and Micklewright (1983).

5. *Statistical tests of Property 2*: Estimates of the smallest eigenvalue
   of the matrix C with confidence bounds.

Estimates of the conditional variance curve and the matrices
cov $v(x)$ and cov v_Δ are obtained by nonparametric regression methods (kernel estimators). A general reference is Härdle (1990). The
particular methods used for the present data analysis are described
in Hildenbrand and Kneip (1993). For more details and references, I
refer to Kneip (1993). The estimates of the matrices $C(x)$ and C rely
on kernel derivative estimation methods.

The average derivative method of Härdle and Stoker (1989) is
used to estimate the matrix C_ρ. The particular version of this method
that is used here is due to Kneip (1993); a concise description is given
in Hildenbrand and Kneip (1993).

All estimates of confidence bounds for the eigenvalues of the
matrices $C(x)$, C_ρ, and C rely on bootstrap techniques. These techniques allow estimation of upper and lower confidence bounds c_{up}
and c_{low} for the smallest eigenvalue λ_{min} of the various matrices such
that, approximately, one obtains

$$\text{Probability} (\lambda_{min} \geq c_{up}) \approx 0.05$$

and

$$\text{Probability} (\lambda_{min} \leq c_{low}) \approx 0.05.$$

These confidence bounds c_{up} and c_{low} can serve as test statistics
for testing positive definiteness with respect to the critical value $\alpha = 0.05$:

1. Reject the hypothesis that the matrix is positive semidefinite if
   $c_{up} < 0$, i.e., if the entire confidence interval for the smallest
   eigenvalue is negative.
2. Reject the hypothesis that the matrix is not positive definite if
   $c_{low} > 0$, i.e., if the entire confidence interval for the smallest
   eigenvalue is positive.

Estimates of the Conditional Variance Curve

In Figures 3.6 and 3.7 are shown estimates of the conditional variance curve for the FES and EBF data. The curves look similar for all
years. All curves show a clear tendency of increasing variance (heteroscedasticity). In looking at these figures, one should keep in mind

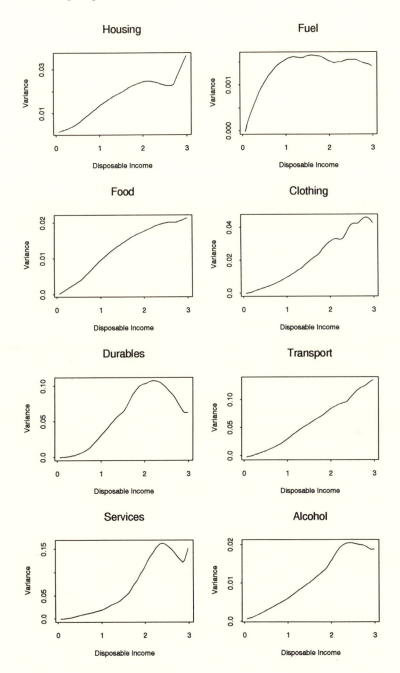

Figure 3.6. *Estimates of the Variance of x-Households' Expenditure on Commodity Aggregates: UK FES, 1984*

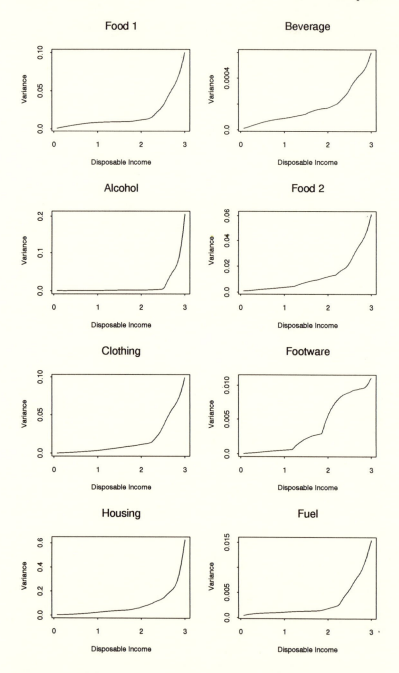

Figure 3.7. *Estimates of the Variance of x-Households' Expenditure on Commodity Aggregates: EBF, 1989*

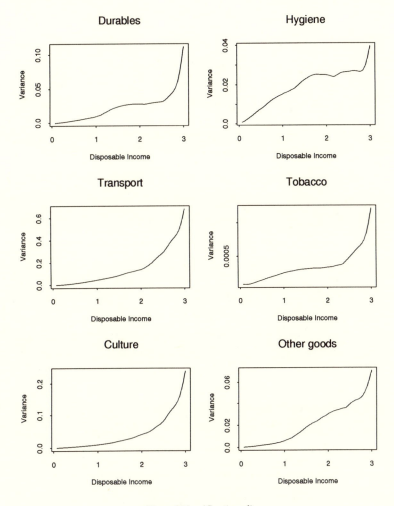

Figure 3.7. *(Continued)*

that for different income levels the sample size is not the same. The estimates are not very reliable for high values of income.

Estimates of the Ellipsoid of Dispersion

In Figures 3.8 through 3.11 are shown estimates of the ellipsoid of dispersion for the FES and EBF data. With the exception of some very few cases, the ellipsoids indicate a clear increase in dispersion. The exception—Housing-Food in FES 1970—disappears in other years.

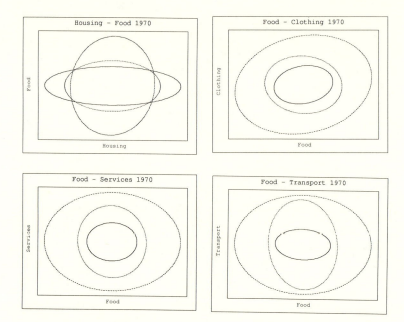

Figure 3.8. *Estimates of Dispersion Ellipsoids for Various Pairs of Commodity Aggregates at the Income Levels 0.5, 1, and 1.5 Times the Mean Income $\bar{x}_t$ for the Year 1970: UK FES*

*Statistical Tests of Property 1**

Table 3.1 shows for the FES and EBF data the *number of rejections* of the hypothesis that the matrix

$$\operatorname{cov} \nu(x + 0.5\bar{x}_t) - \operatorname{cov} \nu(x)$$

is *positive definite* and *is not positive definite* for the values of income $x = 0.5\bar{x}_t$, $\bar{x}_t$, and $1.5\bar{x}_t$.

The hypothesis of increasing dispersion of conditional demand from the income level x to the income level $x + 0.5\bar{x}_t$ is never rejected, neither for the UK nor for the French data. However, the opposite hypothesis, that is, the dispersion is *not* increasing, is not often rejected!

There are more rejections for the opposite hypothesis if one conditions on total expenditure instead of disposable income. This is shown in Table 3.2.

Table 3.3 shows for the FES and EBF data the *number of rejections* of the hypothesis that the matrix $C(x)$ is *positive definite* and *is*

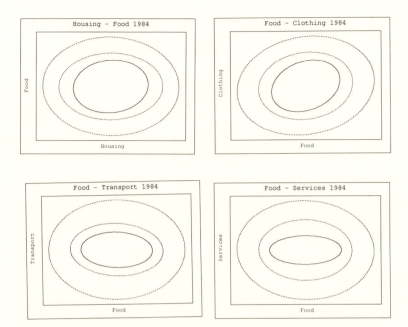

Figure 3.9.   *Estimates of Dispersion Ellipsoids for Various Pairs of Commodity Aggregates at the Income Levels 0.5, 1, and 1.5 Times the Mean Income $\bar{x}_t$ for the Year 1984: UK FES*

not positive definite for the income level $x \cdot \bar{x}_t$ with $x = 0.25, 0.75, 1.25,$ and 2.

Even though Property 1* is only rejected for low and high income levels, the opposite hypothesis, that is to say, Property 1* does not hold, is not sufficiently often rejected in order to conclude that the data support Property 1*. Indeed, too many confidence intervals for the smallest eigenvalue are entirely negative. Moreover, most estimates of the smallest eigenvalue are negative. The situation improves somewhat if one considers Property 1* with respect to total expenditure instead of disposable income, as shown in Table 3.4.

Clearly, just counting the number of rejections gives only a rough image; one should also look at the size and position of the confidence intervals. Having looked at a large number of estimations of confidence intervals with various modifications of the estimation method, I believe that it is fair to summarize the results as follows: Property 1* is rejected for low and high levels of income. For income levels

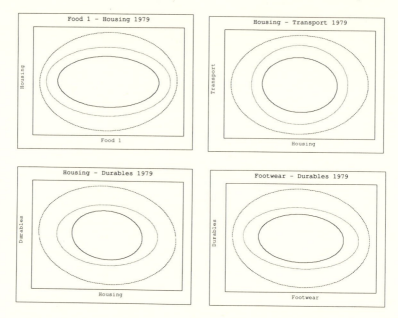

Figure 3.10. *Estimates of Dispersion Ellipsoids for Various Pairs of Commodity Aggregates at the Income Levels 0.5, 1, and 1.5 Times the Mean Income $\bar{x}_t$ for the Year 1979: French EBF*

between $0.5\bar{x}_t$ and $1.5\bar{x}_t$, increasing dispersion is not rejected but the opposite hypothesis is very often not rejected. Thus the data analyzed so far do not support Property 1*. There is a tendency of increasing dispersion of conditional demand and this tendency is more pronounced if one conditions on total expenditure, but this tendency is not as strong as required in Property 1*.

Statistical Tests of Property 1

Table 3.5 gives for the FES and the EBF data the estimates of the smallest eigenvalue with confidence bounds of the matrix C_ρ. As one expects from the previous results, it turns out that the hypothesis of positive definiteness of C_ρ is never rejected; all upper confidence bounds are positive. Furthermore, the opposite hypothesis, that is to say, the matrix C_ρ is *not* positive definite, is always rejected. Indeed, all lower confidence bounds are positive. In this sense the data support well the hypothesis of average increasing dispersion of conditional demand.

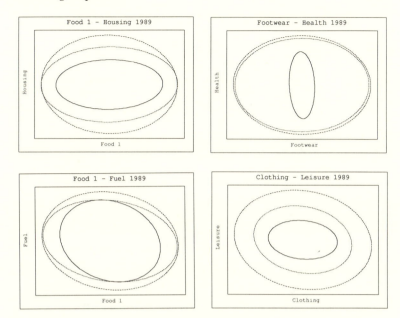

Figure 3.11. *Estimates of Dispersion Ellipsoids for Various Pairs of Commodity Aggregates at the Income Levels 0.5, 1, and 1.5 Times the Mean Income $\bar{x}_t$ for the Year 1989: French EBF*

Without eliminating outliers, the empirical findings are slightly weaker. All upper confidence bounds are positive and for the FES the lower confidence bounds are 4 times out of 17 negative and for the EBF, 1 (out of 3) lower confidence bound is negative.

If one considers Property 1 with respect to total expenditure instead of disposable income, then the hypothesis that the corresponding matrix $\dot{C}_\rho$ is positive definite is *never* rejected and the opposite hypothesis is *always* rejected. All confidence intervals for the smallest eigenvalue of $\dot{C}_\rho$ are strictly positive as shown in Table 3.6.

Statistical Tests of Property 2

As one expects, the hypothesis of a positive definite matrix C has to be rejected. Indeed, for the FES and EBF data the estimates of the smallest eigenvalue of the matrix C are in every year negative and most confidence intervals are entirely negative: 11 (out of 17) for FES and 2 (out of 3) for EBF. If one conditions on total expenditure instead of disposable income, then the confidence interval for the

Table 3.1.   *Number of Rejections*

	(a) FES Number of Rejections (out of 17) of the Hypothesis $\mathrm{cov}\,\nu(x + 0.5\bar{x}_t) - \mathrm{cov}\,\nu(x)$ is		(b) EBF Number of Rejections (out of 3) of the Hypothesis $\mathrm{cov}\,\nu(x + 0.5\bar{x}_t) - \mathrm{cov}\,\nu(x)$ is	
Income x	Positive Definite	Not Positive Definite	Positive Definite	Not Positive Definite
$0.5\bar{x}_t$	0	1	0	0
$\bar{x}_t$	0	0	0	1
$1.5\bar{x}_t$	0	0	0	0

smallest eigenvalue of the matrix $\dot{C}$ is entirely negative for every year in both data sets.

The rejections of positive definiteness of the matrix C can be illustrated for two commodities by drawing the ellipsoids of dispersion. Positive definiteness of the matrix C means that ν_Δ is more dispersed than ν if $\Delta > 0$, i.e.,

$$\mathrm{Ell\,cov}\,\nu \subset \mathrm{Ell\,cov}\,\nu_\Delta.$$

In Figure 3.12 are drawn these ellipsoids for $\Delta = 0$ (solid line), $\Delta = 0.3\bar{x}_t$, and $\Delta = 0.6x_t$ in the case of FES 1969 (Food-Transport) and EBF 1979 (Food 1-Alcohol).

Table 3.2.   *Number of Rejections*

	(a) FES Number of Rejections (out of 17) of the Hypothesis $\mathrm{cov}\,\nu(e + 0.5\bar{e}_t) - \mathrm{cov}\,\nu(e)$ is		(b) EBF Number of Rejections (out of 3) of the Hypothesis $\mathrm{cov}\,\nu(e + 0.5\bar{e}_t) - \mathrm{cov}\,\nu(e)$ is	
Total Expenditure e	Positive Definite	Not Positive Definite	Positive Definite	Not Positive Definite
$0.5\bar{e}_t$	0	16	0	3
$\bar{e}_t$	0	14	0	3
$1.5\bar{e}_t$	0	12	0	2

Table 3.3. *Number of Rejections*

	(a) FES		(b) EBF	
	Number of Rejections (out of 17) of the Hypothesis $C(x)$ is		Number of Rejections (out of 3) of the Hypothesis $C(x)$ is	
Income Level $\bar{x}_t$ Times	Positive Definite	Not Positive Definite	Positive Definite	Not Positive Definite
0.25	4	2	0	0
0.75	0	1	0	0
1.25	0	0	0	0
2	0	0	1	0

If one considers now the hypothesis of positive definiteness of C on the hyperplane $F(p)^{\perp}$, then it turns out that this hypothesis is well supported by the data. In order to show that the matrix C is positive semidefinite on the hyperplane $F(p)^{\perp}$, one considers the orthogonal projection of $\mathbb{R}^K$ onto $F(p)^{\perp}$. Let L denote the matrix representation of this projection. Then the matrix C is positive semidefinite on the hyperplane $F(p)^{\perp}$ if and only if the matrix LCL is positive semidefinite. By definition, the matrix LCL always has an eigenvalue that is equal to zero.

The hypothesis of LCL being positive semidefinite is never rejected, neither for the UK FES nor for the French EBF. Furthermore,

Table 3.4. *Number of Rejections*

	(a) FES		(b) EBF	
	Number of Rejections (out of 17) of the Hypothesis $\dot{C}(e)$ is		Number of Rejections (out of 3) of the Hypothesis $\dot{C}(e)$ is	
Total Expenditure $\bar{e}_t$ Times	Positive Definite	Not Positive Definite	Positive Definite	Not Positive Definite
0.25	0	0	0	0
0.75	0	9	0	1
1.25	0	10	0	1
2	0	3	0	1

Table 3.5. *Estimates of Smallest Eigenvalue with Confidence Bounds and Largest Eigenvalue of C_ρ*

Year	Lower Confidence Bound	Smallest Eigenvalue	Upper Confidence Bound	Largest Eigenvalue	Sample Size
		(a) UK FES ($\times 10^3/\bar{x}_t$)			
1968	2.2	2.7	3.2	40	7098
1969	2.7	3.2	3.8	42	6954
1970	1.9	2.4	2.8	39	6331
1971	2.3	2.8	3.3	43	7171
1972	1.8	2.5	3.2	47	6963
1973	1.7	2.3	3.0	43	7059
1974	1.9	2.7	3.5	43	6626
1975	2.2	2.8	3.5	38	7139
1976	2.0	2.7	3.3	39	7133
1977	1.4	1.9	2.3	43	7124
1978	1.3	1.7	2.1	38	6950
1979	1.0	1.3	1.6	42	6712
1980	1.3	2.2	2.9	42	6889
1981	1.4	1.8	2.2	43	7415
1982	1.4	1.9	2.3	42	7358
1983	1.0	1.3	1.5	40	6915
1984	1.5	2.2	2.9	41	7009
		(b) French EBF ($\times 10^4/\bar{x}_t$)			
1979	1.1	1.4	1.9	473	8501
1984	0.7	0.8	1.0	609	11024
1989	0.5	0.7	0.8	695	8458

the opposite hypothesis, i.e., LCL is not positive semidefinite, is always rejected; all confidence intervals for the smallest nonzero eigenvalue are entirely positive.

If one considers Property 2 with respect to total expenditure e instead of disposable income x, that is to say, one considers the matrix $\dot{C}$, then the same results hold: positive definiteness of $L\dot{C}L$ is never rejected and the opposite hypothesis is always rejected.

Table 3.6. *Estimates* ($\times 10^4/\bar{e}_t$) *of Smallest Eigenvalue with Confidence Bounds and Largest Eigenvalue of* $\dot{C}_\rho$

Year	Lower Confidence Bound	Smallest Nonzero Eigenvalue	Upper Confidence Bound	Largest Eigenvalue	Sample Size
		(a) UK FES			
1968	3.0	4.2	5.4	43	7184
1969	3.5	4.4	5.4	48	7007
1970	2.7	3.3	4.0	44	6391
1971	3.1	4.0	4.9	48	7238
1972	2.5	3.6	4.6	55	7017
1973	2.4	3.5	4.6	53	7125
1974	2.6	3.9	5.1	54	6694
1975	3.0	4.3	5.7	48	7201
1976	2.6	3.8	4.9	42	7203
1977	2.2	3.2	4.3	50	7198
1978	2.1	2.8	3.7	47	7001
1979	1.7	2.2	2.6	50	6777
1980	1.4	3.2	4.6	52	6943
1981	1.9	2.6	3.2	53	7485
1982	1.8	2.7	3.5	57	7427
1983	1.6	2.1	2.7	49	6973
1984	1.7	3.0	4.1	51	7081
		(b) French EBF			
1979	0.79	0.95	1.17	400	10647
1984	0.76	0.86	1.00	431	11978
1989	0.67	0.78	0.85	456	9043

In Table 3.7 are given for the FES and EBFdata the estimates of the smallest nonzero eigenvalue with confidence bounds and the largest eigenvalue for the matrix *LCL*.

Remark: **Errors in the Data.** What can be concluded from the preceding analysis of the household expenditure data? If the distribution of the *x*-households expenditure *data* represents well the distribution

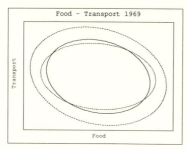
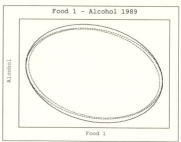

Figure 3.12.   *Ellipsoid of Dispersion,* Ell cov $v(\Delta)$; $\Delta = 0$ *(solid line)*

of the x-households *composite commodity demand*, then the answer is clear: The results of the data analysis support Properties 1 and 2. However, as explained in Section 2.4, there might be errors in the data, and hence these distributions might be different. The question then is: Is it possible that the empirical findings of this section, to a large extent, are due to errors in the data?

In discussing the consequences of possible errors in the data I shall confine myself to the simple case where income x is correctly observed but the vector of composite commodity demand $f^\alpha(x)$ is observed only up to a random error, $f^\alpha(x) + \tilde{u}_{\alpha, x}$. The distribution (on $\mathbb{R}^K$) of the random error $\tilde{u}_{\alpha, x}$ is denoted by $\delta_{\alpha, x}$

Analogously to Section 2.4, I shall consider the expenditure data of x-households as a large random sample of the random variable $(\alpha, u) \mapsto f^\alpha(x) + u$ with respect to the probability distribution $\mu|x \otimes \delta$. The probability measure $\mu|x \otimes \delta$ on $\mathcal{A} \otimes R^K$ is defined by the marginal distribution $\mu|x$ on $\mathcal{A}$ and the conditional distribution $\delta_{\alpha, x}$ given α, x.

One obtains for the covariance matrix of x-households demand with error in the data,

$$\text{cov}_{\mu|x \otimes \delta}\left(f^\alpha(x) + u\right) = \text{cov}_{\mu|x \otimes \delta}\left(f^\alpha(x)\right) + \text{cov}_{\mu|x \otimes \delta}(u)$$
$$+ V(x) + V(x)^\mathsf{T},$$

where $V(x) = \text{cov}_{\mu|x}(f^\alpha(x), \mathbb{E}\tilde{u}_{\alpha, x})$. Consequently, the matrix C_ρ is given by

$$C_\rho = C_{\rho, \text{error}} - \mathcal{U} - \mathcal{V} - \mathcal{V}^\mathsf{T}$$

with

$$C_{\rho, \text{error}} := \int_{\mathbb{R}_+} \partial_x \left(\text{cov}_{\mu|x \otimes \delta}(f^\alpha(x) + u)\right) \rho(x)\, dx,$$

Table 3.7. *Estimates* ($\times 10^4/\bar{x}_t$) *of Smallest Nonzero Eigenvalue with Confidence Bounds and Largest Eigenvalue of LCL*

Year	Lower Confidence Bound	Smallest Nonzero Eigenvalue	Upper Confidence Bound	Largest Eigenvalue	Sample Size
		(a) UK FES			
1968	11.8	17.4	22.7	416	7098
1969	14.9	25.9	35.1	319	6954
1970	16.5	21.9	29.5	353	6331
1971	8.1	15.6	23.6	397	7171
1972	12.3	24.2	33.3	454	6963
1973	13.8	21.9	30.1	463	7059
1974	11.1	20.1	28.1	487	6626
1975	16.7	26.2	34.9	425	7139
1976	9.2	18.8	27.5	393	7133
1977	7.0	12.9	19.4	374	7124
1978	10.6	14.3	17.6	489	6950
1979	6.5	9.9	13.9	584	6712
1980	10.1	14.5	18.5	507	6889
1981	8.5	11.9	15.7	500	7415
1982	8.4	11.2	14.6	498	7358
1983	5.9	8.6	12.1	435	6915
1984	11.8	16.9	22.1	448	7009
		(b) French EBF			
1979	1.0	1.2	1.6	398	9052
1984	0.7	0.8	0.9	498	11023
1989	0.5	0.7	0.7	572	8458

$$\mathcal{U} := \int_{\mathbb{R}_+} \big(\partial_x \, \mathrm{cov}_{\mu|x\otimes\delta}(u)\big)\rho(x)\,dx,$$

and

$$\mathcal{V} =: \int \big(\partial_x V(x)\big)\rho(x)\,dx.$$

The empirical findings support the assumption that the matrix $C_{\rho,\,\mathrm{error}}$ is positive definite. One wants to conclude from this that the matrix C_ρ is positive definite. For this conclusion one needs that the expression $\mathcal{U} + \mathcal{V} + \mathcal{V}^\top$ is negative semidefinite or negligible. What can be said about the structure of the matrices $\mathcal{U}$ and $\mathcal{V}$?

If the random errors $\tilde{u}_{\alpha, x}$ *do not depend on household characteristics* (α, x), then, of course, $\mathcal{U} = 0$ and $\mathcal{V} = 0$. This case does not seem to be very realistic. In general, I find it very plausible that the matrix $\mathcal{U}$ is *positive* semidefinite, that is to say, it models the error structure by the property of average conditional increasing dispersion. This, of course, creates a difficulty if the eigenvalues of $\mathcal{U}$ are not small. Note that the matrix $\mathcal{U}$ is, in fact, positive semidefinite for every decreasing income density ρ on $\mathbb{R}_+$ independently of any specific assumption on the error structure (for a proof, see the Lemma in Section 4.3).

Consequently, if *there is no correlation between the expected error* $\mathbb{E}\tilde{u}_{\alpha, x}$ *and demand* $f^\alpha(x)$ *within the subpopulations of x-households,* i.e., $V(x) = 0$ (e.g., $\mathbb{E}\tilde{u}_{\alpha, x}$ does not depend on α), then the empirical findings, i.e., the positive definiteness of $C_{\rho, \text{error}}$, do not allow a conclusion without a qualification that the matrix C_ρ is positive definite.

The situation, however, is different, if there is a correlation between expected error and demand. The following simple, yet unrealistic, example makes this point clear.

Example: **Deterministic Underreporting.** As in the example in Section 2.4, let

$$\tilde{u}_{\alpha, x} = -D_\tau f^\alpha(x),$$

where D_τ is a diagonal matrix with $\tau_1, \ldots, \tau_K$ on the diagonal. Then one obtains

$$\text{cov}_{\mu|x}\left(f^\alpha(x) - D_\tau f^\alpha(x)\right) = D_{1-\tau}\, \text{cov}_{\mu|x}\left(f^\alpha(x)\right) D_{1-\tau}$$

and hence

$$C_{\rho, \text{error}} = D_{1-\tau} C_\rho D_{1-\tau}.$$

Consequently, C_ρ is positive semidefinite if and only if $C_{\rho, \text{error}}$ is positive semidefinite.

Without specific assumptions on the random error structure nothing can be said on the definiteness of the matrix $\mathcal{V}$. It seems to me, however, implausible that the matrix $\mathcal{V}$ is positive definite, which would lead to an additional difficulty. For example, if the expected error is proportional to demand, i.e., $(\mathbb{E}\tilde{u}_{\alpha, x})_k = -\tau f^\alpha(x)$ for consumption category k, then $\mathcal{V}_{kk} = -\tau \int_{\mathbb{R}_+} \partial_x \text{var}_{\mu|x}(f_k^\alpha(x))\rho(x)\, dx,$

which is likely to be negative, and actually is negative for any decreasing density ρ on $\mathbb{R}_+$. More generally, if one believes that *the expected error* $\mathbb{E}\tilde{u}_{\alpha, x}$ *and demand* $f^\alpha(x)$ *are correlated within the population of x-households*, then it is plausible to assume that $\text{cov}_{\mu|x}(f_k^\alpha(x), \mathbb{E}_k\tilde{u}_{\alpha, x}) <$ 0. To model the error structure by a negative semidefinite matrix $V(x) = \text{cov}_{\mu|x}(f^\alpha(x), \mathbb{E}\tilde{u}_{\alpha, x})$ is surely more demanding. However, this assumption together with a decreasing density ρ would imply that the matrix $\mathcal{V}$ is negative semidefinite, which is favorable for the desired conclusion that C_ρ is positive semidefinite.

In summary, if one takes into account errors in the expenditure data, then the empirical findings do not unambiguously imply Properties 1 and 2. However, I believe that it would be too pessimistic to claim that the observed average increasing dispersion of conditional expenditure, i.e., the positive definiteness of the matrix $C_{\rho, \text{error}}$, is only due to errors in the data.

Metonymy

Finally I shall discuss the crucial question: *Under what circumstances do Properties 1*, 1, and 2, imply Hypotheses 1*, 1, and 2, respectively?*

A distribution μ of household characteristics for which these implications hold shall be called *covariance metonymic*. Thus, metonymy for a distribution μ of household characteristics prevails if the *observable* matrices

$$C(x, p), \qquad C_\rho(p), \quad \text{and} \quad C(p).$$

are good approximations for the *unobservable* matrices

$$\tilde{C}(x, p), \qquad \tilde{C}_\rho(p), \quad \text{and} \quad \tilde{C}(p).$$

To see what is involved by assuming metonymy for a distribution μ, one again considers the distribution $\tilde{v}(\xi, x, p)$.

Hypothesis 1^* says that the dispersion of the distribution $\tilde{v}(x + \Delta, x, p)$ is increasing in Δ, in particular, the matrix

$$\tilde{C}(x, p) = \partial_\xi \text{ cov } \tilde{v}(\xi, x, p)|_{\xi=x}$$

is positive semidefinite.

Property 1^* says that the dispersion of the distribution $\tilde{v}(x, x, p) = v(p|x)$ is increasing in x, in particular, the matrix

$$C(x, p) = \partial_x \text{ cov } \tilde{v}(x, x, p)$$

is positive semidefinite. Hence, if the dispersion of the distribution $\tilde{v}(x, x + \Delta, p)$ were *decreasing* in Δ, in particular, if the matrix

$$\partial_\Delta \operatorname{cov} \tilde{v}(x, x + \Delta, p)|_{\Delta=0} =: D_2 \operatorname{cov} \tilde{v}(x, x, p)$$

were negative semidefinite, then Property 1* would imply Hypothesis 1*, because

$$\partial_x \operatorname{cov} \tilde{v}(x, x, p) = \partial_\xi \operatorname{cov} \tilde{v}(\xi, x, p)|_{\xi=x} + D_2 \operatorname{cov} \tilde{v}(\xi, x, p).$$

Integrating the last equation on both sides with respect to the income distribution yields

$$C_\rho(p) = \tilde{C}_\rho(p) + \int_{\mathbb{R}_+} D_2 \operatorname{cov} \tilde{v}(x, x, p)\rho(x) \, dx.$$

Consequently, if the second matrix on the right hand side is negative semidefinite, then Property 1 implies Hypothesis 1. This implication motivates the following definition:

Definition: **Covariance Metonymy.** The distribution μ of household characteristics is said to be *conditional covariance metonymic* if the distribution $\tilde{v}(x, x + \Delta, p)$ is less dispersed than the distribution $\tilde{v}(x, x, p)$ for sufficiently small $\Delta > 0$, in particular, if the matrix

$$D_2 \operatorname{cov} \tilde{v}(x, x, p)$$

is negative semidefinite for all $x \in \operatorname{supp}(\rho)$. The distribution μ is said to be average covariance metonymic if the matrix

$$\int_{\mathbb{R}_+} D_2 \operatorname{cov} \tilde{v}(x, x, p)\rho(x) \, dx$$

is negative semidefinite.

What is the meaning of this exotic looking definition of covariance metonymy?

The distribution μ is trivially covariance metonymic if the conditional distribution $\mu|x$ does not depend on x, because in that case

$$D_2 \operatorname{cov} \tilde{v}(x, x, p) = 0.$$

Covariance metonymy is a condition on $D_2 \operatorname{cov} \tilde{v}(x, x, p)$ and, hence, is an assumption on the behavior of *different* households in the *same* income situation, whereas Hypothesis 1* is a condition on $D_1 \operatorname{cov} \tilde{v}(x, x, p)$ and, hence, is an assumption on the behavior of the *same* households in *different* income situations. Consequently, Hypothesis 1* and covariance metonymy are quite different assumptions (see the next example). The matrix $D_2 \operatorname{cov} \tilde{v}(x, x, p)$ describes the gap between Property 1* and Hypothesis 1*, because

$$D_2 \operatorname{cov} \tilde{v}(x, x, p) = C(x, p) - \tilde{C}(x, p).$$

To obtain the desired conclusion that Property 1* implies Hypothesis 1*, one has to assume that either *the gap does not matter*, that is to say, that the matrix $D_2 \operatorname{cov} \tilde{v}(x, x, p)$ is negative semidefinite (definition of conditional covariance metonymy) or that *the gap is "sufficiently small"*, that is to say, the positive semidefiniteness is not destroyed by subtracting from the matrix $C(x, p)$ the matrix $D_2 \operatorname{cov} \tilde{v}(x, x, p)$. What is "sufficiently small"? This, of course, depends on the degree of positive definiteness of $C(x, p)$. To simplify the discussion, I consider the extreme case where

$$D_2 \operatorname{cov} \tilde{v}(x, x, p) = 0.$$

This is equivalent to

$$\partial_x \operatorname{cov} \tilde{v}(x, x, p) = \partial_\xi \operatorname{cov} \tilde{v}(\xi, x, p)|_{\xi=x}.$$

Hence

$$|\operatorname{cov} \tilde{v}(x + \Delta, x + \Delta, p) - \operatorname{cov} \tilde{v}(x + \Delta, x, p)| = o(\Delta),$$

that is to say, the observable covariance matrix $\operatorname{cov} \tilde{v}(x + \Delta, x + \Delta, p) = \operatorname{cov} v(p|x + \Delta)$ is a *first order approximation* for the unobservable covariance matrix $\operatorname{cov} \tilde{v}(x + \Delta, x, p)$.

Remark. The local condition $D_2 \operatorname{cov} \tilde{v}(x, x, p) = 0$ becomes quite restrictive if the covariance matrix $\operatorname{cov} \tilde{v}(\xi, x, p)$ is homogeneous of degree zero in (ξ, p), which would follow if individual demand functions $f^\alpha(p, x)$ were homogeneous. Of course, this is typically not the case if f^α describes short-run demand. For homogeneous demand functions, one can show that the local condition $D_2 \operatorname{cov} \tilde{v}(x, x, p) = 0$ implies that $\operatorname{cov} \tilde{v}(\xi, x, p)$ is constant in x. Consequently, in that case, $\operatorname{cov} \tilde{v}(x + \Delta, x + \Delta, p)$ is not only a first order approximation for $\operatorname{cov} \tilde{v}(x + \Delta, x, p)$, but the two covariance matrices are, in fact, identical. Since $\operatorname{cov} \tilde{v}(\xi, x, p) = \operatorname{cov}_{\mu|x}(f^\alpha(p, \xi))$, the independence of these matrices on x then clearly implies a severe restriction on the dependence of the conditional distribution $\mu | x$ on x.

The definition of covariance metonymy, however, does not imply that $\mu | x$ must be independent of x, as the following example shows.

Example: **A Metonymic Distribution.**   Imagine a population consisting of *two types* of households, say females and males. All females (males) in the population have the same demand function $♀(p, x)[♂(p, x)]$. Furthermore, assume that the percentage of females in the population with income x *depends* on x, for example, it is a decreasing function.

In this example the *support* of the conditional distribution $\mu | x$ is independent of x:

$$\text{supp}(\mu | x) = \{♀, ♂\}.$$

However, the conditional *distribution* $\mu | x$ depends on x:

$$\mu | x\{♀\} = \pi(x), \quad \mu | x\{♂\} = 1 - \pi(x).$$

One easily verifies that

$$\text{cov } \tilde{v}(\xi, x, p) = \pi(x)(1 - \pi(x))$$
$$\cdot (♀(p, \xi) - ♂(p, \xi))(♀(p, \xi) - ♂(p, \xi))^{\mathsf{T}}$$

and, hence,

$$D_2 \text{ cov } \tilde{v}(x, x, p) = \pi'(x)(1 - 2\pi(x))$$
$$\cdot (♀(p, x) - ♂(p, x))(♀(p, x) - ♂(p, x))^{\mathsf{T}}.$$

If the two demand functions $♀$ and $♂$ are really different, then the population of this example is covariance metonymic if and only if

$$\pi'(x)(1 - 2\pi(x)) \le 0 \quad \text{for all } x \in \text{supp } \rho.$$

This condition is satisfied if either $\pi(x) \le \frac{1}{2}$ and $\pi'(x) \le 0$ or $\pi(x) \ge \frac{1}{2}$ and $\pi'(x) \ge 0$. Consequently, the population of this example is covariance metonymic if at the lowest income level $\underline{x}$ one has $\pi(\underline{x}) = \frac{1}{2}$ and if $\pi(x)$ is monotone, either monotone increasing or monotone decreasing. The example shows that covariance metonymy does not imply that $\mu | x$ is independent of x and that $D_2 \text{ cov } \tilde{v}(x, x, p)$ can be positive or negative semidefinite depending on x.

Whether Hypothesis 1* is satisfied in this example depends only on the two demand functions ♀ and ♂. Indeed, one easily verifies that

$$\tilde{C}(x, p) = D_1 \operatorname{cov} \tilde{v}(x, x, p) = \pi(x)\big(1 - \pi(x)\big)\big(uw^\mathsf{T} + wu^\mathsf{T}\big),$$

where

$$u = \partial_x ♀(p, x) - \partial_x ♂(p, x)$$

and

$$w = ♀(p, x) - ♂(p, x).$$

Consequently, the matrix $D_1 \operatorname{cov} \tilde{v}(x, x, p)$ is positive semidefinite if and only if $u = \lambda w$ with $\lambda \geq 0$.

In the case of two commodities, the budget identity then implies that the vectors u and w are collinear. They are even positively collinear if the distance between $♀(p, x)$ and $♂(p, x)$ is increasing in x.

Conclusion to Chapter 3

Traditional aggregation theory analyzes the problem of whether the implications of rational individual behavior are preserved—or to what extent they are preserved—if one goes from an individual household to a large population. Thus the key questions are: What is preserved? What is inherited? The accepted view in the literature is that, in general, one loses structure by aggregation. Only with restrictive additional assumptions on the distribution of household characteristics can this loss of structure be avoided.

Following Hicks, I now would like to take the opposite view in claiming that *Wald's Axiom is better justified for aggregate behavior, that is to say, for mean demand, than for individual behavior.* In claiming this, I base my arguments essentially on the hypothesis of increasing dispersion.

Indeed, for an individual household, negative semidefiniteness of the Jacobian matrix $\partial_p f^\alpha(p, x)$ on the hyperplane $f^\alpha(p, x)^\perp$ (hence, Wald's Axiom) *rests entirely* on an assumption (monotonicity) of the Slutsky compensated demand function, i.e., the negative semidefiniteness of the Slutsky substitution matrix $Sf^\alpha(p, x)$. In contrast to this, for a large population, negative semidefiniteness of $\partial_p F(p)$ on the hyperplane $F(p)^\perp$ *rests on two hypotheses*: One is the negative semidefiniteness of the *average* Slutsky substitution matrix, and the other is the hypothesis of increasing dispersion. Now, if one finds Hypothesis 1* or 2 plausible, then the hypothesis of increasing dispersion *adds* something; it *supports* Wald's Axiom for aggregate demand. Of course, we need some assumptions on individual behavior to obtain that the average Slutsky substitution matrix is not arbitrary. However, Wald's Axiom now stands on two feet: the *average substitution matrix* and the *matrix* $Q(x, p)$ or $Q(p)$ that appeared in the proofs of the proposition. These matrices I do not consider as troublemakers, but as supporters of Wald's Axiom! This claim clearly is based on a strong belief in the hypothesis of increasing dispersion.

Notes on Chapter 3

The property of a market demand function, which I called Wald's Strict Axiom, was first formulated in Wald (1936). He formulated his famous "condition (6)" in terms of the inverse of the market demand function and mentioned that this condition is satisfied for an individual demand function that is derived from utility maximization. Also he announced a paper that, however, has never been published, in which he wanted to show that utility maximization implies "condition 6" for market demand functions. Wald used his condition to guarantee uniqueness of the market equilibrium. Uniqueness is essential for his existence proof, which does not rely on a fix-point theorem.

The property of a function that is described by Wald's Axiom is called in the mathematical literature pseudo-monotonicity; see, e.g., Harker and Pang (1990). The example of Figure 3.1 is from Hicks (1956), Figure 5, p. 53.

The concept of the ellipsoid of dispersion is taken from Malinvaud (1980), Chapter 5.2.

Positive semidefiniteness of the covariance matrix of marginal propensity to consume and demand (average propensity to consume, respectively) has been assumed already by several authors; Arrow and Hahn (1971), Shapiro (1977), Jerison (1982, 1984) and Freixas and Mas-Colell (1987) . The latter authors (Freixas and MasColell) call this assumption positive association. As I have shown, this assumption is equivalent to Hypothesis 1. Jerison [(1984), p. 4] was the first person to give a geometrical interpretation of this assumption. He writes "Positive semidefiniteness of the covariance matrix is equivalent to the requirement that the covariance of budget shares multiplied by mean income increases by a positive semidefinite matrix when mean income rises."

I learned various versions of Hypothesis 2 from Jerison. His work greatly influenced the content of this chapter, in particular, Jerison (1982, 1984) and several unpublished notes, one of which contains the implication mentioned in Remark 5. I had many stimulating discussions with Michael Jerison on the subject of this chapter during his visits to the University of Bonn.

The "empirical findings" of the average increasing dispersion of conditional demand with respect to total expenditure was first shown in Härdle, Hildenbrand and Jerison (1991). In this paper the importance of metonymy conditions was made explicit.

An extensive statistical analysis of the UK Family Expenditure Survey and the French Enquête Budget de Famille, only part of which is shown in the figures and tables of this chapter, has been carried out by Wolfgang Härdle, Alois Kneip, and Joachim Engel. Their help and collaboration is greatfully acknowledged.

Chapter 4

The Law of Demand

We ... must now consider this basic proposition,
[the Law of Demand] which remains what it always was, the centre of the whole matter. Here
at least there is no doubt about practical applicability, for on this principle all practical demand
studies are founded.

—J. R. Hicks, *A Revision of Demand Theory*, (1956),
p. 59

In this chapter I discuss the central theme of demand theory: the Law
of Demand for the market demand function. The law asserts that the
market demand function

$$p \longmapsto F(p) := \int_{\mathbb{R} \times \mathcal{A}} f^{\alpha}(p, x) \, d\mu$$

is strictly monotone, i.e., for any two price vectors p and q with $p \neq q$,
one has

$$(p - q) \cdot \big(F(p) - F(q)\big) < 0.$$

That is to say, the vector of price changes and the vector of demand
changes point in opposite directions. (see Figure 4.1)

As I explained in the introduction, one can derive the monotonicity of the market demand function in the μ-model by simply
assuming that the support of the joint distribution of preferences
and income contains only preference relations leading to individual

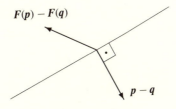

$F(p) - F(q)$

$p - q$

Figure 4.1.

demand functions that are monotone in prices. The class of these preference relations is well-known. For a sufficient condition for monotonicity expressed in terms of utility functions, I refer to the theorem of Mitjuschin and Polterovich in Appendix 4.

In this chapter, however, I want to derive the Law of Demand in the μ-model without making specific assumptions on individual demand functions, that is to say, without simply assuming the Law of Demand on the individual level. I would like to obtain the Law of Demand as a *result of the aggregation procedure*, and not as a property that is preserved from the individual level through aggregation.

I shall assume throughout this chapter the standard assumptions of Chapter 2. From this alone, of course, the Law of Demand will not follow. I have shown in Chapter 3 that in the μ-model, Hypothesis 2 implies Wald's Axiom for the market demand function F. However, between Wald's Axiom and the Law of Demand there is still a substantial gap. Thus, for example, Wald's Axiom does not even imply that the partial market demand curves $p_k \longmapsto F_k(\bar{p}_1, \ldots, p_k, \ldots, \bar{p}_l)$ are downward sloping.

4.1 The Hypothesis of Increasing Spread of Households' Demand

It is well-known that the market demand function F of a consumption sector, which is modeled by a distribution μ of households' characteristics satisfying the standard assumptions of Chapter 2, is monotone if the *average Slutsky income effect matrix*

$$\bar{A}(p) := \int_{\mathbb{R} \times \mathscr{A}} \left(\partial_x f^\alpha(p, x) \right) f^\alpha(p, x)^\top \, d\mu$$

is positive semidefinite.

Indeed, by the standard assumptions, the market demand function

$$F(p) = \int_{\mathbb{R}\times\mathscr{A}} f^\alpha(p, x)\, d\mu$$

is differentiable. Hence, monotonicity of F is equivalent to the negative semidefiniteness of the Jacobian matrix $\partial_p F(p)$ for every price vector p (Appendix 1). Since one can apply the Leibniz rule, the Slutsky decomposition (Appendix 3)

$$\partial_p f^\alpha(p, x) = Sf^\alpha(p, x) - Af^\alpha(p, x)$$

implies that

$$\partial_p F(p) = \int_{\mathbb{R}\times\mathscr{A}_+} Sf^\alpha(p, x)\, d\mu - \int_{\mathbb{R}\times\mathscr{A}_+} Af^\alpha(p, x)\, d\mu$$
$$= \qquad \bar{S}(p) \qquad - \qquad \bar{A}(p).$$

By the standard assumptions the average Slutsky substitution matrix $\bar{S}(p)$ is negative semidefinite. Consequently, if one wants to derive the monotonicity of the market demand function F *without using the substitution effect other than being negative semidefinite* (thus, allowing the possibility of a zero substitution effect), then one needs the average income effect matrix $\bar{A}(p)$ to be positive semidefinite in order to establish that the Jacobian matrix $\partial_p F(p)$ is negative semidefinite.

I now want to look at the matrix $\bar{A}$ in a slightly different way by using again, as in Section 3.1, the distribution $v(p)$ of all households' demand and the hypothetical distribution $\tilde{v}(\Delta, p)$, which is obtained by assuming that the income of every household is increased by $\Delta > 0$.

I shall now describe the way in which the two distributions $\tilde{v}(\Delta, p)$ and $v(p)$ on $\mathbb{R}^l_+$ have to be related in order to obtain a positive semidefinite average expenditure effect matrix $\bar{A}(p)$.

Instead of comparing, as in Chapter 3, the *dispersion* (around the mean) of the hypothetical distribution $\tilde{v}(\Delta, p)$ with the *dispersion* (around the mean) of the distribution $v(p)$, I shall now compare the *spread* (from the origin) of these distributions and formulate the hypothesis that the distribution $\tilde{v}(\Delta, p)$ is "more spread" than the distribution $v(p)$.

I shall now define the partial ordering "to be more spread" for distributions on $\mathbb{R}^l$. First I shall consider one-dimensional distributions. For a distribution v on $\mathbb{R}$, the second moment m^2v is defined by

$$m^2v := \int_{\mathbb{R}} y^2 \, dv.$$

The following Markov inequality is well-known:

$$v\{y \in \mathbb{R} \mid |y| \geq \eta\} \leq \frac{m^2v}{\eta^2} \quad \text{for every } \eta > 0.$$

This inequality justifies the use of the second moment m^2v of a one-dimensional distribution v as a measure of "spread around the origin". This is the same type of justification that was used in Chapter 3 for the variance as a measure of dispersion around the mean, which is based on Tchebychev's inequality.

Thus, a distribution v_1 on $\mathbb{R}$ is called *more spread* than a distribution v_2 on $\mathbb{R}$ if $m^2v_1 \geq m^2v_2$.

One should carefully distinguish between "more dispersed" and "more spread". By the formula

$$m^2v = \text{var } v + (\text{mean } v)^2,$$

it is obvious that there is a difference between "more spread" and "more dispersed". For example, let v_1 be the uniform distribution on the two points 1 and 3 and let v_2 be the uniform distribution on 5 and 6. Then v_1 is more dispersed than v_2, but v_2 is more spread than v_1. For any two distributions v_1 and v_2 with equal mean, v_1 is more spread than v_2 if and only if v_1 is more dispersed than v_2. However, if the absolute value of the mean of v_1 is greater than the absolute value of the mean of v_2, then the relation "v_1 is more dispersed than v_2" implies the relation "v_1 is more spread than v_2".

For two distributions v_1 and v_2 on $\mathbb{R}^l$ one can now define the partial ordering "more spread" by requiring that in any direction the spread is increasing. Thus, consider any linear mapping from $\mathbb{R}^l$ into $\mathbb{R}$, i.e., $y \longmapsto v \cdot y$ for some $v \in \mathbb{R}^l$ with $|v| = 1$. In other words, consider the orthogonal projection of $\mathbb{R}^l$ on the straight line generated by the direction v (see Figure 3 of Chapter 3). It is well-known that the second moment of the one-dimensional image distribution of a distribution v on $\mathbb{R}^l$ under this linear mapping is given by

$$v \cdot (m^2v)v,$$

where $m^2 v$ denotes the $l \times l$ *matrix of second moments* of v, that is to say, the matrix $m^2 v$ is defined by

$$(m^2 v)_{k,j} := \int_{\mathbb{R}^l} y_k y_j \, dv, \qquad 1 \le k, j \le l.$$

Consequently, the distribution v_1 on $\mathbb{R}^l$ is said to be *more spread in the direction v* than the distribution v_2 on $\mathbb{R}^l$ if

$$v \cdot (m^2 v_1) v \ge v \cdot (m^2 v_2) v.$$

This motivates the following definition:

Definition.   The distribution v_1 on $\mathbb{R}^l$ is said to be more spread than the distribution v_2 on $\mathbb{R}^l$ if the matrix

$$m^2 v_1 - m^2 v_2$$

is positive semidefinite.

Every matrix of second moments m^2 of a distribution on $\mathbb{R}^l$, which is not singular,[1] is positive definite. Consequently, one can define an ellipsoid by

$$\text{Ell}(m^2 v) := \{v \in \mathbb{R}^l \mid v \cdot (m^2 v)^{-1} v \le 1\}.$$

This is called the *ellipsoid of spread*. One easily verifies the following property:

Property.   *The distribution v_1 is more spread than the distribution v_2 if and only if*
$$\text{Ell}(m^2 v_2) \subset \text{Ell}(m^2 v_1).$$

The distribution of stars in Figure 4.2 is more spread than the distribution of dots. Indeed, Figure 4.3 shows the corresponding ellipsoids of spread.

In the degenerate case, where the distributions v_1 and v_2 are concentrated on the points y_1 and y_2 in $\mathbb{R}_+^l$, respectively, i.e., $v_1\{y_1\} = 1$ and $v_2\{y_2\} = 1$, the distribution v_1 is more spread than v_2 if and only if $y_1 = \lambda y_2$ with $\lambda \ge 1$.

---

[1] This is not a restrictive assumption in our context. For a singular matrix m^2 one can proceed like in the definition of the ellipsoid of dispersion in Section 3.1.

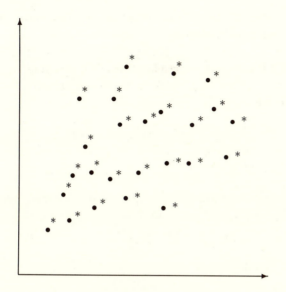

Figure 4.2.

The relation "more spread" can be checked by stratifying the distributions. That is to say, if P_1, P_2, ... is a partition of $\mathbb{R}^l$ and if for every P_i the conditional distribution of ν_1 given P_i is more spread than the conditional distribution of ν_2 given P_i, then the distribution ν_1 is more spread than the distribution ν_2.

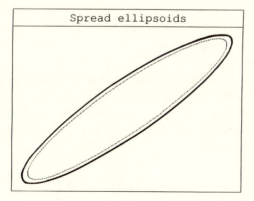

Figure 4.3.

Having defined the partial ordering "more spread," I now can state the following hypothesis:

Hypothesis 3: Increasing Spread of Household Demand.   *The distribution $\tilde{v}(\Delta, p)$ is more spread than the distribution $v(p)$ if $\Delta > 0$. In particular, the matrix*

$$\partial_\Delta m^2 \, \tilde{v}(\Delta, p)|_{\Delta=0} =: \tilde{M}(p)$$

is positive semidefinite.

In terms of the distribution $\tilde{v}(\xi, x, p)$ of Chapter 3, one defines

$$\tilde{M}(x, p) := \lim_{\Delta \to 0} \frac{1}{\Delta} \left(m^2 \, \tilde{v}(x + \Delta, x, p) - m^2 v(p|x) \right).$$

Then one obtains

$$\tilde{M}(p) = \int_{\mathbb{R}_+} \tilde{M}(x, p) \rho(x) \, dx.$$

Remark 1.   Let me emphasize that the hypothesis of increasing spread of household demand does not imply a specific restriction on the behavior of any particular individual household. The hypothesis refers to the whole population of households, which is thought of as being large. If the number of households in the population is smaller than the number l of commodities, then Hypothesis 3 is very restrictive. However, this is not the typical case.

Remark 2.   The hypothesis of increasing spread is defined with respect to a given commodity space $\mathbb{R}^l$. Consider any partition $\mathcal{P}$ of $\{1, \ldots, l\}$ and any base price vector $\bar{p} \in \mathbb{R}^l$ and the corresponding reduced (composite commodity) μ-model, as explained in Section 2.3. If Hypothesis 3 is satisfied, then it is also satisfied for every reduced μ-model. The proof is analogous to the proof of Remark 4 of Chapter 3. Are there any a priori reasons why the hypothesis of increasing spread should be rejected for some level of commodity aggregation but not for another?

Remark 3.   It is interesting to observe that in this case where household demand functions satisfy the budget identity, $p \cdot f(p, x) \equiv x$, Hypothesis 3, the increasing spread of household demand, *is a* *strengthening of* Hypothesis 2, the increasing dispersion of house-hold demand in all directions v that are orthogonal to the market demand $F(p)$. That is to say, *positive semidefiniteness of the matrix* $\tilde{M}(p) := \partial_\Delta m^2 \, \tilde{v}(\Delta, p)|_{\Delta=0}$ *implies positive semidefiniteness of the matrix* $\tilde{C}(p) := \partial_\Delta \operatorname{cov} \tilde{v}(\Delta, p)|_{\Delta=0}$ *on the hyperplane* $F(p)^\perp$.

Indeed, this is a consequence of the following result, which is proved in Appendix 5: If *household demand functions satisfy the budget identity*, then *the matrix* $\tilde{M}(p)$ *is positive semidefinite if and only if*

$$v \cdot \tilde{C}(p)v \geq \frac{1}{2\bar{x}} \left(v \cdot \int_{\mathbb{R}_+ \times \mathcal{A}} x \, \partial_x f^\alpha(p, x) \, d\mu \right)^2$$

for every $v \in \mathbb{R}^l$ *that is orthogonal to* $F(p)$.

Thus, Hypothesis 3, the increasing *spread* of households' de-mand, means that the increase in *dispersion* of households' demand in all directions v that are orthogonal to $F(p)$ *must be sufficiently strong*, as expressed by the preceding inequality.

I do not claim that Hypothesis 3 is *prima facie* plausible as I did in the case of Hypothesis 1* and, in particular, in the case of Hypoth-esis 1. However, it is plausible at least that the diagonal elements of the matrix $\tilde{M}(p)$ are positive. I shall discuss Hypothesis 3 in detail in Section 4.3, where I shall show that Hypothesis 1 in certain circum-stances implies Hypothesis 3. However, the best argument in favor of Hypothesis 3 is, in my opinion, that it is well supported by empirical evidence. I shall give details in the next section.

Now I want to show that Hypothesis 3 implies that the market demand function is monotone.

Proposition 2. *Let μ be a distribution on the space of households' char-acteristics $\mathbb{R}_+ \times \mathcal{A}$ satisfying the standard assumptions. Then Hypothesis 3 implies that the market demand function $F(p) = \int f^\alpha(p, x) \, d\mu$ is monotone.*

Proof. I showed already at the beginning of this section that the market demand function F is monotone if the average income effect matrix

$$\bar{A}(p) = \int_{\mathbb{R}_+ \times \mathcal{A}} \left(\partial_x f^\alpha(p, x) \right) f^\alpha(p, x)^\top d\mu$$

is positive semidefinite. Thus, it remains to show that Hypothesis 3 implies this property of $\bar{A}(p)$. Since

$$m^2 \tilde{v}(\Delta, p) = \int_{\mathbb{R}_+ \times \mathscr{A}} f^\alpha(p, x + \Delta) f^\alpha(p, x + \Delta)^\top d\mu,$$

one obtains for the derivative $\partial_\Delta m^2 \tilde{v}(\Delta, p)$ evaluated at $\Delta = 0$,

$$\tilde{M}(p) = \partial_\Delta m^2 \tilde{v}(\Delta, p)|_{\Delta=0} = \int_{\mathbb{R}_+ \times \mathscr{A}} \partial_x \left(f^\alpha(p, x) f^\alpha(p, x)^\top \right) d\mu$$

$$= \bar{A}(p) + \bar{A}(p)^\top.$$

Thus, Hypothesis 3 is equivalent to the positive semidefiniteness of the matrix $\bar{A}(p)$.   Q.E.D.

I have to admit that Proposition 2 is almost trivial, because I assumed by Hypothesis 3, in only a slightly disguised form, what is needed in the proof. The really hard work in this chapter is to justify Hypothesis 3. This will be done in the next two sections. At this point I just want to emphasize that Hypothesis 3 refers to the *entire population* of households, which typically is quite heterogeneous. Indeed, households are different in their demand behavior, described by different demand functions, and, as a matter of fact, households differ in income.

This remark is important because Hypothesis 3, when applied to a population of households with *identical* income (the population of x-households) *is not well supported* by cross-section data that have been analyzed so far. This will be shown in Section 4.2.

If Hypothesis 3 is applied to the subpopulation of x-households, that is to say, if one postulates increasing spread of x-households' demand, then this amounts to assuming that the matrix

$$\partial_\Delta m^2 \tilde{v}(x + \Delta, x, p)|_{\Delta=0} =: \tilde{M}(x, p)$$

is positive semidefinite. This is equivalent to a strengthening of Hypothesis 1* if all household demand functions satisfy the budget identity. Indeed, the result of Appendix 5 implies in that case that *the matrix $\tilde{M}(x, p)$ is positive semidefinite if and only if*

$$v \cdot \tilde{C}(x, p)v \geq \frac{x}{2} \left(v \cdot \int_{\mathscr{A}} \partial_x f^\alpha(p, x) d\mu|x \right)^2$$

for every v that is orthogonal to $\bar{f}(p, x)$.

This inequality means that the increase in dispersion of x-households' demand in all directions v that are orthogonal to $\bar{f}(p, x)$ *must be sufficiently strong.* As I said before, this strong form of increasing dispersion of x-households' demand is not supported by cross-section data (this claim, of course, is based on an appropriate metonymy condition that one might reject!).

The mathematical result, however, which says that *sufficiently strong increasing dispersion of x-households' demand* (quantified by the foregoing inequality) *implies the Law of Demand for* $\bar{f}(\cdot, x)$, *and, hence, for the market demand function F*, is quite elegant. Unfortunately, as is often the case with elegant results (e.g., Lemma 1 in succeeding text), the required assumption is in conflict with empirical evidence!

It is interesting at this point to consider again the examples of Section 3.2.

1. The trivial example of demand functions, which are linear in income, i.e.,

$$f^\alpha(p, x) = x f^\alpha(p, 1),$$

satisfies the foregoing strong version of Hypothesis 3, because in that case

$$\tilde{M}(x, p) = \frac{2}{x} m^2 v(p|x),$$

which is positive semidefinite.

2. For the example of Grandmont (1992), one obtains by a computation analogous to the one in Chapter 3.2 that

$$\tilde{M}(x, p) = \frac{2}{x} m_\eta^2 \big(f^\alpha(p, x) \big)$$

$$+ \frac{1}{x} \sum_{k=1}^{l} \int_{\mathbb{R}_+^l} \big(f^\alpha(p, x) f^\alpha(p, x)^\top \big) \partial_{\alpha_k} \big(\alpha_k \eta(\alpha) \big) d\alpha.$$

The matrix $m_\eta^2 \big(f^\alpha(p, x) \big)$ of second moments clearly is positive semidefinite. If now the density η of the distribution of α is such that $\log \alpha$ has a sufficiently "flat" density, as explained in Section 3.2, then the second matrix on the right hand side can be neglected and, consequently, the matrix $\tilde{M}(x, p)$ tends to be positive semidefinite.

In both examples it thus turns out that the average demand of all x-households, i.e., the function $\bar{f}(\cdot, x)$, is monotone. Consequently, in these examples, to obtain the Law of Demand for the market demand function F, one does not need any form of heterogeneity of the population in income!

***Remark:* From Monotonicity to the Law of Demand.**   Proposition 2 does not say that Hypothesis 3 implies the Law of Demand for the market demand function F, that is to say, that F is *strictly* monotone. However, the gap between monotonicity and the Law of Demand for F is easily filled.

To obtain the Law of Demand it suffices (Appendix 1) to show that the Jacobian matrix

$$\partial_p F(p) = \bar{S}(p) - \bar{A}(p)$$

is negative definite, not just negative semidefinite. This can be achieved in two ways: either one strengthens Hypothesis 3 or one requires a non-zero average Slutsky substitution effect (compare the discussion for Wald's Strong Axiom in Chapter 3).

In the first case, one assumes that the matrix $\tilde{M}(p)$ is *positive definite*. I call this Hypothesis 3^+. I have shown previously that $\tilde{M}(p) = \bar{A}(p) + \bar{A}(p)^{\mathsf{T}}$. Thus, Hypothesis 3^+ is equivalent to the positive definiteness of the matrix $\bar{A}(p)$. This proves that *Hypothesis 3^+ implies the Law of Demand for the market demand function F.*

In the second case, one assumes that the average Slutsky substitution matrix $\bar{S}(p)$ satisfies

$$v \cdot \bar{S}(p)v < 0$$

for every $v \neq 0$ that is not collinear with p. I call this assumption a *nonzero average substitution effect*.

I have excluded a vector v that is collinear with p because $\bar{S}(p)p = 0$ for all demand functions that satisfy the budget identity.

Thus, by assumption, $v \cdot \bar{S}(p)v$ can only be zero for $v = \lambda p$, but in this case,

$$v \cdot \bar{A}(p)v = \lambda^2 \int \partial \left(p \cdot f^\alpha(p, x) \right) d\mu \cdot \left(p \cdot F(p) \right),$$

which can be assumed to be positive. Hence, I have shown that *Hypothesis 3 and a nonzero average substitution effect implies the Law of Demand.*

The stronger assumption on $\tilde{M}(p)$ or $\bar{S}(p)$ was not assumed from the beginning, even though for a large heterogeneous population these strengthenings seem to me very acceptable. The reason is that in simple *examples* for μ-models where *there is not sufficient heterogeneity* they might not be satisfied.

For example, if all households in the population have the same demand function $f(p, x)$ with $f(p, 0) = 0$ and if income is uniformly distributed on the interval $[0, 1]$, then Hypothesis 3 is satisfied but not Hypothesis 3^+. Indeed, in this case one easily shows that

$$
\begin{aligned}
\tilde{M}(p) &= \bar{A}(p) + \bar{A}(p)^\mathsf{T} \\
&= \int_0^1 \left(\partial_x f(p, x)\right) f(p, x)^\mathsf{T}\, dx + \int_0^1 f(p, x)\left(\partial_x f(p, x)\right)^\mathsf{T} dx \\
&= \int_0^1 \partial_x\left(f(p, x) f(p, x)^\mathsf{T}\right) dx \\
&= f(p, 1) f(p, 1)^\mathsf{T}.
\end{aligned}
$$

Thus, $\tilde{M}(p)$ is positive semidefinite but not positive definite; the rank of the matrix $\tilde{M}(p)$ is equal to 1. This or other examples of similar type are not very relevant for a positive theory of market demand, yet to exclude them from the general theory would be quite awkward.

4.2 Empirical Evidence of Increasing Spread

In this section I want to argue that Hypothesis 3 is well supported by empirical evidence. To do this, I shall proceed, as in Chapter 3, in three steps:

1. First I shall formulate a property of the distribution $v(p)$ of households' demand, called Property 3, which is the "observable" counterpart to Hypothesis 3.
2. Then I shall discuss the empirical support of Property 3.
3. Finally I shall argue under what circumstances Property 3 implies Hypothesis 3.

As with Hypotheses 1 and 2, the "inductive validation" of Hypothesis 3 is based, alas, on an untested metonymy condition.

Average Increasing Spread of Conditional Demand

Consider the *average Δ-shifted conditional second moment* matrix

$$m^2 v(\Delta, p) := \int_{\mathbb{R}_+} m^2 v(p|x + \Delta)\rho(x)\,dx.$$

As the notation indicates, this matrix is just the matrix of second moments of the distribution $v(\Delta, p)$, which was defined in Chapter 3. Clearly, $m^2 v(0, p) = m^2 v(p)$ is the second moment matrix of all households' demand.

The following property of the distribution $v(p)$ of households' demand describes the observable counterpart to Hypothesis 3.

*Property 3: **Average Increasing Spread of Conditional Demand.***   *The distribution $v(\Delta, p)$ is more spread than the distribution $v(p)$ if $\Delta > 0$, i.e., the matrix*
$$m^2 v(\Delta, p) - m^2 v(p),$$
is positive semidefinite for $\Delta > 0$. In particular, the matrix
$$\int_{\mathbb{R}_+} \partial_x m^2\, v(p|x)\rho(x)\,dx =: M(p)$$
is positive semidefinite.

It is important to remark that—in contrast to Hypothesis 3—if Property 3 is satisfied for every subpopulation of a partition of the entire population, then the entire population does not necessarily satisfy Property 3. Thus, Property 3 is not additive!

Property 3, the average increasing spread of conditional demand, is formulated in terms of the conditional distribution $v(p|x)$ of x-households' demand, which is obtained by stratifying the population of households by disposable income x. Alternatively, one can also stratify the population by total expenditure $e = p \cdot f(p, x)$. In this case, one considers for every total expenditure level e, the conditional distribution of $v(p)$ on the expenditure set

$$B(p, e) = \{y \in \mathbb{R}_+^l \mid p \cdot y = e\}.$$

These conditional distributions are denoted by $\dot{v}(p|e)$. The density of the distribution of total expenditure is denoted by $\dot{\rho}$. Note that the density $\dot{\rho}$ is now price-dependent, because $\dot{\rho}$ is the density of the image distribution of μ under the mapping $(x, \alpha) \mapsto p \cdot f^\alpha(p, x)$.

Average increasing spread of conditional demand with respect to total expenditure then means that the matrix

$$\dot{M}(p) := \int_{\mathbb{R}_+} \partial_e m^2 \, \dot{v}(p|e)\dot{\rho}(e)\, de$$

is positive semidefinite.

Both matrices, $M(p)$ and $\dot{M}(p)$, can be estimated from cross-section demand data; results are given in the next section. From the point of view of statistical analysis, the matrix $\dot{M}(p)$ has an advantage over the matrix $M(p)$: The estimates of $\dot{M}(p)$ are more reliable than the estimates of $M(p)$, because there is less noise in the data if one conditions on total expenditure rather than on disposable income. However, for a deductive derivation of the Law of Demand, one needs Hypothesis 3, and the observable counterpart to this hypothesis is Property 3; hence, one has to consider the matrix $M(p)$ and not the matrix $\dot{M}(p)$.

There is, of course, a link between these two matrices. For example, if all x-households spend the same amount, i.e., $e^\alpha(p, x) = e(p, x)$ is independent of α, then

$$\partial_x m^2 \, v(p|x) = \partial_e m^2 \, \dot{v}\, (p|e(p, x)) \cdot \partial_x e(p, x),$$

and hence

$$M(p) = \int_{\mathbb{R}_+} \partial_x e(p, x)\partial_e m^2 \, \dot{v}\, (p|e(p, x))\, \rho(x)\, dx.$$

On the other hand,

$$\dot{M}(p) = \int_{\mathbb{R}_+} \partial_e m^2 \, \dot{v}(p|e)\dot{\rho}(e)\, de$$

$$= \int_{\mathbb{R}_+} \partial_e m^2 \, \dot{v}\, (p|e(p, x))\, \rho(x)\, dx.$$

If the marginal propensity to save is positive, then $\partial_x e(p, x) < 1$. In this case one expects that the increase in spread is more pronounced if one conditions on total expenditure rather than on disposable income.

Empirical Support of Property 3

The definition of Property 3 refers to the microeconomic μ-model, and hence elementary commodities are involved. Individual household demand data on elementary commodities are not available. The family household expenditure data that are available refer to expenditure (in current prices) on consumption categories, as explained in Section 2.4. An empirical test of Property 3 using family expenditure surveys can only be made for a reduced μ-model, which was defined in Section 2.3. Obviously, if the microeconomic μ-model (with commodity space $\mathbb{R}^l$) satisfies Property 3, then *every* reduced μ-model must satisfy Property 3. Thus, if Property 3 is falsified for at least one reduced μ-model, then Property 3 is falsified for the microeconomic μ-model. It is clear that for a reduced μ-model, Property 3 can only be tested *at the prevailing price system* with respect to which the expenditure data are obtained. In this section, where I present the data analysis, I shall drop into the notation the price vector p, because this is always the prevailing price vector. Thus, $v(x)$, v_Δ, $M(x)$, and M denote $v(p|x)$, $v(\Delta, p)$, $M(x, p)$, and $M(p)$, respectively.

The following empirical findings for the UK Family Expenditure Survey and the French Enquête Budget de Famille, refer each to a reduced model. The composite commodities in each case are explained in Section 2.4. I consider 9 composite commodities for the UK data and 14 for the French data. Surely one could choose different numbers or types of composite commodities, but the data are available in this form and this is the only reason I have chosen for the present data analysis $K = 9$ for the UK FES data and $K = 14$ for the French EBF data. Alternative aggregation levels should also be analyzed.

The results of the statistical data analysis of the UK FES and the French EBF are presented in the following order:

1. *Estimates of the conditional second moment curve:* $x \mapsto m^2 v(x)_{hh}$
   for a selection of composite commodities h.
2. *Estimates of the ellipsoid of spread of conditional demand:*

$$\text{Ell } m^2 v(x)$$

   for different income levels x and for a selection of pairs of composite commodities.
3. *Estimates of the increase in spread of the Δ-shifted distribution v_Δ:*
   - Ell $m^2 v_\Delta$ for a selection of pairs of composite commodities
   - Eigenvalues of the matrix $m^2 v_\Delta - m^2 v$
   for different values of Δ.
4. *Statistical test of Property 3:* Estimates of the smallest eigenvalue with confidence bounds of the matrix M.

Estimates of the conditional second moment curves and the matrix $m^2 v(x)$ are obtained by nonparametric regression methods (kernel estimators). A general reference is Härdle (1990). The particular methods used for the present data analysis are described in Hildenbrand and Kneip (1993). For more details and references, I refer to Kneip (1993). The estimation of $m^2 v_\Delta$ is easily obtained by standard procedures. The estimates of the matrix M rely on kernel derivative estimation methods.

The average derivative method of Härdle and Stoker (1989) is used to estimate the matrix M. The particular version of this method that is used here is due to Kneip (1993); a concise description is given in Hildenbrand and Kneip (1993).

All estimates of confidence bounds for the eigenvalues of the matrices $M(x)$ and M rely on bootstrap techniques. These techniques allow estimation of upper and lower confidence bounds c_{up} and c_{low} for the smallest eigenvalue λ_{min} of the various matrices such that, approximately, one obtains

$$\text{Probability } (\lambda_{min} \geq c_{up}) \approx 0.05$$

and

$$\text{Probability } (\lambda_{min} \leq c_{low}) \approx 0.05.$$

These confidence bounds c_{up} and c_{low} can serve as test statistics for testing positive definiteness with respect to the critical value $\alpha = 0.05$:

1. Reject the hypothesis that the matrix is positive semidefinite if $c_{up} < 0$, i.e., if the entire confidence interval for the smallest eigenvalue is negative.
2. Reject the hypothesis that the matrix is not positive definite if $c_{low} > 0$, i.e., if the entire confidence interval for the smallest eigenvalue is positive.

In the computation of all estimates that refer to disposable income, outliers have been eliminated from the data. All households who spend more than three times their disposable income have been eliminated. If the estimates refer to total expenditure, no outliers are eliminated.

Estimates of the Conditional Second Moment Curve

In Figures 4.4 through 4.7 are shown estimates of the conditional second moment curve for the FES and EBF data. The curves look similar in all years. All curves show a distinctive increasing tendency. This, of course, is not surprising because

$$m^2 v(x)_{hh} = \text{var } v(x)_{hh} + (\text{mean } v(x)_h)^2$$

and the estimates of the conditional variance curves of Section 3.3, Figures 3.6 and 3.7, and the statistical Engel curves (Section 2.4, Figure 2.6) have an increasing tendency. In looking at these figures, one should keep in mind that for different income levels the sample size is not the same. The estimates are not very reliable for very low and high values of income.

Estimates of the Ellipsoid of Spread of Conditional Demand

In Figures 4.8 through 4.11 are shown estimates of the ellipsoid of spread for various pairs of commodity aggregates at the income levels 0.5, 1.0, and 1.5 times mean income $\bar{x}_t$ for the FES (1970 and 1984) and EBF (1979 and 1989). The figures look similar in other years. With only few exceptions, the data show a distinctive increase in spread between the income levels 0.5, 1.0, and 1.5 for every pair of composite commodities.

The hypothesis of increasing spread of x-household's demand, i.e., the hypothesis that the matrix $\partial_x m^2 v(x) = M(x)$ is positive semidefinite for every income level x on the relevant domain of the income distribution, is not supported by the data. Although the hypothesis of a positive semidefinite matrix $M(x)$ is not often rejected, the opposite hypothesis is, however, in most cases rejected.

Estimates of the Increase in Spread of the Δ-Shifted Distribution v_Δ

In Figures 4.12 and 4.13 are shown estimates of the ellipsoid of spread of the Δ-shifted distribution v_Δ for $\Delta = 0$ (solid line), $\Delta = 0.2\bar{x}_t$, and $\Delta = 0.4\bar{x}_t$. For both data sets, all pairs of composite commodities, and all years (with only few exceptions), the ellipsoid of spread Ell m^2 is contained in the ellipsoid of spread Ell $m^2 v_\Delta$ if $\Delta = 0.2$ and 0.4. The increase in spread is, however, in some directions very weak.

If one considers the matrix

$$m^2 v_\Delta - m^2 v, \qquad \Delta > 0,$$

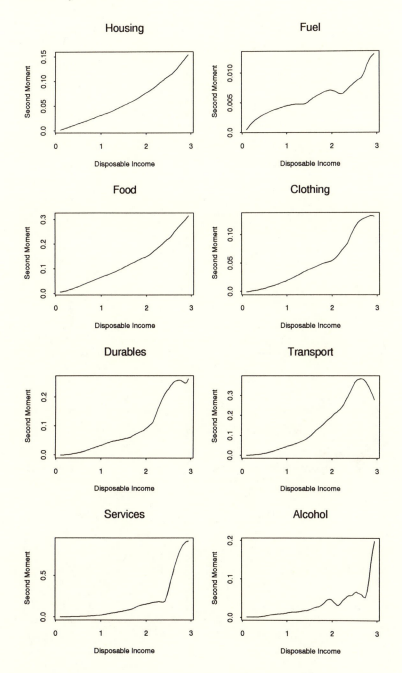

Figure 4.4. *Estimates of the Second Moment of x-Households' Expenditure on Commodity Aggregates: UK FES, 1979*

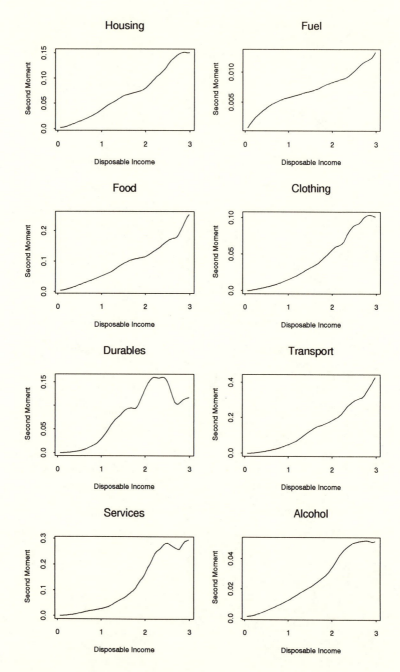

Figure 4.5.   *Estimates of the Second Moment of x-Households' Expenditure on Commodity Aggregates: UK FES, 1984*

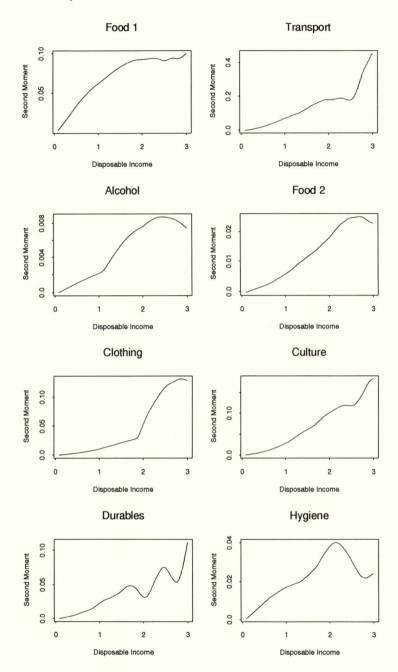

Figure 4.6. *Estimates of the Second Moment of x-Households' Expenditure on Commodity Aggregates: French EBF, 1979*

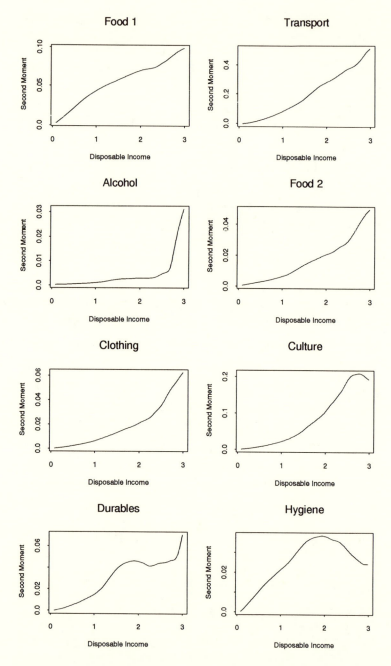

Figure 4.7. *Estimates of the Second Moment of x-Households' Expenditure on Commodity Aggregates: French EBF, 1989*

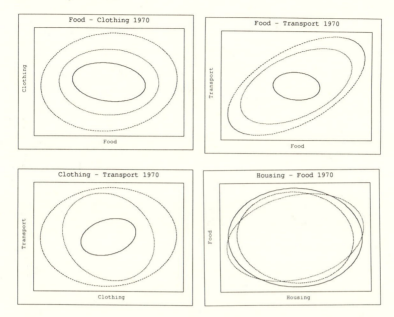

Figure 4.8. *Estimates of the Ellipsoid of Spread for Various Pairs of Composite Commodities at the Income Levels 0.5, 1.0, and 1.5 Times the Mean Income $\bar{x}_t$ for the year 1970: UK FES*

and the estimates of the eigenvalues of this matrix for $\Delta = 0.2$ and 0.4, then the smallest eigenvalue is sometimes negative, yet very small as compared to the largest eigenvalue. All eigenvalues other than the smallest one turn out to be positive, however, several are very small.

Table 4.1 gives the estimates of the smallest and largest eigenvalues of the matrix $m^2 v_\Delta - m^2 \Delta$ for $\Delta = 0.2$ and 0.4 for the FES and EBF data.

The results shown in Table 4.1 improve if one conditions on total expenditure instead of disposable income. Only very few estimates of the smallest eigenvalue of the matrix $m^2 \dot{v}_\Delta - m^2 \dot{v}$ are then negative.

Statistical Test of Property 3

In Table 4.2 are given the estimates of the smallest eigenvalues with confidence bounds and the largest eigenvalues of the matrix M for the FES and EBF data. The hypothesis of average increasing spread of conditional demand, i.e., the hypothesis of a positive definite matrix

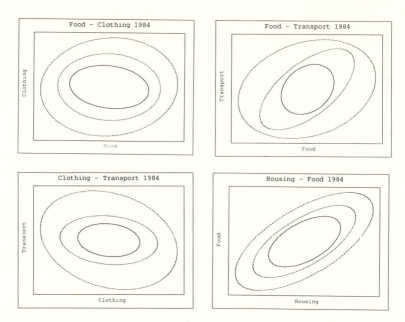

Figure 4.9.   *Estimates of the Ellipsoid of Spread for Various Pairs of Composite Commodities at the Income Levels 0.5, 1.0, and 1.5 Times the Mean Income $\bar{x}_t$ for the year 1984: UK FES*

M, is *never rejected*. Indeed, the upper confidence bound for the smallest eigenvalue is always positive. Furthermore, and more importantly, the opposite hypothesis, that is to say, the matrix *M* is not positive definite, is *always rejected* for the UK FES and the French EBF, because all lower confidence bounds for the smallest eigenvalue are positive. Recall that in computing these estimates, "outliers" have been eliminated from the sample; all households who spend three times more than their disposable income have been eliminated. If one does not eliminate the outliers, then for the UK FES all upper confidence bounds still are positive, yet 3 (out of 17) lower confidence bounds are negative. For the French EBF all lower confidence bounds are still positive. Estimates also have been carried out by various modifications of the estimation procedure. The particular estimates, of course, change slightly, but the general findings are the same. *The hypothesis of average increasing spread of conditional demand is well supported by both data sets for the years analyzed so far.*

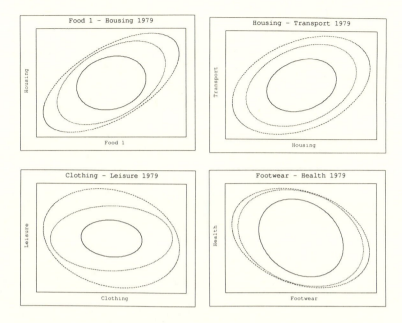

Figure 4.10. *Estimates of the Ellipsoid of Spread for Various Pairs of Composite Commodities at the Income Levels* 0.5, 1.0, *and* 1.5 *Times the Mean Income* $\bar{x}_t$, *for the Year 1979: French EBF*

If one conditions on total expenditure instead of on disposable income, that is to say, if one considers the matrix $\dot{M}$, then one obtains the same result: The hypothesis of a positive definite matrix $\dot{M}$ is never rejected and the opposite hypothesis is always rejected. Table 4.3 shows the estimates in the case of total expenditure. In this case no outliers are eliminated.

***Remark.* Errors in the Data.** What can be concluded from the preceding analysis of the household expenditure data? If the distribution of the expenditure *data* of the x-households represents well the distribution of the x-households' *composite commodity demand*, then the answer is clear: The results of the data analysis support Property 3. However, as explained in Section 2.4, there might be errors in the data, and hence these distributions might be different. The question then is: Is it possible that the empirical findings of this section are due to a large extent to errors in the data?

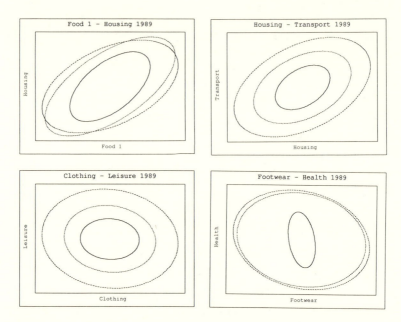

Figure 4.11. *Estimates of the Ellipsoid of Spread for Various Pairs of Composite Commodities at the Income Levels 0.5, 1.0, and 1.5 Times the Mean Income $\bar{x}_t$ for the Year 1989: French EBF*

In discussing the consequences of possible errors in the data, I shall confine myself, as in the remark of Section 3.3, to the simple case where income x is correctly observed yet the vector of composite commodity demand $f^\alpha(x)$ is observed only up to a random error, $f^\alpha(x) + \tilde{u}_{\alpha,x}$. The distribution (on $\mathbb{R}^K$) of the random error $\tilde{u}_{\alpha,x}$ is denoted by $\delta_{\alpha,x}$

Analogously to Section 3.4, I shall consider the expenditure data of x-households as a large random sample of the random variable $(\alpha, u) \mapsto f^\alpha(x) + u$ with respect to the probability distribution $\mu|x \otimes \delta$. The probability measure $\mu|x \otimes \delta$ on $\mathcal{A} \otimes \mathbb{R}^K$ is defined by the marginal distribution $\mu|x$ on $\mathcal{A}$ and the conditional distribution $\delta_{\alpha,x}$ given α, x.

One obtains for the second moment matrix of x-households' demand with error in the data

$$m^2_{\mu|x\otimes\delta}\big(f^\alpha(x) + u\big) = m^2_{\mu|x\otimes\delta}\big(f^\alpha(x)\big) + m^2_{\mu|x\otimes\delta}(u) + W(x) + W(x)^\top,$$

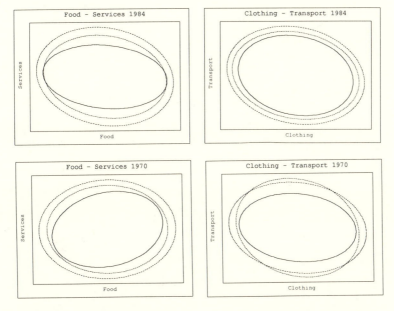

Figure 4.12. *Ellipsoid of Spread* Ell $m^2 v_\Delta$: *FES, 1970 and 1984;* $\Delta = 0$ *Solid Line*

where $W(x) = \mathbb{E}_{\mu|x}(f^\alpha(x), \mathbb{E}\tilde{u}_{\alpha,x}^\top)$. Consequently, the matrix M is given by

$$M = M_{\text{error}} - \mathcal{R} - \mathcal{W} - \mathcal{W}^\top$$

with

$$M_{\text{error}} := \int_{\mathbb{R}_+} \partial_x \left(m_{\mu|x \otimes \delta}^2 (f^\alpha(x) + u) \right) \rho(x) \, dx$$

$$\mathcal{R} := \int_{\mathbb{R}_+} \left(\partial_x m_{\mu|x \otimes \delta}^2 (u) \right) \rho(x) \, dx$$

and

$$\mathcal{W} := \int \left(\partial_x W(x) \right) \rho(x) \, dx.$$

The empirical findings support the assumption that the matrix M_{error} is positive definite. One wants to conclude from this that the matrix M is positive definite. For this conclusion one needs that the expression $\mathcal{R} + \mathcal{W} + \mathcal{W}^\top$ is negative semidefinite or negligible. What can be said about the structure of the matrices $\mathcal{R}$ and $\mathcal{W}$?

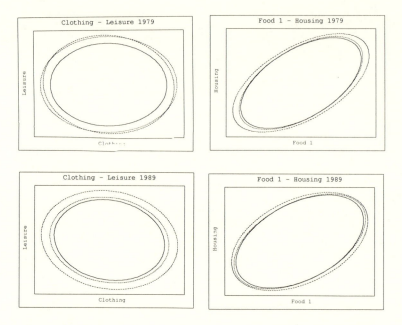

Figure 4.13.   *Ellipsoid of Spread,* Ell $m^2 v_\Delta$: *EBF, 1979 and 1989;* $\Delta = 0$ *Solid Line*

If the random errors $\tilde{u}_{\alpha, x}$ *do not depend on household character-istics* (α, x), then, of course, $\Re = 0$. This case seems to be not very realistic. In general, I find it more plausible that the matrix $\Re$ is *pos-itive* semidefinite, that is to say, to model the error structure by the property of increasing spread. This, of course, creates a difficulty if the eigenvalues of $\Re$ are not small. Note that the matrix $\Re$ is, in fact, positive semidefinite for every decreasing income density ρ on $\mathbb{R}_+$ independently of any specific assumption on the error structure (for a proof, see the lemma in Secton 4.3).

The situation, however, is different, if there is a correlation between expected error and demand. The following simple, yet un-realistic, example makes this point clear.

***Example*: Deterministic Underreporting.**   As in the example of Section 2.4, let

$$\tilde{u}_{\alpha, x} = -D_\tau f^\alpha(x),$$

Table 4.1. *Estimates* ($\times 10^4 / \bar{x}_t$) *of the Smallest and Largest Eigenvalue of the Matrix* $m^2 v_\Delta - m^2 v$

Year	$\Delta = 0.2$		$\Delta = 0.4$	
	Largest Eigenvalue	Smallest Eigenvalue	Largest Eigenvalue	Smallest Eigenvalue
(a) UK FES				
1968	487	0.8	1059	6.8
1969	602	15	1072	12
1970	588	7	1138	13
1971	647	−11	1343	10
1972	628	3	1192	12
1973	510	5	1055	1
1974	470	9	1037	10
1975	449	−3	980	9
1976	514	3	1054	3
1977	487	2	1059	−1
1978	476	0.5	1035	3
1979	514	2	1067	4
1980	479	4	929	17
1981	488	4	981	4
1982	518	1	1046	4
1983	435	−1.6	893	−1.0
1984	629	−1.5	1148	5
(b) French EBF				
1979	443	−0.1	956	0.6
1984	532	0.1	1108	0.3
1989	583	0.1	1188	−1.6

where D_τ is a diagonal matrix with $\tau_1, \ldots, \tau_K$ on the diagonal. Then one obtains

$$m^2_{\mu|x} \left(f^\alpha(x) - D_\tau f^\alpha(x) \right) = D_{1-\tau} m^2_{\mu|x} \left(f^\alpha(x) \right) D_{1-\tau},$$

and hence

$$M_{\text{error}} = D_{1-\tau} M D_{1-\tau}.$$

Table 4.2. *Estimates ($\times 10^4 / \bar{x}_t$) of Smallest Eigenvalue with Confidence Bounds and Largest Eigenvalue of the Matrix M*

Year	Lower Confidence Bound	Smallest Eigenvalue	Upper Confidence Bound	Largest Eigenvalue	Sample Size
(a) UK FES					
1968	7.9	14.0	20.0	2316	7098
1969	11.0	22.8	32.7	2210	6954
1970	10.6	17.1	24.5	2301	6331
1971	4.5	12.8	21.5	2225	7171
1972	8.5	20.9	30.6	2294	7059
1973	10.3	19.1	27.8	2193	7059
1974	8.6	18.0	26.5	2206	6626
1975	13.2	23.4	32.7	2203	7139
1976	5.8	15.4	24.5	2181	7133
1977	3.1	9.8	16.8	2176	7124
1978	7.7	11.8	15.1	2143	6950
1979	3.5	7.3	11.6	2243	6712
1980	7.1	11.7	15.9	2045	6889
1981	5.2	9.0	12.9	2050	7415
1982	5.0	8.1	11.8	2131	7358
1983	1.8	4.9	8.7	2106	6915
1984	7.9	13.6	19.0	2193	7009
(b) French EBF					
1979	0.99	1.23	1.62	2107	9052
1984	0.69	0.78	0.90	2265	11023
1989	0.53	0.64	0.74	2418	8458

Consequently, M is positive semidefinite if and only if M_{error} is positive semidefinite.

Without specific assumptions on the random error structure, nothing can be said on the definiteness of the matrix $\mathcal{W}$. Clearly, for unbiased errors, i.e., $\mathbb{E}\tilde{u}_{\alpha, x} = 0$, it follows that $\mathcal{W} = 0$. For biased errors with $\mathbb{E}\tilde{u}_{\alpha, x} < 0$, it seems to me, however, implausible that the matrix $\mathcal{W}$ is positive definite, which would lead to an additional diffi-

Table 4.3. *Estimates ($\times 10^4/\bar{e}_t$) of the Smallest Eigenvalue of $\dot{M}$, Upper and Lower Confidence Bounds*

Year	Lower Confidence Bound	Smallest Eigenvalue	Upper Confidence Bound	Largest Eigenvalue	Sample Size
		(a) UK FES			
1968	26.5	35.0	42.6	2641	7184
1969	29.6	36.8	43.4	2652	7007
1970	21.3	26.5	31.2	2625	6391
1971	24.3	31.7	38.1	2621	7238
1972	14.4	35.0	49.9	2613	7017
1973	20.8	30.1	38.2	2570	7125
1974	20.3	31.6	41.5	2541	6694
1975	24.5	36.5	47.3	2590	7201
1976	20.7	30.9	40.0	2590	7203
1977	19.6	27.5	34.9	2571	7198
1978	16.0	21.7	27.3	2567	7001
1979	12.4	16.4	19.7	2538	6777
1980	13.9	27.9	39.0	2570	6943
1981	16.0	20.6	25.1	2540	7485
1982	14.8	21.4	27.0	2517	7427
1983	11.7	14.5	17.3	2536	6973
1984	13.6	23.6	31.3	2502	7081
		(b) French EBF			
1979	1.11	1.33	1.63	2416	10645
1984	0.79	0.91	1.01	2508	11976
1989	0.62	0.72	0.82	2521	9038

culty. For example, if the expected error is proportional to demand, i.e., $(\mathbb{E}\tilde{u}_{\alpha,x})_k = -\tau f^\alpha(x)$ for consumption category k, then

$$\mathcal{W}_{kk} = -\tau \int_{\mathbb{R}_+} \partial_x m_{\mu|x}^2 (f_k^\alpha(x))\rho(x)\,dx,$$

which is likely to be negative, and actually is negative for any decreasing density ρ on $\mathbb{R}_+$.

More generally, one obtains for the matrix $\mathcal{W}$,

$$\mathcal{W} = \mathcal{V} + \int \partial_x \big(\bar{f}(x) \bar{u}(x)^{\mathsf{T}} \big) \rho(x) \, dx,$$

where $\bar{u}(x)$ denotes the expected errors of all x-households, i.e., $\bar{u}(x) = \mathbb{E}_{\mu|x \otimes \delta} u$, $\bar{f}(x)$ denotes the mean demand of all x-households, and the matrix $\mathcal{V}$ has been defined in the Remark in Section 3.3 by

$$\mathcal{V} = \int \partial_x \left(\operatorname*{cov}_{\mu|x} \big(f^\alpha(x), \mathbb{E}\tilde{u}_{\alpha,x} \big) \right) \rho(x) \, dx.$$

It was argued in Chapter 3 that there is a tendency for the matrix $\mathcal{V}$ to be negative semidefinite. If now one assumes that $\bar{u}(x) = -\tau \bar{f}(x)$, then one obtains

$$\int \partial_x \big(\bar{f}(x) \bar{u}(x)^{\mathsf{T}} \big) \rho(x) \, dx = -\tau \int \partial_x \big(\bar{f}(x) \bar{f}(x)^{\mathsf{T}} \big) \rho(x) \, dx$$

$$= -\tau \, B(\bar{f}, \rho).$$

The matrix $B(\bar{f}, \rho)$ is analyzed in detail in Appendix 6. It is shown that this matrix has a clear tendency to be positive semidefinite. Consequently, under the foregoing assumptions, the matrix $\mathcal{W}$ has a tendency to be negative semidefinite, which is in favor of the desired conclusion that the matrix M is positive semidefinite.

In summary, if one takes into account errors in the expenditure data, then the empirical findings do not unambiguously imply Property 3. However, I believe that it would be too pessimistic to claim that the observed average increasing spread of conditional expenditure, i.e., the positive definiteness of the matrix M_{error}, is only due to errors in the data.

Average Second Moment Metonymy

It now remains to link Hypothesis 3, the increasing spread of households' demand, to the "empirical fact" expressed by Property 3, the average increasing spread of conditional demand. The question thus is: *Under what circumstances does Property 3 imply Hypothesis 3?*

The answer is easily given if one formulates Hypothesis 3 and Property 3 in terms of the distribution $\tilde{\nu}(\xi, x, p)$.

Hypothesis 3 expresses that the matrix $\tilde{M}(p)$, i.e.,

$$\int_{\mathbb{R}_+} D_1 m^2 \, \tilde{\nu}(x, x, p) \rho(x) \, dx,$$

is positive semidefinite.

Property 3 says that the matrix $M(p)$, i.e.,

$$\int_{\mathbb{R}_+} \partial_x m^2 \tilde{v}(x, x, p)\rho(x)\, dx$$

is positive semidefinite. Because

$$\partial_x m^2 \tilde{v}(x, x, p) = D_1 m^2 \tilde{v}(x, x, p) + D_2 m^2 \tilde{v}(x, x, p),$$

it is now clear what is needed to obtain the desired implication: The positive semidefiniteness should not be destroyed by subtracting from the matrix $M(p)$ the matrix

$$G := \int_{\mathbb{R}_+} D_2 m^2 \tilde{v}(x, x, p)\rho(x)\, dx.$$

This matrix describes the gap between Property 3 and Hypothesis 3 because $G = M(p) - \tilde{M}(p)$. If the matrix G were negative semidefinite, there would be no problem. Unfortunately, I can see no argument in favor of negative semidefiniteness. Therefore, one needs an assumption on the distribution μ that implies that the gap is "small" or, in other words, that the matrix G can be *neglected*.

This leads to the following definition:

Definition: **Average Second Moment Metonymy.** The distribution μ of household characteristics is said to be average second moment metonymic if

$$\int_{\mathbb{R}_+} D_2 m^2 \tilde{v}(x, x, p)\rho(x)\, dx = 0,$$

that is to say, $\tilde{M}(p) = M(p)$.

An obvious sufficient condition for this metonymy assumption is that the conditional distribution $\mu|x$ of x-households demand functions does not depend on x, because in this case,

$$D_2 m^2 \tilde{v}(x, x, p) = 0 \quad \text{for every } x.$$

This local condition for every x is quite strong. Indeed, if the household's demand functions $f^\alpha(p, x)$ are homogeneous in p, x—which, for example, is the case if they satisfy the Weak Axiom of Revealed Preference—then it follows that the spread $m^2 \tilde{v}(\xi, x, p)$ is constant in x, that is to say, $m^2 v(p, x + \Delta) = m^2 \tilde{v}(x + \Delta, x + \Delta, p)$ is not just an approximation for the unobservable spread $m^2 \tilde{v}(x + \Delta, x, p)$, but is actually identical to it.

The following statements might be helpful for understanding the content of the definition of average second moment metonymy.

1. The condition in the definition of average second moment metonymy, i.e.,

$$M(p) = \tilde{M}(p),$$

is equivalent to

$$\int_{\mathbb{R}_+} \left(\partial_x \int_{\mathcal{A}} f^\alpha(p, x) f^\alpha(p, x)^\top d\mu | x \right) \rho(x) \, dx$$

$$= \int_{\mathbb{R}_+} \left(\int_{\mathcal{A}} \partial_x \left(f^\alpha(p, x) f^\alpha(p, x)^\top \right) d\mu | x \right) \rho(x) \, dx.$$

Thus, average second moment metonymy means that *on average* (over ρ) one can interchange differentiation ∂_x and integration with respect to $\mu | x$ for the product function $f_k^\alpha(p, x) f_j^\alpha(p, x)$. This clearly is a restriction on the dependence on x of the conditional distribution $\mu | x$.

2. The condition $M(p) = \tilde{M}(p)$ is equivalent to the assumption that the *observable* second moment matrix

$$m^2 v(\Delta, p) = \int_{\mathbb{R}_+} m^2 v(p | x + \Delta) \rho(x) \, dx$$

is a *first order approximation* for the *unobservable* second moment matrix

$$m^2 \tilde{v}(\Delta, p) = \int_{\mathbb{R}_+} m^2 \tilde{v}(x + \Delta, x, p) \rho(x) \, dx,$$

that is to say,

$$|m^2 v(\Delta, p) - m^2 \tilde{v}(\Delta, p)| = o(\Delta).$$

This is definitely less restrictive than requiring that for *every* expenditure level, $m^2 v(p | x + \Delta)$ is a first order approximation for $m^2 \tilde{v}(x + \Delta, x, p)$, i.e.,

$$|m^2 v(p | x + \Delta) - m^2 \tilde{v}(x + \Delta, x, p)| = o(\Delta).$$

Remark. For a given population of households, one might well reject the condition of average second moment metonymy, yet accept it for suitably stratified subpopulations. Now, if Property 3 holds for every metonymic subpopulation, then Hypothesis 3 is satisfied for the *entire* population! Indeed, Property 3 for each metonymic subpopulation implies Hypothesis 3 for each subpopulation. Since Hypothesis 3 is additive, one obtains the sought-after result.

Example 1 of Section 2.1 illustrates this remark. Recall that the population of households consists of two types with demand functions f^1 and f^2, respectively. The fraction of x-households of type f^1 is equal to $\pi(x)$, which depends on x. In this example one obtains

$$\int D_2 m^2 \, \tilde{v}(x, x, p) \rho(x) \, dx$$

$$= \int \left(f^1(p, x) f^1(p, x)^\mathsf{T} - f^2(p, x) f^2(p, x)^\mathsf{T} \right) \pi'(x) \rho(x) \, dx.$$

This matrix can, but need not, be negligible.

Thus, the entire population might not be average second moment metonymic, but the subpopulations of each type are trivially average second moment metonymic.

SUMMARY OF SECTION 4.2 Under the untested hypothesis of average second moment metonymy, Hypothesis 3 is a logical consequence of Property 3, which was shown to be well supported by cross-section data. Clearly for this "inductive validation" of Hypothesis 3 one does not need that the matrix $\int D_2 m^2 \, \tilde{v}(x, x, p) \rho(x) \, dx$ in the definition of metonymy is *exactly* zero, because this matrix describes the gap between the "empirical fact" expressed by Property 3 and Hypothesis 3. The aim of this section *is not to establish the identity* of the two matrices

$$M(p) = \int_{\mathbb{R}_+} \partial_x m^2 \, v(p|x) \rho(x) \, dx \quad \text{and} \quad \tilde{M}(p) = D_1 m^2 \, \tilde{v}(0, p),$$

but rather to argue that the positive definiteness of the first matrix implies the same property for the second matrix. For this implication the difference $M - \tilde{M}$ need not to be zero.

One might well reject average second moment metonymy for a given population, but still accept Hypothesis 3. If, however, one wants to justify Hypothesis 3 by cross-section data, hence by Property 3, then metonymy comes into play.

4.3   Deductive Validation of Hypothesis 3

Hypothesis 3 and its observable counterpart, Property 3, require an explanation; they cannot be considered as *prima facie* plausible. Indeed, Property 3, for example, says that, on average, the spread of conditional demand is increasing, i.e., the matrix

$$\int \partial_x m^2 \, v(p|x)\rho(x)\,dx$$

is positive semidefinite. I mentioned in the last section that the positive semidefiniteness of the matrix $\partial_x m^2 \, v(p|x)$ is not well supported by the data. Thus it is not clear why the *average* of these matrices should be positive semidefinite. It is exactly this that has to be explained.

Let me compare the present case with that of Property 1, which says that, on average, the *dispersion* of conditional demand is increasing, i.e.,

$$\int \partial_x \operatorname{cov} v(p|x)\rho(x)\,dx$$

is positive semidefinite. Here the situation is different, because the positive semidefiniteness of the matrices $\partial_x \operatorname{cov} v(p|x)$ is *not* rejected by the data: The estimate of the matrix $\operatorname{cov} v(p|x_2) - \operatorname{cov} v(p|x_1)$ for various values of $x_1 < x_2$ turned out to be positive definite. For details I refer to Chapter 3. Hence it is plausible that the average with respect to the expenditure distributions of the matrices $\partial_x \operatorname{cov} v(p|x)$ is, in fact, positive semidefinite.

In this section I want to find a "theoretical explanation" for Hypothesis 3. What does this mean? I would like to identify a characteristic feature of the μ-model—some kind of heterogeneity of the population—that can easily be described, is interpretable, and implies, hence explains (?), Hypothesis 3. For this kind of explanation of Hypothesis 3—which is called deductive validation—it is essential, as I shall show, that the population of households is heterogeneous in demand behavior (preferences or demand functions) *as well as in income*.

One way to explain Hypothesis 3 consists in explaining Property 3, because, under average second moment metonymy, this then implies Hypothesis 3.

Deductive Validation of Property 3

Even though Property 3 is well supported by the cross-section data that have been analyzed so far, one still would like to "understand" why this is so. A purely empirically minded reader might find, I am afraid, the following discussion a superfluous mathematical exercise.

Thus, I leave aside for the moment the argument of empirical evidence and concentrate on deriving Property 3 deductively from certain alternative assumptions.

The following result explains Property 3 in the special case where the income distribution is given by a decreasing density ρ on $\mathbb{R}_+$ (see Figure 4.14), that is to say, for *every* x *and* ξ with $x \leq \xi$ one has $\rho(x) \geq \rho(\xi)$. For example, a uniform distribution on the interval $[0, z]$ has a decreasing density on $\mathbb{R}_+$, but not the uniform distribution on the interval $[y, z]$ with $0 < y < z$. Furthermore, I shall assume that the distribution $v(p|0)$ is concentrated on 0, or equivalently, $m^2 v(p|0) = 0$. If x represents total expenditure, then this assumption trivially holds.

Lemma 1. *If the density ρ is a decreasing function on $\mathbb{R}_+$, and if $m^2 v(p|0) = 0$, then the matrix*

$$M(p) := \int_{\mathbb{R}_+} \partial_x m^2 \, v(p|x)\rho(x) \, dx$$

is positive semidefinite.

The assumption in Lemma 1 is very powerful; one does not need any property of the conditional distribution $v(p|x)$ other than that

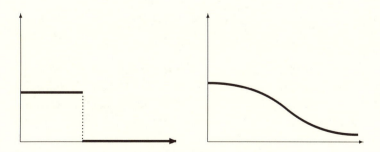

Figure 4.14.   *Decreasing Densities ρ*

$m^2 v(p|x)$ depends smoothly on x, which is part of the standard assumptions. The "explanation" of Property 3, given by Lemma 1, meets the formal requirement of a deductive validation; the assumption of a decreasing density is easily described, easy to interpret, and implies Property 3.

Proof.   Assume first that the density ρ is, in addition, differentiable on $\text{supp}(\rho) = [0, z]$. Then, since $m^2 v(p|0) = 0$, one obtains by partial integration,

$$M = \rho(z)m^2 v(p|z) - \int_0^z m^2 v(p|x)\rho'(x)\,dx.$$

Since $m^2 v(p|x)$ is positive semidefinite for all x in $\text{supp}(\rho)$, one obtains from the assumption $\rho'(x) \leq 0$ that the matrix M is positive semidefinite.

Assume now that ρ is a decreasing function on the interval $[0, z]$ with $\rho(z) = 0$, yet not necessarily differentiable. Now,

$$v \cdot Mv = \int_0^z \partial_x \big(v \cdot m^2 v(p|x)v\big)\rho(x)\,dx.$$

Since ρ is decreasing, the "second mean value theorem" implies the existence of a "mean value" ξ, $0 \leq \xi \leq z$, such that

$$v \cdot Mv = \rho(0)\int_0^\xi \partial_x \big(v \cdot m^2 v(p|x)v\big)\,dx$$

and hence

$$= \rho(0)v \cdot m^2 v(p|\xi)v \geq 0.$$

For a decreasing density ρ on $\mathbb{R}_+$, one obtains the result by a limit argument.   Q.E.D.

One would like, of course, to have an explanation of Property 3 for more general income distributions than those with a decreasing density. For example, for lognormal densities or for densities that look like those in Figure 2.9, which are estimated from UK cross-section data.

In this general case, one needs a new assumption. I now shall base the explanation of Property 3 on Property 1 of Chapter 3, which says that, *on average*, the *dispersion* of conditional demand is increasing, that is to say, the matrix

$$C_\rho = \int \partial_x \operatorname{cov} v(p|x)\rho(x)\,dx$$

is positive semidefinite.

Property 1 seems to me *prima facie* plausible for *all* expenditure distributions. Surely one can construct distributions on the space $\mathbb{R}_+ \times \mathcal{A}$ of households' characteristics that will not lead to a positive semidefinite matrix C_ρ, yet to exclude these in modelling a real consumption sector of an economy seems to me well justified. However the reader feels about the *prima facie* plausibility of Property 1, I choose now Property 1 as an *assumption*. Thus, I assume Property 1 not just in case of a decreasing density—where the assumption is empty as the proof of Lemma 1 shows—but also in the case of distributions that look like those in Figure 2.9. After all, any deductive validation has to start somewhere.

Recall that I want to explain that the matrix

$$ M = \int \partial_x m^2 \, v(p|x)\rho(x)\,dx $$

is positive semidefinite. Since

$$ m^2 v(p|x) = \operatorname{cov} v(p|x) + \bar{f}(p, x)\bar{f}(p, x)^\top, $$

one obtains

$$ M = C_\rho + B(\bar{f}, \rho), $$

where

$$ B(\bar{f}, \rho) := \int_{\mathbb{R}_+} \partial_x \big(\bar{f}(p, x)\bar{f}(p, x)^\top \big)\rho(x)\,dx. $$

Consequently, it only remains to argue that *the postulated positive semidefiniteness of the matrix C_ρ is not destroyed by adding to it the matrix $B(\bar{f}, \rho)$.*

If the matrix $B(\bar{f}, \rho)$ were positive semidefinite, there would be no problem; Property 1 would imply Property 3. Here are two trivial examples:

First, if all cross-section Engel curves $\bar{f}_k(p, \cdot)$ are linear, i.e., $\bar{f}(p, x) = x\bar{f}(p, 1)$, then for *any* income distribution the matrix $B(\bar{f}, \rho)$ is positive semidefinite. This, however, is too special a case to serve as an explanation of Property 3.

Second, if the income density ρ is a decreasing function on $\mathbb{R}_+$, then for *any cross-section demand function* $\bar{f}$, the matrix $B(\bar{f}, \rho)$ is positive semidefinite (same proof as in Lemma 1). In this case, however, by Lemma 1, one already has an explanation for Property 3.

These are the opposite extreme cases. In the first case, an extremely restrictive assumption is made on the shape of the statistical Engel curves, whereas no restriction is needed on the income distribution. In the second case, an extremely restrictive assumption is made on the shape of the income distribution, whereas no assumption is made on the statistical Engel curves. The interesting question, of course, is, whether a simultaneous weakening of the extreme assumptions on the shape of the statistical Engel curves *and* the shape of the income distribution leads to a positive semidefinite matrix $B(\bar{f}, \rho)$. This, indeed, is possible.

Details are given in Appendix 6. Here I just summarize the essential result.

Let me start by assuming that every statistical Engel curve is a polynomial. This is not a restrictive assumption as long as one does not bound the degree of the polynomials, because by Weierstrass' theorem, *every continuous function on a compact interval can be uniformly approximated by polynomials*. Since statistical Engel curves are only defined on the relevant domain of the income distribution, which is a compact interval, Weierstrass' theorem can be applied.

This assumption on the shape of the statistical Engel curves clearly weakens the extreme assumption of the first example, where the degree of the polynomials was assumed to be equal to 1.

Next I shall formulate a restriction on the shape of the income distribution. Consider the $n \times n$ "matrix of moments" of the income distribution

$$M(n, \rho) := \left((i + j) m_{i+j-1} \right)_{i, j=1, \ldots, n},$$

where $m_i := \int x^i \rho(x)\, dx$ denotes the ith moment of the income distribution.

An income distribution is said to be *leaning of degree n* if

$$\det M(m, \rho) > 0 \quad \text{for every } m \le n,$$

or equivalently, if the "matrix of moments" $M(n, \rho)$ is positive definite.

An income distribution with a decreasing density on $\mathbb{R}_+$ is leaning of degree n, for every n. Thus "decreasing" is the extreme form of "leaning".

To be leaning of degree n, for small n, however, is a much less restrictive assumption on the income distribution. For example, if

$n = 2$, then

$$M(2, \rho) = \begin{pmatrix} 2m_1 & 3m_2 \\ 3m_2 & 4m_3 \end{pmatrix}$$

is positive definite if

$$\frac{m_1 \cdot m_3}{m_2^2} > \frac{9}{8}.$$

This inequality is not very restrictive because *any* density on $\mathbb{R}_+$ satisfies (by Hölder's inequality)

$$\frac{m_1 \cdot m_3}{m_2^2} \geq 1.$$

For a general income distribution, it is not easy to visualize the condition on the "matrix of moments" that defines the degree of leaning. If one chooses, however, a parametric functional form for the density ρ, then one can formulate this condition in terms of the parameter of the functional form. This is illustrated by the following example.

Example: **The Lognormal Distribution.** The density of the lognormal distribution with parameter μ and σ in $\mathbb{R}$ is given by

$$\rho(x) = \frac{1}{\sqrt{2\pi\sigma^2}} \cdot \frac{1}{x} \exp\left\{ -\frac{(\ln x - \mu)^2}{2\sigma^2} \right\}.$$

It is shown in the Appendix 6 that the positive definiteness of the matrix $M(n, \rho)$ depends only on the parameter σ. One can show that the *lognormal distribution is leaning of degree n if the coefficient of variation (i.e., $\sqrt{e^{\sigma^2} - 1}$) is sufficiently large.* Table 4.4 shows the critical values of σ^2 and of the coefficient of variation as a function of the degree of leaning n. The estimated coefficient of variation of the expenditure distributions that are shown in Figure 2.9 are about 0.7.

Figure 4.15 shows the normalized lognormal densities (mean $=$ 1, i.e., $\mu = -\sigma^2/2$) for $\sigma^2 = 0.12$, 0.22, and 0.3; $\sigma^2 = 0.4$ corresponds to a coefficient of variation of 0.7.

Figure 4.16 shows the normalized lognormal densities in space view for different values of σ.

The following result shows that polynomial statistical Engel curves and a sufficiently leaning income distribution lead to a positive semidefinite matrix $B(\bar{f}, \rho)$.

Table 4.4.

Degree n of Leaning	Minimal σ^2	Minimal Coefficient of Variation
2	0.118	0.35
3	0.216	0.49
4	0.272	0.56
5	0.304	0.60
6	0.324	0.62

Lemma 2. *If the statistical Engel curves are polynomials of degree n and if the distribution of income is leaning of degree n, then the matrix $B(\bar{f}, \rho)$ is positive semidefinite.*

For a proof and more details I refer to Appendix 6. This result shows under what circumstances—formulated in terms of the shape of the statistical Engel curves and the shape of income distribution—one has a deductive validation of Property 3. Indeed, the

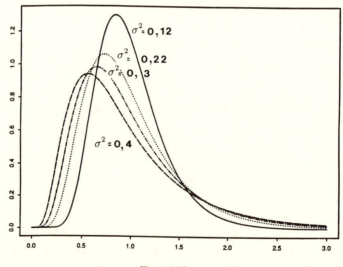

Figure 4.15.

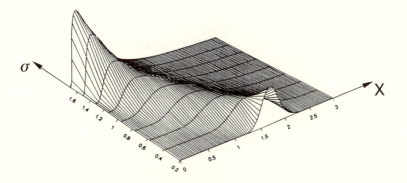

Figure 4.16.

decomposition

$$M = C_\rho + B(\bar{f}, \rho)$$

then leads to the conclusion that Property 1 implies Property 3.

Even though in this section I am not concerned with empirical evidence, it still might be interesting to know up to what integer n the matrix of moments $M(n, \rho)$ is positive definite for the observed income distributions, like those in Figure 2.9.

Surprisingly enough, this simple question is not easily answered. Figure 2.9 suggests that one should estimate the required moments of the income distribution *nonparametrically*, i.e., without assuming that the densities have a certain functional form (e.g., lognormal with parameter σ, μ). The largest income in the given data, however, typically varies a lot from year to year. For example, in the UK Family Expenditure Survey the largest expenditure varies during the years 1968 to 1983 from 8.3 to 16.6 times mean expenditure. The estimates of higher moments of the income distribution are consequently not very good.

On the other hand, if one estimates the moments of the income distribution *parametrically*, using one of the standard functional forms (including the lognormal distribution), then all estimates that have been done so far lead to

$$\det M(n, \rho) > 0 \quad \text{for } n \text{ at least up to 5.}$$

It thus seems that the degree of leaning of the income distribution, expressed by the positive definiteness of the matrix $M(5, \rho)$, is a well supported empirical fact. Is this empirical fact helpful for a deductive validation of Property 3? The answer is positive, provided one can approximate the Engel curves sufficiently well by polynomials of degree 5. This clearly depends to a large extent on the degree of aggregation of the "commodity aggregates".

Deductive Validation of Hypothesis 3

Up to now I have tried to give a deductive validation of Property 3. Under average second moment metonymy this then implies a deductive validation of Hypothesis 3.

Now I want to show the difficulties that one encounters if one wants a direct deductive validation of Hypothesis 3.

It is natural to base an explanation of Hypothesis 3 on Hypothesis 1, which says that, on average, the *dispersion* of x-households' demand is increasing, i.e., the matrix

$$\tilde{C}_\rho(p) = \int_{\mathbb{R}_+} D_1 \operatorname{cov} \tilde{v}(x, x, p) \rho(x) \, dx$$

is positive semidefinite. Hypothesis 1 is easy to interpret and can be considered as *prima facie* plausible.

To link Hypothesis 1 to Hypothesis 3, which says that the matrix $\tilde{M}(p) = D_1 m^2 \, \tilde{v}(0, p)$ is positive semidefinite, I shall now show the following decomposition of the matrix $\tilde{M}(p)$, which is analogous to the previous decomposition of the matrix $M(p)$:

$$\tilde{M}(p) = \tilde{C}_\rho(p) + \tilde{U}(p) + \tilde{U}(p)^\mathsf{T},$$

where

$$\tilde{U}(p) := \int_{\mathbb{R}_+} \bar{\partial}_x f(p, x) \bar{f}(p, x)^\mathsf{T} \rho(x) \, dx$$

and

$$\bar{\partial}_x f(p, x) := \int_{\mathcal{A}} \partial_x f^\alpha(p, x) \, d\mu | x$$

denotes the vector of average propensities to consume of x-households.

Note that $\bar{\partial}_x f(p, x)$ is, in general, different from $\partial_x \bar{f}(p, x)$. Hence, the matrix $\tilde{U}(p) + \tilde{U}(p)^\mathsf{T}$ is not equal to the matrix $B(\bar{f}, \rho)$ of the previous section.

The decomposition easily follows from the definition of the co-variance matrix

$$m^2 \tilde{v}(x + \Delta, x, p) = \text{cov } \tilde{v}(x + \Delta, x, p)$$

$$+ \int_{\mathcal{A}} f^\alpha(p, x + \Delta) \, d\mu | x \int_{\mathcal{A}} f^\alpha(p, x + \Delta) \, d\mu | x^{\mathsf{T}}.$$

By taking the derivative with respect to Δ and evaluating this derivative at $\Delta = 0$, one obtains

$$D_1 m^2 \, \tilde{v}(x, x, p) = D_1 \text{ cov } \tilde{v}(x, x, p)$$

$$+ \bar{\partial}_x f(p, x) \bar{f}(p, x)^{\mathsf{T}} + \bar{f}(p, x) \bar{\partial}_x f(p, x)^{\mathsf{T}}.$$

By integration over x with respect to the expenditure distribution, one obtains the claimed decomposition:

$$\tilde{M}(p) = \tilde{C}_\rho(p) + \tilde{U}(p) + \tilde{U}(p)^{\mathsf{T}}.$$

Consequently, to obtain a deductive validation of Hypothesis 3, one has to argue that the postulated positive semidefiniteness of *the matrix* $\tilde{C}(p)$ is not destroyed by adding the matrix $\tilde{U}(p)$ and its transpose.

If the matrix $\tilde{U}(p)$ were positive semidefinite, there would be no problem: Hypothesis 1 would imply, in that case, Hypothesis 3.

A rather straightforward way to obtain a positive semidefinite matrix $\tilde{U}$ consists in requiring that the vectors $\bar{f}(p, x)$ and $\bar{\partial}_x f(p, x)$ be collinear for all expenditure levels x on the relevant domain of the expenditure distribution. However, why should the average propensities to consume and the average demand of x-households be collinear?

The explanation of Hypothesis 3, which is based on Hypothesis 1 and the collinearity of $\bar{f}(p, x)$ and $\bar{\partial}_x f(p, x)$, does not seem to me fully satisfactory, even though, as I shall show now, it works well in the two examples for μ-models that I discussed in the previous sections.

1. The example of households' demand functions f^α, which are linear in income, is easy. Indeed, if

$$f^\alpha(p, x) = x \cdot f^\alpha(p, 1),$$

then $\partial_x f^\alpha(p, x) = (1/x) f^\alpha(p, x)$, and hence

$$\bar{\partial}_x f(p, x) = \int_{\mathcal{A}} \partial_x f^\alpha(p, x) \, d\mu | x$$

$$= \frac{1}{x} \int_{\mathcal{A}} f^\alpha(p, x) \, d\mu | x = \frac{1}{x} \bar{f}(p, x).$$

Thus, the vectors $\bar{\partial}_x f(p, x)$ and $\bar{f}(p, x)$ are collinear for every x.

2. In the example of Grandmont (see Chapter 2), one first computes households' marginal propensity to consume:

$$\partial_x f^\alpha(p, x) = \frac{1}{x} f^\alpha(p, x) - \frac{1}{x} \sum_{k=1}^{l} \alpha_k \partial_{\alpha_k} f^\alpha(p, x).$$

Thus, in this example, *individual* households' marginal propensity to consume, $\partial_x f^\alpha(p, x)$, and demand, $f^\alpha(p, x)$, are, in general, not collinear. If one now computes the *average* marginal propensity to consume of all x-households, i.e.,

$$\bar{\partial}_x f(p, x) = \int_{\mathbb{R}^l} \partial_x f^\alpha(p, x) \eta(\alpha) \, d\alpha,$$

one obtains from the preceding expression for the marginal propensity to consume and partial integration that

$$\bar{\partial}_x f(p, x) = \frac{1}{x} \bar{f}(p, x) + \frac{1}{x} \sum_{k=1}^{l} \int_{\mathbb{R}^l} f^\alpha(p, x) \partial_{\alpha_k} (\alpha_k \eta(\alpha)) \, d\alpha.$$

Hence, if the density η (which might depend on x) of the distribution of α is such that $\log \alpha$ has a sufficiently flat density, then the second term on the right hand side becomes arbitrarily small. Thus, in that case, the vectors $\bar{\partial}_x f(p, x)$ and $\bar{f}(p, x)$ are "approximately" collinear. This then implies that the matrix $\tilde{U}$ is "approximately" positive definite.

Notes on Chapter 4

This chapter is an outgrowth of Hildenbrand (1983). In this paper I showed that the mean demand function of a population of households having all the same demand function satisfying the Weak Axiom of Revealed Preference is monotone provided the density of the expenditure distribution is decreasing on $\mathbb{R}_+$. This result is a special case of Proposition 3, because this population is trivially metonymic, and, hence, Lemma 1 implies Hypothesis 3.

The approach taken in this chapter follows that of Hildenbrand (1989) and Härdle, Hildenbrand, and Jerison (1991), which emphasizes the importance of heterogeneity in demand behavior.

Alois Kneip convinced me that one should phrase the positive semidefiniteness of the average Slutsky expenditure effect matrix $\bar{A}(p)$ in terms of the statistical notion of second moments of households' demand. His suggestion led to the definition of Hypothesis 3, as given previously. He also observed that Grandmont's model (1992) satisfies Hypothesis 3 asymptotically.

As an analogy to the concept of "increasing dispersion" of Chapter 3, I defined "increasing spread" without knowing whether the term is used elsewhere with a different meaning.

The result that shows that Hypothesis 3 is stronger than Hypothesis 2 of Chapter 3 if the budget identity is satisfied is due to A. Kneip (unpublished). His proof is given in Appendix 5.

An extensive data analysis of the UK FES and the French EBF has been carried out at the Sonderforschungsbereich 303 at the University of Bonn. Only parts of this data analysis are presented here. I would like to thank Alois Kneip, Wolfgang Härdle, and Joachim Engel for their collaboration. The main difference between the results in Hildenbrand (1989), Härdle, Hildenbrand, and Jerison (1991), and Hildenbrand and Kneip (1993) and those given here is that the previous results were obtained by conditioning on total expenditure, whereas I emphasized the conditioning on disposable income in this book.

The definition of average second moment metonymy is the same as that in Härdle, Hildenbrand, and Jerison (1991).

The important decomposition $M = C_\rho + B(\bar{f}, \rho)$ was used before in several papers, e.g., Hildenbrand (1989) and Härdle et al. (1991).

The results on the structure of the matrix $B(\bar{f}, \rho)$ are taken from Grodal and Hildenbrand (1992). A first attempt to estimate the matrix $B(\bar{f}, \rho)$ from Family Expenditure Data was made in Hildenbrand and Hildenbrand (1986). This matrix, however, is typically very ill-conditioned. Therefore, I have changed slightly the approach: I use the data analysis of family expenditure surveys to analyze the matrix C_ρ, and treat the matrix $B(\bar{f}, \rho)$ as explained in the preceding text. For more details and references, see Appendix 6.

Appendix **1**
Monotone Functions

Let F denote a function of a subset D of $\mathbb{R}^n$ into $\mathbb{R}^n$.

Definition. The function F is called *monotone on* D if

$$(p - q) \cdot (F(p) - F(q)) \leq 0 \quad \text{for every } p, q \in D.$$

The function F is called *strictly monotone on* D if

$$(p - q) \cdot (F(p) - F(q)) < 0 \quad \text{for every } p, q \in D \text{ with } p \neq q.$$

Sometimes in the literature monotonicity is defined by the opposite inequality. The preceding definition extends to n dimensions the notion of a monotonically *decreasing* function.

Consider an n-commodity demand–supply system $[F(\cdot), S(\cdot)]$, $p \in \mathbb{R}^n_+$, and the corresponding *excess demand*

$$E(p) := F(p) - S(p), \qquad p \in \mathbb{R}^n_+.$$

In competitive demand–supply analysis, one is interested in "equilibria" of the competitive price adjustment process. Neglecting the actual price adjustment process one can define—as a shortcut—the following "equilibrium" concepts.

Definition. A vector $p^* \in \mathbb{R}^n_+$ is called an *equilibrium* for the excess demand function E if $E(p^*) = 0$. The set of all equilibria is denoted by $\text{Eq}(E)$.

A vector $p^* \in \mathbb{R}^n_+$ is called a *free-disposal equilibrium* for the excess demand function E if $E(p^*) \leq 0$ and $p^* \cdot E(p^*) = 0$. The set of all free-disposal equilibria is denoted by $\text{FEq}(E)$.

Clearly

$$\text{Eq}(E) \subset \text{FEq}(E).$$

For a free-disposal equilibrium one does not insist that all markets are balanced, i.e., $F_h(p^*) = S_h(p^*)$ for all commodities h; one only requires that demand not exceeds supply. However, if supply is larger than demand for a particular commodity h, then the equilibrium price p^*_h must be zero. Thus, a free-disposal equilibrium p^* is an equilibrium if $p^* \gg 0$. A free-disposal equilibrium is called, in the mathematical literature, a solution to the "nonlinear complementarity problem".

The problem of *existence, determinateness,* and *computability* of (free-disposal) equilibria is greatly simplified if the excess demand function E is monotone. Since the subject of this book is not existence, stability, and computability of competitive (short-run) equilibria, I shall give no proofs for this claim. The following two theorems show some useful implications of monotonicity. More details can be found in the paper by Harker and Pang (1990).

Theorem 1. *Let $E: \mathbb{R}^n_+ \to \mathbb{R}^n$ be continuous and strictly monotone on $\mathbb{R}^n_+$. Then there is at most one free-disposal equilibrium. Furthermore, if there exists a vector $\tilde{p} \in \mathbb{R}^n_+$ such that $E(\tilde{p}) \leq 0$, then there exists a (unique) free-disposal equilibrium.*

If, in addition, the function E is continuously differentiable and if the equilibrium $p^* \gg 0$, then the equilibrium p^* is globally stable with respect to the Walrasian tâtonnement process, i.e., for every vector $\tilde{p} \gg 0$, the solution of the differential equation

$$\partial_t p(t) = E\left(p(t)\right), \quad \text{with } p(0) = \tilde{p},$$

converges for $t \to \infty$ to the equilibrium p^*.

Theorem 2. *Let $E: \mathbb{R}^n_+ \to \mathbb{R}^n$ be continuous and monotone on $\mathbb{R}^n_+$. Then the set $\text{Eq}(E) \cap \mathbb{R}^n_{++}$ and the set $\text{FEq}(E)$ of free-disposal equilibria are convex (possibly empty). Furthermore, if there exists a vector $\tilde{p} \in \mathbb{R}^n_+$ such that $E(\tilde{p}) \ll 0$, then the set $\text{FEq}(E)$ of free-disposal equilibria is nonempty, compact, and convex.*

The following characterization of monotonicity for differentiable functions has been used throughout the book.

Lemma.   *Let F be a continuously differentiable function of an open convex subset D of $\mathbb{R}^n$ into $\mathbb{R}^n$. Then the following two properties are equivalent:*

  (i) *$(p - q) \cdot (F(p) - F(q)) \leq 0$ for every $p, q \in D$.*
  (ii) *The Jacobian matrix $\partial F(p)$ is negative semidefinite for every $p \in D$.*

Furthermore, if the Jacobian matrix $\partial F(p)$ is negative definite for every $p \in D$, then it follows that F is strictly monotone on D.

Proof.   (i) $\Rightarrow$ (ii). Given any $p, q \in D$, let $v = p - q$ and $p(\alpha) = \alpha p + (1 - \alpha)q$, $0 \leq \alpha \leq 1$.
   Define the function $g: [0, 1] \longmapsto \mathbb{R}$ by

$$g(\alpha) = v \cdot (F(p(\alpha)) - F(q)).$$

Then we obtain $g(0) = 0$, $g(1) = (p - q) \cdot (F(p) - F(q))$, and the derivative $g'(\alpha) = v \cdot \partial F(p(\alpha))v$.
   Assume now property (i). Then, for $\alpha > 0$,

$$g(\alpha) = \frac{1}{\alpha} (p(\alpha) - q) \cdot (F(p(\alpha)) - F(q)) \leq 0.$$

Since $g(0) = 0$, $g(\alpha) \leq 0$ for $\alpha > 0$, we obtain that $g'(0) \leq 0$, which implies property (ii), because $g'(0) = v \cdot \partial F(q)v$ and p, q are arbitrary vectors in D.
   (ii) $\Rightarrow$ (i). Conversely assume property (ii). Then $g'(\alpha) = v \cdot \partial F(p(\alpha))v \leq 0$. Since $g(0) = 0$ and $g'(\alpha) \leq 0$ for all $\alpha \in [0, 1]$, it follows that $g(1) \leq 0$, which implies property (i).
   Furthermore, because $g(0) = 0$, it follows that $g(1) < 0$ if $g'(\alpha) < 0$, $\alpha \in [0, 1]$. This proves that a negative definite Jacobian matrix $\partial F(p)$, $p \in D$, implies strict monotonicity on D.   Q.E.D.

Remark.   The preceding proof also gives the following implication, which has been used in Chapter 2: *Let U be a neighborhood of $\bar{q}$. If for every $p \in U$,*

$$(p - \bar{q}) \cdot (F(p) - F(\bar{q})) \leq 0,$$

then the Jacobian $\partial F(\bar{q})$ is negative semidefinite.
   The converse, of course, is not correct, i.e., if $\partial F(\bar{q})$ is negative semidefinite then one cannot conclude that there is a neighborhood U of $\bar{q}$ such that the foregoing inequality holds.

Appendix **2**
Wald's Axiom

Let F be a function of the subset D of $\mathbb{R}^n$ into $\mathbb{R}^n$.

Definition. The function F satisfies Wald's Axiom on D if for every $p, q \in D$,

$$(p - q) \cdot F(q) \leq 0 \quad \textit{implies} \quad (p - q) \cdot F(p) \leq 0.$$

The function F satisfies Wald's Strict Axiom on D if for every $p, q \in D$ with $p \neq q$,

$$(p - q) \cdot F(q) \leq 0 \quad \textit{implies} \quad (p - q) \cdot F(p) < 0.$$

Wald's Axiom is called in the mathematical literature, pseudo-monotonicity. Clearly, monotonicity implies Wald's Axiom, because monotonicity of F requires that

$$(p - q) \cdot F(p) \leq (p - q) \cdot F(q).$$

Many results that have been established for monotone functions F can also be shown if F satisfies only Wald's Axiom. For example, Theorem 2 of Appendix 1 still holds if monotonicity is replaced by Wald's Axiom. However, because Wald's Axiom *is not additive*, it does not follow that the *excess demand* $E(p) = F(p) - S(p)$ of a demand–supply system $[F(\cdot), S(\cdot)]$ satisfies Wald's Axiom if the demand function F satisfies Wald's Axiom and if $-S(p)$ is monotone or even price-independent. To make use of Wald's Axiom for the demand function F in a competitive demand–supply analysis, one needs some additional properties of the demand function F. For example, if

$$p \cdot F(p) = \text{constant},$$

171

that is to say, if total expenditure of the population of households is price-independent, then Wald's Axiom for demand function F implies that the set of equilibria of an excess demand function with fixed supply is convex.

Proposition. *Let F be a continuous function of $\mathbb{R}^n_{++}$ into $\mathbb{R}^n$ with*

$$p \cdot F(p) \equiv c > 0,$$

which satisfies Wald's Axiom. Let y be any vector in $\mathbb{R}^n_{++}$. Then the solution set

$$\text{Eq}(F, y) = \{p \in \mathbb{R}^n_{++} \mid F(p) = y\}$$

is convex.

Proof. Let $Q = \{p \in \mathbb{R}^n_{++} \mid p \cdot y = c\}$. For every solution of $F(p) = y$ we have $p \in Q$. Let $E(p) = F(p) - y$. From Wald's Axiom for F we obtain for $p, q \in Q$,

$$p \cdot E(q) \le 0 \text{ implies } q \cdot E(p) \ge 0. \tag{$*$}$$

We now show that

$$\text{Eq}(F, y) = \bigcap_{q \in Q} \{p \in Q \mid p \cdot E(q) \ge 0\}.$$

Since the intersection of convex sets is convex, this identity implies the convexity of $\text{Eq}(F, y)$ (possibly empty).

Now, let $p^* \in \text{Eq}(F, y)$, i.e., $E(p^*) = 0$ and $p^* \in Q$. Hence, for every $q \in Q$, $q \cdot E(p^*) = 0$ and we obtain from $(*)$ that $p^* E(q) \ge 0$.

To prove the converse inclusion, let $\bar{p} \in Q$ be such that $\bar{p} \cdot E(q) \ge 0$ for every $q \in Q$.

Let $p_\lambda = \lambda q + (1 - \lambda) \bar{p}$ for some arbitrary $q \in Q$. Then $p_\lambda \in Q$ and $0 = p_\lambda E(p_\lambda) = \lambda q E(p_\lambda) + (1 - \lambda) \bar{p} \cdot E(p_\lambda)$. Because $\bar{p} \cdot E(p_\lambda) \ge 0$, we obtain

$$q \cdot E(p_\lambda) \le 0.$$

Hence, for λ converging to zero, we obtain by continuity of E that

$$q \cdot E(\bar{p}) \le 0.$$

Thus we proved that for every $q \in Q$, $q \cdot E(\bar{p}) \le 0$, which implies that $E(\bar{p}) \le 0$. Because $\bar{p} \cdot E(\bar{p}) = 0$ and $\bar{p} \gg 0$, we obtain $E(\bar{p}) = 0$.
Q.E.D.

Remark. Convexity of the solution set $\mathrm{Eq}(F, y)$ by itself is not very useful. However, in applications, one can often show that the set of solutions is finite (e.g., for regular economies). Finiteness and convexity of $\mathrm{Eq}(F, y)$ however, then, imply uniqueness of the solution.

The following result characterizes Wald's Axiom in terms of the Jacobian matrix $\partial F(p)$.

Lemma. *Let F be a continuously differentiable function of an open convex subset D of $\mathbb{R}^n$ into $\mathbb{R}^n$ such that $F(p) \neq 0$, $p \in D$. Then the following two properties are equivalent:*

(i) *F satisfies Wald's Axiom on D.*
(ii) *The Jacobian matrix $\partial F(p)$ is negative semidefinite on the hyperplane $F(p)^{\perp}$ for every $p \in D$, i.e., $v \cdot \partial F(p)v \leq 0$ for every v with $v \cdot F(p) = 0$.*

Furthermore, if $\partial F(p)$ is negative definite on $F(p)^{\perp}$ for every $p \in D$, then it follows that F satisfies Wald's Strict Axiom on D.

Proof. (i) $\Rightarrow$ (ii). Let $q \in D$ and $v \perp F(q)$. We can assume that $p = v + q \in D$. Define $p(\alpha) = \alpha p + (1 - \alpha)q$, $0 \leq \alpha \leq 1$.

The function g in the proof of the Lemma in Appendix 1 now becomes

$$g(\alpha) = v \cdot F(p(\alpha)), \qquad \alpha \in [0, 1].$$

Then one obtains $g(0) = 0$ and $g'(\alpha) = v \cdot \partial F(p(\alpha))v$. We have to show that $g'(0) \leq 0$.

Since $(p(\alpha) - q) \cdot F(q) = \alpha v \cdot F(q) = 0$, one obtains from Wald's Axiom $(p(\alpha) - q) \cdot F(p(\alpha)) \leq 0$. Because $g(\alpha) = (1/\alpha)(p(\alpha) - q) \cdot F(p(\alpha))$, $0 \leq \alpha \leq 1$, we obtain $g(\alpha) \leq 0$, $0 \leq \alpha \leq 1$, and $g(0) = 0$, which implies $g'(0) \leq 0$.

(ii) $\Rightarrow$ (i). The proof of this implication[1] is more delicate than the corresponding proof in Appendix 1.

Let $p, q \in D$ be such that $(p - q) \cdot F(q) \leq 0$. Define, as before, $p(\alpha) = \alpha p + (1 - \alpha)q$, $v = p - q$, and $g(\alpha) = v \cdot F(p(\alpha))$, $0 \leq \alpha \leq 1$. We have to show that $g(1) \leq 0$.

We shall now show that the assumption $g(1) > 0$ leads to a contradiction. Indeed, because $g(0) \leq 0$, the assumption $g(1) > 0$

---

[1] The proof is due to Reinhard John. I thank him for the permission to present his proof.

implies the existence of τ with $0 \le \tau < 1$ such that $g(\tau) = 0$ and $g(\alpha) > 0$ for $\tau < \alpha \le 1$.

This implies that $(g'(\alpha))/(g(\alpha))$ is unbounded near τ. Indeed,

$$\partial_\alpha (\log g(\alpha)) = \frac{g'(\alpha)}{g(\alpha)}.$$

If α approaches τ, then $\log(g(\alpha))$ approaches $-\infty$ and, hence, its derivative is unbounded.

Next we show that $(g'(\alpha))/(g(\alpha))$ is bounded near τ, which leads to the contradiction.

Let

$$v_\alpha := v - \lambda(\alpha) F(p(\tau)),$$

where

$$\lambda(\alpha) := \frac{g(\alpha)}{F(p(\tau)) \cdot F(p(\alpha))}, \qquad \tau < \alpha, \alpha \text{ near } \tau.$$

One obtains $v_\alpha \cdot F(p(\alpha)) = 0$ and, hence, by property (ii) it follows that

$$v_\alpha \cdot \partial F(p(\alpha)) v_\alpha \le 0.$$

This inequality and the definition of v_α then lead to

$$v \cdot \partial F(p(\alpha)) v \le g(\alpha) \varphi(\alpha),$$

where

$$\begin{aligned}
\varphi(\alpha) = \frac{1}{F(p(\tau)) F(p(\alpha))} \Big[& F(p(\alpha)) \cdot \partial F(p(\tau)) v \\
& + v \cdot \partial F(p(\alpha)) F(p(\tau)) \\
& - \lambda(\alpha) F(p(\tau)) \cdot \partial F(p(\alpha)) F(p(\tau)) \Big].
\end{aligned}$$

The function φ remains bounded as α tends to τ. Since $g'(\alpha) = v \cdot F(p(\alpha)) v$, it follows that $(g'(\alpha))/(g(\alpha))$ is bounded near τ.

Thus we have shown that the asssumption $g(1) > 0$ leads to a contradiction. Consequently, we have shown that (ii) implies (i).

It remains to show that Wald's Strict Axiom holds if $\partial F(p)$ is negative definite on $F(p)^\perp$, $p \in D$. For this we have to show that $g(1) < 0$.

If $g(\alpha) = 0$, i.e., $v \cdot F(p(\alpha)) = 0$, then, by assumption, $v \cdot \partial F(p(\alpha)) v < 0$ and, hence, $g'(\alpha) < 0$. Because $g'(\alpha) < 0$ whenever $g(\alpha) = 0$, the graph of the function g has a strictly negative slope whenever it touches the horizontal axis. Consequently, $g(0) \le 0$ implies $g(1) < 0$. \hfill Q.E.D.

Appendix **3**

The Weak Axiom of
Revealed Preference and
the Slutsky Decomposition

An individual *demand function* f associates to every strictly positive price vector $p \in \mathbb{R}^n_{++}$ and every positive income level x a commodity vector $f(p, x) \in \mathbb{R}^n$. We shall always assume that in this appendix a demand function satisfies the *budget identity* $p \cdot f(p, x) \equiv x$.

Definition. An individual demand function f satisfies the Weak Axiom of Revealed Preference if for every (p, x) and (p', x'),

$$p \cdot f(p', x') \leq x \quad \text{implies} \quad p' \cdot f(p, x) \geq x'.$$

Figure A3.1 illustrates a demand function that does not satisfy the axiom.

In this appendix we want to characterize the Weak Axiom of Revealed Preference for a differentiable demand function f in terms of the Jacobian matrix $\partial_p f(p, x)$. Before doing this, we recall the definition of the Slutsky substitution matrix Sf.

For every continuously differentiable demand function f and every reference vector $\bar{y} = f(\bar{p}, \bar{x})$, one defines the Slutsky *compensated demand* function $g_{\bar{y}}$ by

$$p \longmapsto g_{\bar{y}}(p) = f(p, p \cdot f(\bar{p}, \bar{x})).$$

175

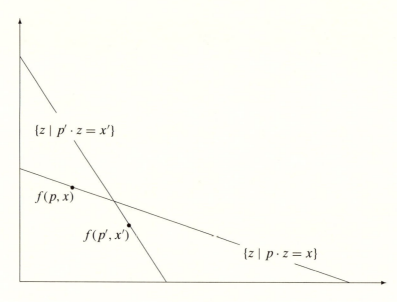

Figure A3.1

The Jacobian matrix $\partial_p g_{\bar{y}}(\bar{p})$ of g at the price vector $\bar{p}$ is called the *Slutsky substitution matrix*, which is denoted by $Sf(\bar{p}, \bar{x})$.

Thus one defines

$$Sf(\bar{p}, \bar{x}) := \partial_p f(p, p \cdot f(\bar{p}, \bar{x}))|_{p=\bar{p}}.$$

Differentiating the Slutsky compensated demand function $g_{\bar{y}}$, one obtains

$$\partial_{p_j} g_{\bar{y}i}(\bar{p}) = \partial_{p_j} f_i(\bar{p}, \bar{x}) + \partial_x f_i(\bar{p}, \bar{x}) f_j(\bar{p}, \bar{x}).$$

The second matrix on the right hand side, i.e., $\partial_x f(\bar{p}, \bar{x}) f(\bar{p}, \bar{x})^\mathsf{T}$ is denoted by $Af(\bar{p}, \bar{x})$ and is called the *matrix of income effects*. Thus we obtain the **Slutsky decomposition of $\partial_p f(p,x)$:**

$$\partial_p f(p, x) = Sf(p, x) - Af(p, x).$$

Theorem.   *Let $f(p, x)$ be a continuously differentiable demand function. Then the following three properties of f are equivalent:*

(i) *f satisfies the Weak Axiom of Revealed Preference.*

(ii) *f is homogenous in* (p, x) *and for every* (p, x), *the Jacobian matrix* $\partial_p f(p, x)$ *is negative semidefinite on the hyperplane* $f(p, x)^\perp$, *i.e.,*

$$v \cdot \partial_p f(p, x) v = \sum_{i,j=1}^{n} v_i v_j \, \partial_{p_j} f_i(p, x) \leq 0$$

for every $v \in \mathbb{R}^n$ *with* $v \cdot f(p, x) = 0$.

(iii) *For every* (p, x), *the Slutsky substitution matrix* $Sf(p, x)$ *of* f *is negative semidefinite, i.e.,*

$$v \cdot Sf(p, x) v \leq 0 \quad \textit{for every } v \in \mathbb{R}^n.$$

Proof. (i) $\Longrightarrow$ (ii). First we show that the Weak Axiom of Revealed Preference implies homogeneity of f.

Consider (p, x) and $(p', x') = (\lambda p, \lambda x)$, $\lambda > 0$. To show $f(p, x) = f(p', x')$ it suffices to show that

$$q \cdot \big(f(p, x) - f(p', x')\big) \leq 0$$

for every strictly positive vector q. Indeed, this implies $f(p, x) - f(p', x') \leq 0$, and the budget identity yields $p \cdot (f(p, x) - f(p', x')) = 0$; hence, $f(p, x) = f(p', x')$.

To show the preceding inequality for the vector q, we can assume that $q \cdot f(p', x') = x$. Define $p_\alpha := \alpha q + (1 - \alpha) p, \alpha \in [0, 1]$. Then we obtain $p_\alpha \cdot f(p', x') = x$ because $q \cdot f(p', x') = x$ and $p \cdot f(p', x') = x$.

The weak axiom now implies $p' \cdot f(p_\alpha, x) \geq x'$ or, equivalently, $p \cdot f(p_\alpha, x) \geq x$. Because $x = p_\alpha \cdot f(p_\alpha, x) = \alpha q \cdot f(p_\alpha, x) + (1 - \alpha) p \cdot f(p_\alpha, x)$, we obtain $q \cdot f(p_\alpha, x) \leq x$ for every $\alpha \in [0, 1]$. By continuity of f, this implies $q \cdot f(p, x) \leq x$. Hence we obtain the inequality

$$q \cdot \big(f(p, x) - f(p', x')\big) \leq 0.$$

Thus we have shown that the Weak Axiom of Revealed Preference implies homogeneity of f.

Choose now any (p, x) and let $v \in \mathbb{R}^n$ be orthogonal to $f(p, x)$ [written as $v \perp f(p, x)$]. We have to show that $v \cdot \partial_p f(p, x) v \leq 0$.

We can assume that $p + v$ is strictly positive. Let $p(\alpha) = p + \alpha v$ and define the function η

$$\eta(\alpha) = v \cdot f(p(\alpha), x), \qquad 0 \leq \alpha \leq 1.$$

Then $\eta(0) = 0$ and $\eta'(\alpha) = v \cdot \partial_p f(p(\alpha), x) v$. We have to show that $\eta'(0) \leq 0$. It follows from property (i) that $\eta(\alpha) \leq 0$ for $\alpha > 0$. To see this, note that $v \perp f(p, x)$ implies $p(\alpha) \cdot f(p, x) = x$. Hence property (i) implies that $p \cdot f(p(\alpha), x) \geq x$. Since

$$\eta(\alpha) = \frac{1}{\alpha}(p(\alpha) - p) \cdot f(p(\alpha), x) = \frac{1}{\alpha}(x - p \cdot f(p(\alpha), x)),$$

we obtain $\eta(\alpha) \leq 0$. This and $\eta(0) = 0$ imply $\eta'(0) \leq 0$, i.e., $v \cdot \partial_p f(p, x)v \leq 0$.

(ii) $\Longrightarrow$ (iii). The following identities are well-known and follow readily from the definitions:

$Af(p, x)u = 0$ if $u \cdot f(p, x) = 0$ (by definition of Af)   (A3.1)

$Sf(p, x)p = 0$ (by homogeneity)   (A3.2)

$(\partial_p f(p, x))^{\mathsf{T}} p = -f(p, x)$ (by the budget identity).   (A3.3)

We assume now that (ii) holds at p, x and show that $Sf(p, x)$ is negative semidefinite. Because $p \cdot f(p, x) = x \neq 0$, every $v \in \mathbb{R}^n$ can be written in the form

$$v = u + \beta p,$$

where $u \cdot f(p, x) = 0$ and $\beta = v \cdot f(p, x)/x$. Thus,

$$v \cdot Sf(p, x)v = v \cdot Sf(p, x)u + \beta v \cdot Sf(p, x)p$$

$$= v \cdot Sf(p, x)u \quad \text{[by property (A3.2)]}$$

$$= u \cdot Sf(p, x)u + \beta p \cdot Sf(p, x)u.$$

Now, $u \cdot Sf(p, x)u = u \cdot (\partial_p f(p, x))u$ [by property (A3.1)] and $p \cdot Sf(p, x)u = 0$ if $u \cdot f(p, x) = 0$ [by properties (A3.1) and (A3.3)]. Consequently, we obtain

$$v \cdot Sf(p, x)v = u \cdot (\partial_p f(p, x))u \leq 0$$

by property (ii). This proves the claimed implication.

(iii) $\Longrightarrow$ (i). We first show that f is homogenous in (p, x). For this it suffices to show that $Sf(p, x)p = 0$ for every (p, x). The budget identity implies that $p^{\mathsf{T}} Sf(p, x) = 0$. Hence,

$$p \cdot (Sf(p, x) + Sf(p, x)^{\mathsf{T}}) p = 0.$$

Since $Sf(p, x) + Sf(p, x)^{\mathsf{T}}$ is a symmetric and negative semidefinite matrix, it follows that $(Sf(p, x) + Sf(p, x)^{\mathsf{T}}) p = 0$; hence, $Sf(p, x)p = 0$.

Since the function f is homogenous in (p, x), it suffices to prove property (i) for the case $x = x' = 1$. Thus, we assume that $Sf(p, 1)$ is negative semidefinite for every $p \in \mathbb{R}^n_{++}$.

Consider $p, q \in \mathbb{R}^n_{++}$ such that $q \cdot f(p, 1) \leq 1$. We have to show that $p \cdot f(q, 1) \geq 1$. Let $p(\alpha) = \alpha q + (1 - \alpha)p$ and define the function

$$\eta(\alpha) = (q - p) \cdot f(p(\alpha), 1).$$

Since $\eta(1) = (q - p) \cdot f(q, 1) = 1 - p \cdot f(q, 1)$, we have to show that $\eta(1) \leq 0$.

By assumption we have $q \cdot f(p, 1) \leq 1$; hence, $\eta(0) \leq 0$. Consider now the derivative of η,

$$\eta'(\alpha) = v \cdot \partial_p f(p(\alpha), 1)v,$$

where $v = q - p$. By Slutsky decomposition we obtain

$$\eta'(\alpha) = v \cdot Sf(p(\alpha), 1)v - v \cdot Af(p(\alpha), 1)v$$

and, hence, by property (iii), we have

$$\eta'(\alpha) \leq -v \cdot Af(p(\alpha), 1)v.$$

Since $v \cdot Af(p(\alpha), 1)v = (v \cdot f(p(\alpha), 1))(v \cdot \partial_x f(p(\alpha), 1))$, we obtain

$$\eta'(\alpha) \leq -\eta(\alpha)v \cdot \partial_x f(p(\alpha), 1).$$

We will show that this inequality implies that $\eta(1) \leq 0$. Assume to the contrary that $\eta(1) > 0$. Then there is an open interval $(\tau, 1)$ such that $\eta(\alpha) > 0$ for $\alpha \in (\tau, 1)$ and $\eta(\tau) = 0$. On this interval $\log \eta(\alpha)$ is well defined and we obtain

$$\partial_\alpha(\log \eta(\alpha)) = \frac{\eta'(\alpha)}{\eta(\alpha)} \leq -v \cdot \partial_x f(p(\alpha), 1), \quad \alpha \in (\tau, 1). \quad \text{(A3.4)}$$

As α approaches τ, $\ln \eta(\alpha)$ approaches $-\infty$; hence, its derivative is unbounded. The right hand side of (A3.4) is continuous, hence bounded on the interval $[\tau, 1]$, so we obtain a contradiction. Thus $\eta(1) \leq 0$.   Q.E.D.

This appendix is based on Kihlstrom, Mas-Colell, and Sonnenschein (1976), Hildenbrand, and Jerison (1989), and John (1991).

Monotonicity of Individual Demand Functions

It is well-known that the *preference maximization hypothesis* alone does not imply *monotonicity* of an individual demand function $f^{\succsim}(p, x)$.

Recall that the function $f^{\succsim}(\cdot, x)$ is called *monotone* if

$$(p - q) \cdot \left(f^{\succsim}(p, x) - f^{\succsim}(q, x) \right) \leq 0$$

for every $p, q \in \mathbb{R}^n_{++}$.

Monotonicity, however, follows if the demand function $f^{\succsim}$ is derived from a *homothetic* preference relation, i.e., $z \precsim y$ if and only if $\lambda z \precsim \lambda y$, $\lambda > 0$. In this section we want to analyze to what extent the assumption of homotheticity can be relaxed.

If $f^{\succsim}$ is differentiable, one obtains the Slutsky decomposition of the Jacobian of $f^{\succsim}(\cdot, x)$ (see Appendix 3):

$$\partial_p f^{\succsim}(p, x) = Sf^{\succsim}(p, x) - Af^{\succsim}(p, x).$$

Preference maximization implies that the Slutsky substitution matrix $Sf^{\succsim}(p, x)$ is negative semidefinite (and symmetric).

Now, the income effect matrix

$$Af^{\succsim}(p, x) = \left(\partial_w f^{\succsim}(p, x) \right) f^{\succsim}(p, x)^{\mathsf{T}}$$

is positive semidefinite if and only if the vectors $f^{\succsim}(p, x)$ and $\partial_x f^{\succsim}(p, x)$ are collinear, which is the case if and only if the preference relation $\succsim$ is homothetic. Thus, only in the homothetic case do the income effects not cause any difficulty for the Jacobian matrix $\partial_p f^{\approx}(p, x)$ to be negative semidefinite. If, however, the income effect matrix $Af^{\approx}$ is no longer positive semidefinite, then to obtain monotonicity of $f^{\approx}(\cdot, x)$ one needs a *sufficiently strong substitution effect* to guarantee that the difference

$$Sf^{\approx}(p, x) - Af^{\approx}(p, x)$$

is still negative semidefinite.

We now give a *sufficient condition* for monotonicity for a differentiable individual demand function; however, the sufficient condition is formulated in terms of a *concave utility function*. Thus, the sufficient condition is not ordinal (invariant under monotone transformations of utility). It is possible to formulate a sufficient condition in terms of preferences, but this is more delicate; for details I refer to Kannai (1989).

Theorem. [Mitjuschin and Polterovich (1978)]. *Let $f(p, x)$ denote a C^1 demand function that is derived from a C^2, monotone, and concave utility function u. If*

$$\sigma(z) = -\frac{z \cdot \partial^2 u(z)z}{z \cdot \partial u(z)} < 4, \qquad z \in \mathbb{R}^n_{++},$$

then the function $f(\cdot, x)$ is strictly monotone, i.e.,

$$(p - q) \cdot (f(p, x) - f(q, x)) < 0$$

for every $p, q \in \mathbb{R}^n_{++}$, $p \neq q$, and $x > 0$.

Remark. Concavity of the utility function u implies that the matrix $\partial^2 u(z)$ of second derivatives of u is negative semidefinite. Thus, together with monotonicity of the utility function [i.e., $\partial u(z) \gg 0$], we obtain $\sigma(x) \geq 0$.

If the utility function u is, in addition, homogenous of degree α, $0 < \alpha \leq 1$, then

$$\sigma(z) = 1 - \alpha < 4.$$

Indeed, by the Euler equation,

$$\alpha u(z) = \partial u(z) \cdot z,$$

we obtain

$$\alpha \, \partial u(z) = \partial^2 u(z)z + \partial u(z);$$

hence,

$$-z \cdot \partial^2 u(z)z = z \cdot \partial u(z)(1 - \alpha),$$

that is

$$\sigma(z) = 1 - \alpha.$$

Proof. Since $f(p, x)$ is homogenous in p, x, it suffices to show that $f(p, 1)$ is strictly monotone. For this, it suffices to show that the Jacobian matrix $\partial_p f(p, 1)$ is negative definite for all $p \in \mathbb{R}^n_{++}$.

Consider the function $g \colon \mathbb{R}^n_{++} \longmapsto \mathbb{R}^n_{++}$ defined by

$$g(z) = \frac{1}{z \cdot \partial u(z)} \cdot \partial u(z), \qquad z \in \mathbb{R}^n_{++}.$$

The function g is the inverse of the function $f(p, 1)$, that is to say,

$$g(f(p, 1)) = p \quad \text{for every } p \in \mathbb{R}^n_{++}.$$

Indeed, given $p \in \mathbb{R}^n_{++}$, $f(p, 1)$ is a solution of the system of equations

$$\partial_i u(z) - \lambda p_i = 0, \qquad i = 1, \ldots, n,$$

$$p \cdot z = 1.$$

Hence,

$$f_i(p, 1) \, \partial_i u(f(p, 1)) - \lambda p_i f_i(p, 1) = 0, \qquad i = 1, \ldots, n,$$

and we obtain

$$f(p, 1) \cdot \partial u(f(p, 1)) - \lambda p \cdot f(p, 1) = 0.$$

Since $p \cdot f(p, 1) = 1$, we obtain

$$p_i = \frac{\partial_i u(f(p, 1))}{f(p, 1) \cdot \partial u(f(p, 1))} = g_i(f(p, 1)).$$

Since g is the inverse function of $f(\cdot, 1)$, it follows that the Jacobian matrix $\partial_z g(z)$ at $z = f(p, 1)$ is the inverse matrix of the Jacobian matrix $\partial_p f(p, 1)$. Consequently, $\partial_p f(p, 1)$ is negative definite for all $p \in \mathbb{R}^n_{++}$ if (and only if) $\partial_z g(z)$ is negative definite for all $z \in \mathbb{R}^n_{++}$.

We shall now prove that

$$v \cdot \partial_z g(z)v < 0, \qquad v \in \mathbb{R}^n, v \neq 0.$$

We have to compute the Jacobian of g:

$$\partial_j g_i(z) = \partial_{z_j}\left(\frac{1}{z \cdot \partial u(z)} \cdot \partial_i u(z)\right)$$

$$= \frac{1}{z \cdot \partial u(z)} \cdot \partial_{ij}^2 u(z)$$

$$- \frac{1}{(z \cdot \partial u(z))^2}\left(\partial_i u(z)\, \partial_j u(z) + \partial_i u(z) \sum_{h=1}^n z_h\, \partial_{jh}^2 u(z)\right).$$

Thus, we obtain for the Jacobian $\partial_z g(z)$ in matrix notation,

$$\partial_z g(z) = \frac{1}{z \cdot \partial u(z)}\, \partial^2 u(z)$$

$$- \frac{1}{(z \cdot \partial u(z))^2}\left[\partial u(z)\, \partial u(z)^{\mathsf{T}} + \partial u(z)(\partial^2 u(z)z)^{\mathsf{T}}\right].$$

To shorten the notation let $(z \cdot \partial u(z))^{-1} = \gamma > 0$. Thus we obtain

$$v \cdot \partial g(z)v = \gamma v \cdot \partial^2 u(z)v - \gamma^2(v \cdot \partial u(z))^2 - \gamma^2(v \cdot \partial u(z))(v \cdot \partial^2 u(z)z).$$

If $v \cdot \partial u(z) = 0$, then

$$v \cdot \partial g(z)v = \gamma v \cdot \partial^2 u(z)v,$$

which is indeed negative, because $v \cdot \partial u(z) = 0$ and since f being differentiable implies that the utility function u is strictly quasiconcave, which is exactly what we need.

If $v \cdot \partial u(z) \neq 0$, it suffices to consider v such that

$$v \cdot \partial u(z) = z \cdot \partial u(z) = \frac{1}{\gamma}.$$

Consequently we obtain

$$v \cdot \partial g(z)v = \gamma\left(v \cdot \partial^2 u(z)v - v \cdot \partial^2 u(z)z\right) - 1.$$

Since

$$v \cdot \partial^2 u(z)v - v \cdot \partial^2 u(z)z$$

$$= \left(v - \tfrac{1}{2}z\right) \cdot \partial^2 u(z)\left(v - \tfrac{1}{2}z\right) - \tfrac{1}{4}z\, \partial^2 u(z)z$$

$$\leq -\tfrac{1}{4}z \partial^2 u(z)z \quad \text{by concavity of the utility function } u.$$

Hence

$$v \cdot \partial g(z) v \leq -\frac{1}{4} \frac{z \cdot \partial^2 u(z) z}{z \cdot \partial u(z)} - 1 < 0$$

by assuming $\sigma(z) < 4$.   Q.E.D.

Remark.   For an *additive* utility function

$$u(z_1, \ldots, z_n) = u_1(z_1) + \cdots + u_n(z_n),$$

a sufficient condition for $\sigma(z) < 4$ is

$$-\frac{z_h u_h''(z_h)}{u_h'(z_h)} < 4 \quad \text{for every } z_h \text{ and } h = 1, \ldots, n.$$

Let now x be a random variable that takes the values $z_1, \ldots, z_n$ with probabilities $\pi_1, \ldots, \pi_n$, respectively. If v is a von Neumann–Morgenstern utility, then

$$u(z) = \sum_{h=1}^{n} \pi_h v(z_h)$$

is the expected utility of z. In this situation, the expression

$$-\frac{z_h v''(z_h)}{v'(z_h)}$$

is called the *coefficient of relative risk aversion*. To assume that the coefficient of relative risk aversion is always less than 4 might be justifiable.

This appendix is based on Mitjuschin and Polterovich (1978) and Mas-Colell (1991).

Appendix 5

Spread and Dispersion

In this appendix I show that Hypothesis 3, "increasing spread of households' demand", of Chapter 4 implies Hypothesis 2, "increasing dispersion of households' demand", of Chapter 3 provided the demand functions satisfy the budget identity.

Proposition. *The matrix $\tilde{M}(p)$ is positive semidefinite if and only if*

$$v \cdot \tilde{C}(p)v \geq \frac{1}{2\bar{x}} \left(v \cdot \int_{\mathbb{R}_+ \times \mathscr{A}} x\, \partial_x f^\alpha(p, x)\, d\mu \right)^2 \qquad (*)$$

for every $v \in \mathbb{R}^l$ that is orthogonal to $F(p)$.

This proposition has been proved by A. Kneip (unpublished). I thank him for the permission to reproduce his proof.

Proof. First it is shown that *the matrix*

$$\tilde{M}(p) = \int_{\mathbb{R}_+ \times \mathscr{A}} \left(f^\alpha(p, x) f^\alpha(p, x)^\top \right) d\mu$$

is positive semidefinite if and only if $\tilde{M}(p)$ is positive semidefinite on the hyperplane $z^\perp$, with $z = \tilde{M}(p)p$.

By definition of $\tilde{M}(p)$, one obtains from the budget identity,

$$z = F(p) + \int_{\mathbb{R}_+ \times \mathscr{A}} x\, \partial_x f^\alpha(p, x)\, d\mu.$$

The vector p is not orthogonal to z, because $p \cdot z = 2\bar{x} > 0$. Therefore, any vector $v \in \mathbb{R}^l$ can be written as

$$v = w + \beta p \quad \text{with } w \perp z.$$

185

Since

$$v \cdot \tilde{M}v = w \cdot \tilde{M}w + \beta^2 p \cdot \tilde{M}p + 2\beta w \cdot \tilde{M}p$$
$$= w \cdot \tilde{M}w + 2\beta^2 \bar{x},$$

it follows that the matrix $\tilde{M}(p)$ is positive semidefinite if it is positive semidefinite on the hyperplane $z^\perp$.

For any $u \in \mathbb{R}^l$ such that $u \perp F(p)$, let

$$v = \gamma p + u.$$

The vector v is orthogonal to $z = \tilde{M}(p)p$ if and only if $\gamma = -(u \cdot y)/(2\bar{x})$ with $y = \int x \partial_x f^\alpha(p, x) \, d\mu$. Now,

$$v \cdot \tilde{M}(p)v = u \cdot \tilde{M}(p)u + \gamma^2 p \cdot \tilde{M}(p)p + 2\gamma u \cdot \tilde{M}p.$$

Because $u \perp F(p)$, it follows that

$$u \cdot \tilde{M}(p)u = u \cdot \tilde{C}(p)u.$$

Furthermore, $p \cdot \tilde{M}(p)p = 2\bar{x}$ and $u \cdot \tilde{M}(p)p = u \cdot y$ because $u \perp F(p)$. Thus,

$$v \cdot \tilde{M}(p)v = u \cdot \tilde{C}(p)u + 2\gamma^2 \bar{x} + 2\gamma u \cdot y.$$

Substituting $\gamma = -(u \cdot y)/(2\bar{x})$, i.e., assuming $v \perp z$, yields

$$v \cdot \tilde{M}(p)v = u \cdot \tilde{C}(p)u - \frac{1}{2\bar{x}}(u \cdot y)^2. \tag{1}$$

From equation (1) now follows the claim of the proposition. Indeed, for every $u \perp F(p)$, let $v = \gamma p + u$ with $\gamma = -(u \cdot v)/(2\bar{x})$. Then $v \perp z$ and equation (1) holds. Positive semidefiniteness of $\tilde{M}(p)$ then implies that the right hand side of the equation is nonnegative, i.e., the inequality (∗) holds. Conversely, it suffices to show that $v \cdot \tilde{M}v \geq 0$ for $v \perp z$. Any such v can be written as $v = \gamma p + u$ with $\gamma = -(u \cdot y)/(2\bar{x})$. Thus, the equation (1) holds and the inequality (∗) implies that $v \cdot \tilde{M}v \geq 0$.   Q.E.D.

The Structure

of the Matrix $B(\bar{f}, \rho)$

In Section 4.3, I showed that the matrix $B(\bar{f}, \rho)$ plays an essential role in deriving the law of demand from the hypothesis of increasing dispersion.

The matrix $B(\bar{f}, \rho)$ is defined by the density ρ of the income distribution and the cross-section Engel function $\bar{f}(p, \cdot): \text{supp}(\rho) \longrightarrow \mathbb{R}^l$,

$$B(\bar{f}, \rho)_{ij} := \int \partial_x \big(\bar{f}_i(p, x)\, \bar{f}_j(p, x)\big)\rho(x)\, dx, \qquad i, j = 1, \dots, l$$

or, in matrix notation,

$$B(\bar{f}, \rho) := \int \partial_x \big(\bar{f}(p, x)\, \bar{f}(p, x)^\top\big)\rho(x)\, dx.$$

I shall always assume that the support $\text{supp}(\rho)$ of the density ρ is an interval $[0, b]$ or $\mathbb{R}_+$, and that the cross-section Engel function $\bar{f}(p, \cdot)$ is differentiable on this interval and $\bar{f}(p, 0) = 0$. Because I shall analyze the matrix $B(\bar{f}, \rho)$ for a fixed price vector p, I shall shorten the notation, and write $\bar{f}(x)$ and F instead of $\bar{f}(p, x)$ and $F(p) = \int \bar{f}(p, x)\rho(x)\, dx$.

The goal of this appendix is to show under what circumstances the matrix $B(\bar{f}, \rho)$ is either positive semidefinite or, at least, positive semidefinite on the hyperplane $F^\perp = \{z \in \mathbb{R}^l \mid z \cdot F = 0\}$.

I discussed in Section 4.3 two special cases where the matrix $B(\bar{f}, \rho)$ is positive semidefinite: if the function $\bar{f}$ is linear, i.e., $\bar{f}(x) = xc$ with $c \in \mathbb{R}^l$, and if the density ρ is a decreasing function on $\mathbb{R}_+$.

Indeed, in the first case one obtains

$$B(\bar{f}, \rho)_{ij} = \int 2x c_i c_j \rho(x)\, dx$$

$$= 2\bar{x} c_i c_j.$$

Hence $v \cdot B(\bar{f}, \rho)v = 2\bar{x}(v \cdot c)^2 \geq 0$.

In the second case, consider first a differentiable density on the interval $(0, b)$; hence $\rho'(x) \leq 0$.

By partial integration one obtains

$$B(\bar{f}, \rho) = -\int_0^b \bar{f}(p, x)\bar{f}(p, x)^{\mathsf{T}} \rho'(x)\, dx + \bar{f}(p, b)\bar{f}(p, b)^{\mathsf{T}} \rho(b)$$

because $\bar{f}(p, 0) = 0$. The matrix $\bar{f}(p, x)\bar{f}(p, x)^{\mathsf{T}}$ is positive semidefinite; consequently, $\rho'(x) \leq 0$ implies that the matrix $B(\bar{f}, \rho)$ is positive semi-definite.

For a general decreasing density ρ, the proof is analogous to the proof of Lemma 1 in Chapter 4.

These simple cases are, however, not very useful, because cross-section Engel curves $\bar{f}_k$ are typically not linear and the density of an income distribution is, in general, not decreasing for low expenditure levels.

I shall now show that the positive semidefiniteness of the matrix $B(\bar{f}, \rho)$ depends only on the density ρ if all cross-section Engel curves are polynomials. This is an acceptable assumption as long as the degree of these polynomials is not too much restricted (Weierstrass approximation theorem).

The following proposition shows that the positive semidefiniteness of the matrix $B(\bar{f}, \rho)$ depends on the density ρ and the *linear function space* $\mathscr{L}(\bar{f})$, which is generated by the cross-section Engel curves $\bar{f}_k, k = 1, \ldots, l$:

$$\mathscr{L}(\bar{f}) := \operatorname{span}\{\bar{f}_k \mid k = 1, \ldots, l\} \subset C^1(\operatorname{supp}(\rho)).$$

For any collection of differentiable functions g_i of $\operatorname{supp}(\rho)$ into $\mathbb{R}$ $(i = 1, \ldots, n)$ consider the linear function space

$$\mathscr{L}(g) = \operatorname{span}\{g_1, \ldots, g_n\} \subset C^1(\operatorname{supp}(p))$$

and the $n \times n$ matrix

$$B(g, \rho) := \left(\int \partial_x \big(g_i(x)g_j(x)\big)\rho(x)\, dx \right)_{i,j}.$$

Proposition A1. *The $l \times l$ matrix $B(\bar{f}, \rho)$ is positive semidefinite (on the hyperplane $F^\perp$) for every $\bar{f}$ with $\bar{f}_k \in \mathcal{L}(g)$, $k = 1, \ldots, l$, if and only if the $n \times n$ matrix $B(g, \rho)$ is positive semidefinite (on the hyperplane $G^\perp$, where $G = \int g(x)\rho(x)\,dx$).*

Proof. Let $\bar{f}$ be such that $\bar{f}_k \in \mathcal{L}(g)$, i.e., $\bar{f}_k(x) = \sum_{i=1}^{n} \alpha_i^k g_i(x)$ for some $\alpha_1^k, \ldots, \alpha_n^k$ in $\mathbb{R}$. Hence,

$$B(\bar{f}, \rho)_{hk} = \int \partial_x \left(\left(\sum_{i=1}^{n} \alpha_i^h g_i(x) \right) \left(\sum_{i=1}^{n} \alpha_i^k g_i(x) \right) \right) \rho(x)\,dx$$

$$= \sum_{i=1}^{n} \sum_{j=1}^{n} \alpha_i^h \alpha_j^k \int \partial_x \big(g_i(x)g_j(x) \big) \rho(x)\,dx.$$

Let $C = (\alpha_i^k)$ denote the $n \times l$ matrix of coefficients of $\bar{f}$. Then one obtains in matrix notation,

$$B(\bar{f}, \rho) = C^\top B(g, \rho)C.$$

Consequently, $B(\bar{f}, \rho)$ is positive semidefinite if $B(g, \rho)$ has this property. Furthermore, if $B(\bar{f}, \rho)$ is positive semidefinite for every function $\bar{f}$ with $\bar{f}_k \in \mathcal{L}(g)$, then it follows that $B(g, \rho)$ is positive semidefinite. Since $F_k = \sum_{i=1}^{n} \alpha_i^k \int g_i(x)\rho(x)\,dx$, one obtains that $v \in F^\perp$ if and only if $Cv \in G^\perp$. Consequently, $B(g, \rho)$ is positive semidefinite on the hyperplane $G^\perp$ if and only if $B(\bar{f}, \rho)$ is positive semidefinite on the hyperplane $F^\perp$ for every $\bar{f}$ with $\bar{f}_k \in \mathcal{L}(g)$. Q.E.D.

In Section 4.3, I defined the $n \times n$ *matrix of moments* of the density ρ by

$$M(n, \rho) := \big((i + j)m_{i+j-1} \big)_{i,j},$$

where $m_i := \int x^i \rho(x)\,dx$ denotes the ith moment of the density ρ.

If one considers the functions $g_1(x) = x$, $g_2(x) = x^2$, $\ldots$, $g_n(x) = x^n$, then one obtains

$$M(n, \rho) \equiv B(g, \rho).$$

Thus Proposition 1 implies the following corollary.

Corollary. *Assume that all cross-section Engel curves $\bar{f}_k$ are polynomials of degree n. Then a sufficient condition for positive semidefiniteness (on the hyperplane $F^\perp$) of the matrix $B(\bar{f}, \rho)$ is that the matrix of moments $M(n, \rho)$ is positive semidefinite (on the hyperplane $(m_1, \ldots, m_n)^\perp$).*

In Section 3.3, I called a density ρ "leaning of degree n" if the matrix of moments $M(n, \rho)$ is positive definite.

The extreme form of leaning is a decreasing density, because such a density is leaning of any degree. Indeed, $M(n, \rho) = B(g, \rho)$ if $g_1(x) = x, \ldots, g_n(x) = x^n$, and I have shown previously that the matrix $B(g, \rho)$ is positive semidefinite if the density ρ is decreasing. To be leaning of degree n for small n clearly is a much less restrictive assumption.

Unfortunately, for a general density ρ I do not know simple sufficient conditions that imply that this density is leaning of degree n. However, if one chooses a parametric functional form for the density ρ, then one can characterize the parameter values that lead to densities that are leaning of degree n.

Consider, for example, the densities of the lognormal distribution with parameters μ and σ

$$\rho(x|\mu, \sigma) = \frac{1}{\sqrt{2\pi\sigma^2}} \cdot \frac{1}{x} \exp\left\{-\frac{(\ln x - \mu)^2}{2\sigma^2}\right\}.$$

The coefficient of variation ($\sqrt{\text{var}}$/mean) of this density is given by $\sqrt{e^{\sigma^2} - 1}$.

Proposition A2. *Let ρ be the density of the lognormal distribution with parameters μ and σ. Then the positive definiteness of the matrix of moments $M(n, \rho)$ depends only on the parameter σ and, hence, on the coefficient of variation of ρ. For every integer n there exists a bound $k(n)$ such that a coefficient of variation larger than $k(n)$ implies that the density ρ is leaning of degree n.*

In Table A6.1 are shown the critical values of σ^2 and the bound $k(n)$ for the coefficient of variation for $n = 2, \ldots, 6$.

Proof. The h-th moment m_h for the lognormal density with parameter μ and σ is given by

$$m_h = e^{h\mu + (h^2\sigma^2/2)}.$$

Let $\alpha = e^\mu$ and $\beta = e^{\sigma^2/2}$. For the matrix of moments $M(n, \rho)$ one then obtains

$$M(n, \rho)_{ij} = (i + j)\alpha^{(i+j-1)}\beta^{(i+j-1)^2}, \qquad 1 \leq i, j \leq n.$$

Table A6.1.

Degree n of Leaning	Critical Value of σ^2	Bound $k(n)$ for the Coefficient of Variation
2	0.118	0.35
3	0.216	0.49
4	0.272	0.56
5	0.304	0.60
6	0.324	0.62

Consider now the $n \times n$ matrix $N(n, \rho)$ defined by

$$N(n, \rho)_{ij} = (i + j)\beta^{2(1+ij-(i+j))}, \qquad 1 \le i, j \le n.$$

It is well known that a symmetric matrix is positive definite if and only if the determinants of all successive principal minors are positive. Consequently, if one shows that

$$\text{sign det } M(m, \rho) = \text{sign det } N(m, \rho)$$

for all m, then it follows that the matrix $M(n, \rho)$ is positive definite if and only if the matrix $N(n, \rho)$ has this property.

By definition of the determinant one has

$$\det M(m, \rho) = \sum_{\pi} \text{sign}(\pi) \prod_{i=1}^{m} M_{i,\pi(i)}$$

and

$$\det N(m, \rho) = \sum_{\pi} \text{sign}(\pi) \prod_{i=1}^{m} N_{i,\pi(i)},$$

where the summation is taken over all permutations π of $\{1, 2, \ldots, m\}$.

Consider the quotient

$$Q(\pi) = \frac{\text{sign}(\pi) \prod_{i=1}^{m} M_{i,\pi(i)}}{\text{sign}(\pi) \prod_{i=1}^{m} N_{i,\pi(i)}}.$$

Then one obtains

$$Q(\pi) = \prod_{i=1}^{m} \alpha^{i+\pi(i)-1} \cdot \prod_{i=1}^{m} \beta^{(i^2+\pi(i)^2-1)}$$

$$= \alpha^{2\sum_{i=1}^{m} i - m} \cdot \beta^{2\sum_{i=1}^{m} i^2 - m}.$$

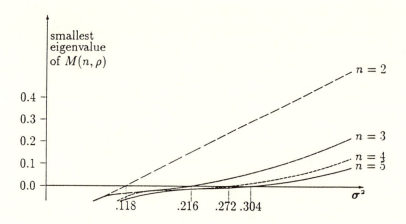

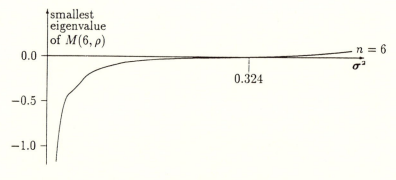

Figure A6.1

Consequently, $Q(\pi)$ is positive and independent of the permuta-
tion π. Hence

$$\text{sign det } M(m, \rho) = \text{sign det } N(m, \rho).$$

Since the matrix $N(n, \rho)$ does not depend on the parameter μ,
it follows that the positive definiteness of the matrix of moments
$M(n, \rho)$ only depends on the parameter β and hence on the

coefficient of variation, which is equal to $\sqrt{e^{\sigma^2} - 1}$. It follows from the definition of the matrix $N(n, \rho)$, that the positive definiteness of $N(n - 1, \rho)$ implies the positive definiteness of $N(n, \rho)$ provided β is sufficiently large, because the element $N(n, \rho)_{n,n}$ grows much faster with increasing β than the other elements of $N(n, \rho)$.   Q.E.D.

In Figure A6.1 are plotted[1] the *smallest eigenvalue* of the matrix of moments $M(n, \rho)$ as a function in the parameter σ^2 for $n = 1, \dots, 6$. The smallest eigenvalue does not decrease abruptly for values of the coefficient of variation that are slightly below the bound $k(n)$.

In Figure A6.2 are plotted the smallest eigenvalues relative to the hyperplane $(m_1, \dots, m_n)^{\perp}$ of the matrix of moments $M(n, \rho)$, i.e., the number

$$\min_{v \in m^{\perp}} \frac{v \cdot M(n, \rho)v}{v \cdot v}$$

as a function in the parameter σ^2 for $n = 2, \dots, 6$.

This appendix is based on Chiapori (1985) and Grodal and Hildenbrand (1992).

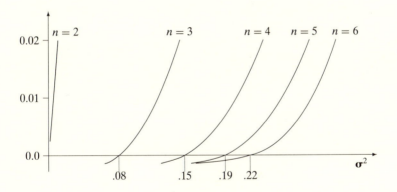

Figure A6.2.

[1]The computations of Figures A6.1 and A6.2 have been carried out by C. Folkertsma.

References

Anderson, T. W., and Dasgupta, S. (1963). Some Inequalities on Characteristic Roots of Matrices. *Biometrika* 50, 522–524.

Arrow, K. J., and Hahn, F. M. (1971). *General Competitive Analysis*. San Francisco: Holden-Day.

Atkinson, A. B., and Micklewright, J. (1983). On the Reliability of Income Data in the Family Expenditure Survey 1970–1977. *The Journal of the Royal Statistical Society* 146, 1: 33–61.

Blaug, M. (1980). *The Methodology of Economics*. Cambridge: Cambridge University Press.

Becker, G. S. (1962). Irrational Behavior and Economic Theory. *Journal of Political Economy* 70, 1–13.

Caldwell, B. J. (1982). *Beyond Positivism: Economic Methodology in the Twentieth Century*. London: George Allen & Unwin.

Chiappori, P. A. (1985). Distributions of Income and the "Law of Demand." *Econometrica* 53, 109–127.

Debreu, G. (1974). Excess Demand Functions. *Journal of Mathematical Economics* 1, 15–23.

Engel, E. (1861). Die Getreidepreise, die Ernteerträge und der Getreidehandel im preussischen Staate. *Zeitschrift des Königlichen preussischen statistischen Bureaus* I, 249–289.

Farquhar, H., and Farquhar, A. B. (1891). *Economic and Industrial Delusions* New York.

FES, Family Expenditure Survey, Reports for 1957–1985. Department of Employment (1958–1986), Ed. London: Her Majesty's Stationary Office.

Freixas, X., and Mas-Colell, A. (1987). Engelcurves leading to the Weak Axiom in the Aggregate. *Econometrica* 55, 515–531.

Friedman, M. (1953). *Essays in Positive Economics*. Chicago: University of Chicago Press.

Grodal, B., and Hildenbrand, W. (1992). *Cross-Section Engelcurves, Expenditure Distributions and the Law of Demand*. Essays in Honor of H. S. Houthakker, L. Philips and L. D. Taylor, Eds. Dordrecht: Kluwer Academic Publisher.

Grandmont, J. M. (1992). Transformation of the Commodity Space, Behavioral Heterogeneity, and the Aggregation Problem. *Journal of Economic Theory* 57(1), 1–35.

Härdle, W. (1990). *Applied Nonparametric Regression*. Econometric Society Monograph Series 19. Cambridge: Cambridge University Press.

Härdle, W., and Stoker, T. (1989). Investigating Smooth Multiple Regression by the Method of Average Derivatives. *Journal of the Amerian Statistical Association* 84, 986–995.

Härdle, W., Hildenbrand, W., and Jerison, M. (1991). Empirical Evidence on the Law of Demand. *Econometrica* 59, 1525–1549.

Harker, P. T., and Pang, J.-S. (1990). Finite-Dimensional Variational Inequality and Nonlinear Complementarity Problems: A Survey of Theory, Algorithms and Applications. *Mathematical Programming* 48, 161–220.

Hicks, J. R. (1946). *Value and Capital*, 2nd ed. London: Oxford University Press (Clarendon).

Hicks, J. R. (1956). *A Revision of Demand Theory*. London: Oxford University Press.

Hildenbrand, K., and Hildenbrand, W. (1986). On the Mean Income Effect: A Data Analysis of the U.K. Family Expenditure Survey. *Contributions to Mathematical Economics in Honor of Gérard Debreu*, W. Hildenbrand and A. Mas-Colell, Eds. Amsterdam: North-Holland, pp. 247–268.

Hildenbrand, W. (1983). On the Law of Demand. *Econometrica* 5, 997–1019.

Hildenbrand, W. (1989). Facts and Ideas in Microeconomic Theory. *European Economic Review* 33, 251–276.

Hildenbrand, W., and Jerison, M. (1989). The Demand Theory of the Weak Axiom of Revealed Preferences. *Economics Letters* 29, 209–213.

Hildenbrand, W., and Kneip, A. (1993). Family Expenditure Data, Heteroscedasticity and the Law of Demand. *Ricerche Economiche* 47, pp. 137–165.

Hutchison, T. W. (1938). *The Significance and Basic Postulates of Economic Theory*. New York: Augustus M. Kelley.

Jerison, M. (1982). The Representative Consumer and the Weak Axiom when the Distribution of Income is Fixed. Report DP 150, SUNY Albany.

Jerison, M. (1984). Aggregation and Pairwise Aggregation of Demand When the Distribution of Income is Fixed. *Journal of Economic Theory* 33(1), 1–31.

John, R. (1991). The Weak Axiom of Revealed Preferences and Homogeneity of Demand Functions. *SFB 303, Discussion Paper No. A-345, Universität Bonn.*

Kannai, Y. (1989). A Characterization of Monotone Individual Demand Functions. *Journal of Mathematical Economics* 18, pp. 87–94.

Kemsley, W. F., Redpath, R. U., and Holmes, M., Eds. (1980). *Family Expenditure Survey Handbook*. London: Her Majesty's Stationery Office.

Keynes, J. N. (1891). *The Scope and Method of Political Economy*. Reprint (1955), New York: Kelley & Millman.

Kihlstrom, R., Mas-Colell, A., and Sonnenschein, H. (1976). The Demand Theory of the Weak Axiom of Revealed Preferences. *Econometrica* 44(5), 971–978.

Kneip, A. (1993). *Heterogeneity of Demand Behavior and the Space of Engel Curves*. To appear.

Koopmans, T. C. (1957). *Three Essays on the State of Economic Science*. New York: McGraw-Hill.

Malinvaud, E. (1980). *Statistical Methods of Econometrics*. Amsterdam: North-Holland Publishing Company.

Malinvaud, E. (1991). *Voies de la Recherche Macroéconomique*. Paris: Editions Odile Jacob.

Mantel, R. (1979). Homothetic Preferences and Community Excess Demand Functions. *Journal of Economic Theory* 12, 197–201.

Marshall, A. (1920). *Principles of Economics*. London: Macmillan.

Mas-Colell, A. (1991). On the Uniqueness of Equilibrium Once Again. *Equilibrium Theory and Applications: Proceedings of the Sixth International Symposium in Economic Theory and Econometrics*, W. A. Barnett, B. Cornet, C. d'Aspremont,

J. J. Gabszewicz, and A. Mas-Colell, Eds. Cambridge: Cambridge University Press, pp. 275–296.

Mitjuschin, L. G., and Polterovich, W. M. (1978). Criteria for monotonicity of demand functions. *Ekonomika i Matematicheskie Metody* 14, 122–128 (in Russian).

Robbins, L. (1935). *An Essay on the Nature and Significance of Economic Science*. London: MacMillan and Co., Limited.

Samuelson, P. A. (1938). A Note on the Pure Theory of Consumer's Behaviour. *Economica* 5, 61–71.

Shapiro, P. (1977). Aggregation and the Existence of Social Utility Function. *Journal of Economic Theory* 16, 480–487.

Slutsky, E. (1915). Sulla teoria del bilancio del consomatore. *Giornale degli Economisti*, Vol. 51, pp. 1–26. English trans. in: Readings in Price Theory, G. Stigler, and K. E. Boulding, Eds. Chicago University Press, 1952.

Sonnenschein, H. (1973). Do Walras' Identity and Continuity Characterize the Class of Community Excess Demand Functions? *Journal of Economic Theory* 6, 345–354.

Sonnenschein, H. (1974). Market Excess Demand Functions. *Econometrica* 40, 549–563.

Stigler, G. S. (1954). The Early History of Empirical Studies of Consumer Behavior. *The Journal of Political Economy* XLII.

Wald, A. (1936). Über die Produktionsgleichungen der ökonomischen Wertlehre, *Ergebnisse eines mathematischen Kolloquiums*. Karl Menger, Ed., 7 (1934–35), pp. 1–6.

Author Index

Subject Index